WOLF'S NICK

THE DEATH OF EVELYN FOSTER

by

Michael James

First published in Great Britain in 2015 by Tyne Green.
This edition published in 2016 by Amazon and Kindle.

A CIP catalogue record for this book
is available from the British Library.

ISBN 978-0-956 1843-7-5

AUTHOR'S NOTE

My interest in the story of Evelyn Foster's death is fourfold. I am a Northumbrian, my first girlfriend came from Otterburn, I have known something of the tragedy for years and, wherever the truth of it may lie, had and have sympathy for Miss Foster's family.

In considering whether to write this book I was aware of walking a path others had already walked. With approximately the same material to work with, they reached different conclusions. The common denominator seemed to be that the police of the time had made mistakes. I don't think anyone could reasonably dispute it, but thankfully both police procedures and expertise, in Northumberland and the UK, have moved on since the 1930s—although they are still far from perfect.

To give a fresh perspective, I decided to try an approach not taken previously. The result is that accursed hybrid, 'faction'. On the fictional side, I have set six characters in Newcastle Law School and the Criminology Department of Durham University. On the factual side, as far as I know, all the evidence I have presented and which they discuss is a true account of what happened. Geographical and historical references are also as accurate as my knowledge allows.

Evelyn Foster, an Otterburn girl, died on 7 January 1931 as a result of shock induced by severe burning. She and her car, a Hudson Super-Six, were burned the previous evening in an area of bleak moorland called Wolf's Nick, some six miles southeast of Otterburn alongside the A696 Newcastle-Jedburgh road. The how, where and when of her death are known. The questions are: who, and why?

The cover features a photograph taken across Todcrag Moss from due north. Wolf's Nick is the dip in the horizon just left of centre. The A696 runs right to left below the hill (a lighter-coloured area). It is the view, not much changed today, that shepherd Sidney Henderson would have had.

BY THE SAME AUTHOR:

The Pleasure Dome
Secession
Winds of Change
Caransay

In memory of my Mum and Dad

and

to any surviving kin of the
Foster family of Otterburn

OTTERBURN AND AREA: PLACE NAMES

(not to scale)

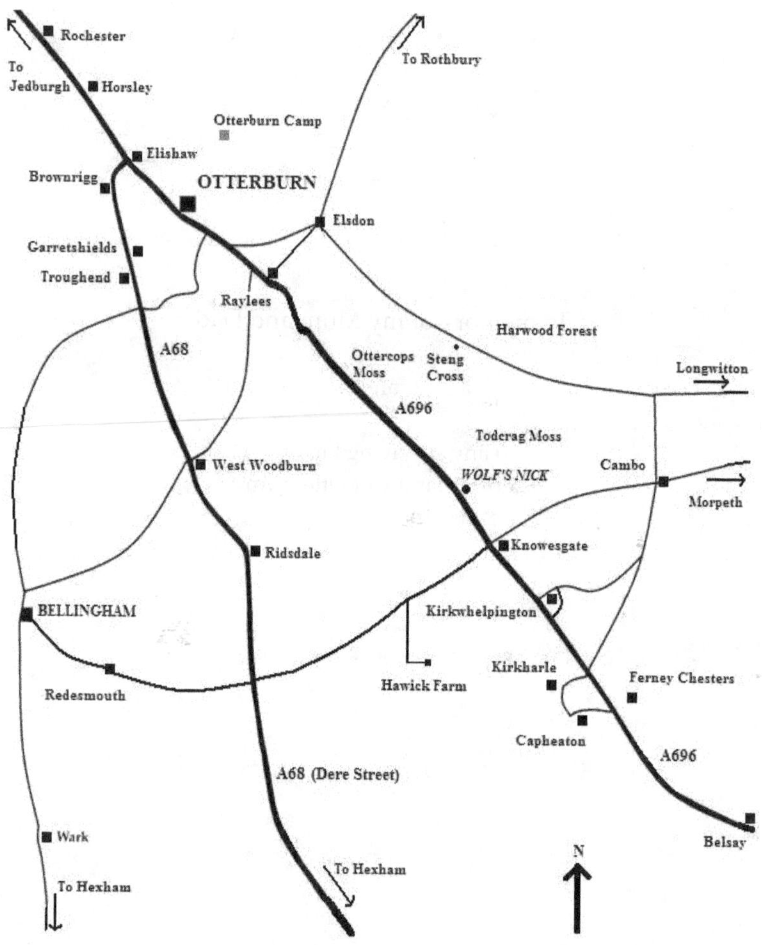

OTTERBURN VILLAGE, 1931

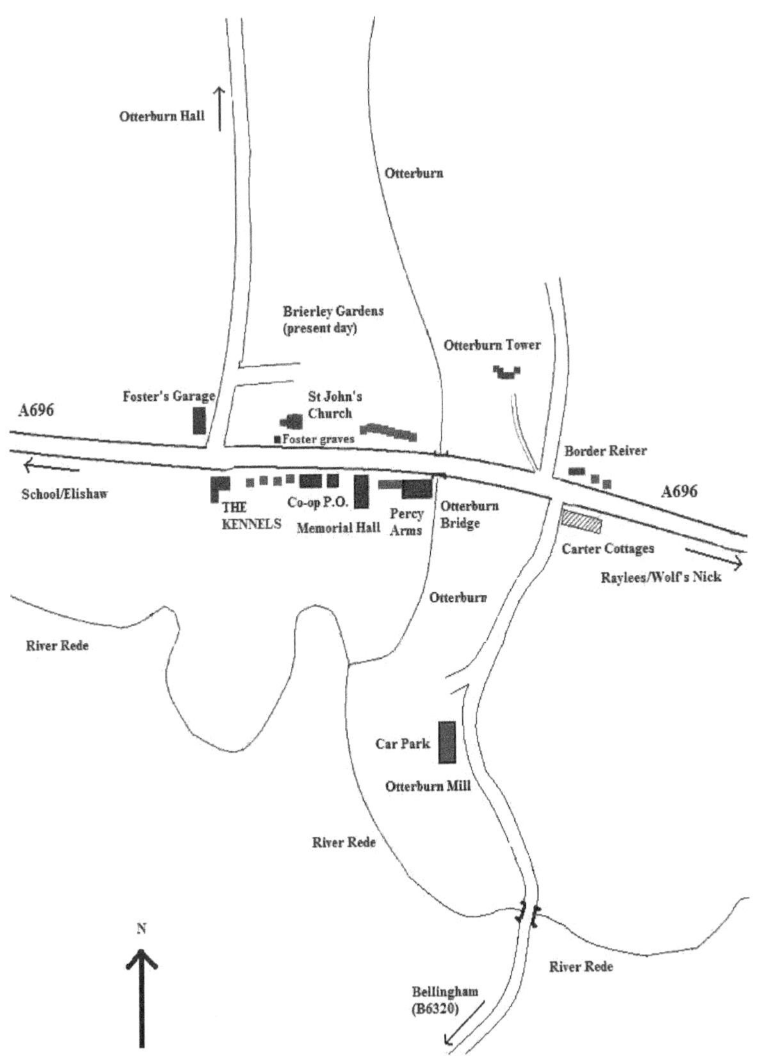

CHAPTER ONE

Otterburn, Northumberland
The present day, 6 January

Among my friends, many of whom are now inevitably scattered, are a married couple who believe the hotel which hosted their wedding reception twenty years ago is as nice now as it was then. It is not. It has not received a lick of paint or new carpet in those twenty years. My friends see it through the delusive prism of their wedding day, and who can blame them? It is not as though things have soured. Quite the reverse; they have a solid marriage and are entitled to look back with fondness.

Standing here today, I wish I could borrow that prism. I am looking at something which is as hauntingly sad as one of those old black-and-white snapshots—I'm sure you'll be familiar with them—the ones that make you think of Brownie box cameras and black curtains and less cluttered, simpler days. The kind that inspire, at best, nostalgia; at worst, intimations of mortality. Some are strictly family fare, their subjects fixed in unnatural poses; as unnatural as today's selfies will be a few decades hence (if they aren't unnatural the moment they are taken). Others may be of more general interest, indeed to a historian may be a goldmine, but I am not a historian. I do not rule out (I'm not quite a Philistine) that many may be works of art, but they are dismal on the sunniest of days, grainy and creased relics of a distant moment in time. And all too often they carry a health warning on a well-loved cliché. They tell us that if a picture can paint a thousand words, every one of them may as well be gibberish if it comes without a setting or a fourth dimension.

But this is no old snapshot. It is full-blown dilapidated reality.

I am looking at what, in its glory days, was the Percy Arms hotel, and before that the Murray Arms, a 17th century coaching inn standing on the south side of the A696 in Otterburn, a road which to the unobservant passer-through gives the impression that the place is no more than the one-street village it used to be. Here is one of the dominant buildings on that road—*the* dominant building if you exclude the Church of St John the Evangelist—and it is a sadly collapsing wreck. The forecourt is lichen-covered, the paint along the frontage, once a creamy-yellow and fronted by cheery umbrella-shaded tables, is dirty and pockmarked, the window boxes sprout dead weeds, the panes above are grimy and cobweb-coated. The Percy Arms, stretching as it does along the road like an abandoned engine shed, has never since its early days been a thing of beauty. But now it looks ashamed to be there at all.

Even the birds flitting between trees over the Otter Burn seem to be avoiding it, although I'm sure come springtime there'll be lots of pickings from guttering and slates and window sills to help them line their nests and feed their young.

There is a discreet sign in a window near the entrance. It says *Pride Hotels Ltd, trading as the Percy Arms*, is in liquidation. It does not give a sale price. I learn later it is open to offers of £300,000, anything up to £800,000 depending which agent you look at, but much scaled-down from its early days on the market (£975,000). This includes a building to the rear, almost as shabby, which was used as a 16-bedroom care home and is being touted, 'subject to planning permission', as having the potential to add more letting rooms to the hotel's armoury. It seems to me that down-sizing might be a better option, shaving the hotel to a twelve-bedroom village inn, something closer to what it once was, but who am I to judge?

The Percy Arms came to the end of its tether, or at least this part of its recent history, in December 2012 following local flooding, a succession of power outages and consequent booking cancellations. A family who have spent many years in America have expressed interest, along with buying one of the village's other two hotels, also closed: Otterburn Hall (which has its own chequered history). There has been, I'm told, some local difficulty with the Parish Council over footpaths and rights of access, I hope now resolved: you can always trust bureaucracy, even well-meaning bureaucracy, to get in the way of a good idea.

Meantime, where do the villagers go to have a drink and socialise of an evening? There is nothing within three miles, and that would mean confronting drink-driving limits. Otterburn Tower (establishment No. 3, which stands in its own grounds opposite and quite close to the Percy Arms) is no convivial local pub. It is not an establishment where working men and women would feel comfortable, not in their working clothes anyway. It does not pretend to be. It is handsome, upmarket; probably for local people the place for a meal out on special occasions, anniversaries and the like. But here is a case of what goes around comes around. Not too many years ago Otterburn Tower itself was a rat-infested dump, now converted at presumably great expense to a Country House Hotel and rechristened (again) Otterburn Castle.

So hope lives eternal, and I hope the Percy Arms does not prove to be the exception to the rule. (*Note: the hotel was in fact resurrected in 2016.*)

But it is not just a case of dominant buildings and eyesores. The loss of such a place in such a community is much the same as having a major organ removed; a lung, or a kidney. (You notice I do not say a beating heart, since that would imply death. Otterburn is not dead but simply lacking a functioning part or two.) And this, my friends, is not to mention the loss of two dozen hard-to-come-by jobs. Which, in a remote rural community, in a catchment of a few hundred people, is a lot of jobs.

I peer through a murky window in the west end of the building. The remnants of two bars flank the dining room; torn carpets, plywood, dirty bar stools, dusty chairs, some beer taps still on display, optics hanging over empty bars, even smudged glasses with dregs of wine. The dining room is set up ready for dinner, blue and white cloths and bits of cutlery on the tables. Desolation and decay. The axe must have fallen with shocking suddenness; a phone-call, despair, tears, the arrival of staff one morning to find they were no longer needed. What would be the point of tidying up? Why bother anymore? Or maybe they'd been given the bad news the previous evening and told not to turn up. Or maybe rumours of impending disaster had been rife for weeks. I don't know.

But to get nearer to the point: *memories*.

Twenty-five years ago, in one of these bars, my father, Matthew Armstrong senior, bought me my first official, i.e. legal, alcoholic drink. It was around New Year, and we were on a day visit from Hexham to follow the hounds. There were still hounds then, both foxhounds and beagles I think, which along with their human and equine followers enjoyed *proper* hunts for foxes and hares. Otter-hunting along the River Rede had ended long before, and—I know this is where I'm exposed as a hypocrite—thank goodness. I like otters, adore them in fact, but foxes are vermin, or are fast becoming so, and hares make palatable eating. The Tone Inn, a few miles from here down Dere Street, used to make, and maybe still makes, an excellent game pie featuring those self-same hares. And I hope it isn't too long before a rabid 'urban' fox turns up at the Palace of Westminster, runs amok, and is graceless enough to tear morsels out of those Members who voted to ban the sport.

You'll have to forgive me. I'm a country boy at heart. We have some strangely unconventional ideas.

And apropos of all that, although I make my living as a student and teacher of law, I think in many ways the law's an ass and those who make it bigger asses; asses who seem to live in determined ignorance of one of the biggest laws of all: that of unintended consequences. Including the unintended consequence of encouraging wild animals to roam around people's back yards and gardens, taking a less than healthy interest in the pet rabbit in its hutch or the baby in its pram.

You remember the Australian dingo case, don't you? The death by dingo of baby Azaria Chamberlain?

For dingo, read fox.

Call it cynical or worse, but that's the way I am. Or can be.

This room, though, this now eerily forlorn bar in the west wing of the building, was where on my Dad's insistence I forced a schooner of sherry down—and kept smiling. In truth, I found it much less drinkable than the (unofficial, illegal) beers—Newcastle 'Broon' and Exhibition of Blue Star fame—I'd been drinking for three years by then. He meant well, I don't doubt it, and being a kind and thoughtful man would have assumed it would lodge as something special in my memory bank. And he was half right. Although it may have been like swallowing a medicine or sugar solution, it *was* special in a way. I haven't had one since.

It was also in the way of a celebration, since my Dad was pleased I had successfully negotiated my first term in what was then the University of Newcastle upon Tyne's Faculty of Law. I remember him smiling and saying, "It's a better choice than drug dealing, son. Maybe not quite so lucrative, but not quite so criminal either."

It was in this room that he went on to tell me the story of Evelyn Foster, a story that did indeed lodge as something special in my memory bank. Perhaps the Hunt was meeting on the morning of Twelfth Night, if that isn't a contradiction. I don't remember. Perhaps it was the date that jogged his memory.

Evelyn Foster, you see, fell upon very hard times indeed on the Twelfth Night of 1931. She died the following morning: what would have been, without a blessed dose of morphine, an agonising death.

When term starts after the Christmas-New Year break I have it in mind to introduce her story to a handful of my postgraduate students at Newcastle Law School. Get their imaginative—their *deductive*—juices flowing. I will enjoy seeing what they make of it. I hope.

Meantime, here I am on another Twelfth Night, 6th January, a day before the eighty-some anniversary of Evelyn's death, paying if you will a kind of homage; and looking at another rural catastrophe, another arrow in the heart of rural life.

Mournfully I turn away and climb into my car, a reconditioned 1974 Triumph TR6 roadster, cripplingly expensive to maintain on a humble tutor's salary. But we sometimes indulge ourselves on the things we love, don't we? Is there a better way of spending money?

Heading southeast, back to the city of Newcastle-upon-Tyne via Knowesgate and Kirkwhelpington, Belsay and Ponteland (Pon*tee*land), I pass Raylees and climb the steepish hill to Ottercops Moss, which merges further along the road into Todcrag Moss. These are place-names with which, if you persevere, you will become familiar. To my far left, against the stark backdrop of Harwood Forest, lie the remains of Steng Cross, a relic of Saxon times and a boundary marker along an ancient drover's track, and above it the gaunt outline of Winter's Gibbet, or *Stob*. The gibbet, which is about to be replaced, is a grim reminder of old-style justice and punishment, raw and pitiless and in its way artistic. It is where in 1791 the body of William Winter was suspended in chains. Mr Winter was a vagrant hanged with two female faws (tinware and crockery vendors) at The Westgate in Newcastle for killing a local woman, an old shopkeeper named Margaret Crozier. His rotting corpse was allowed to swing on its gallows for many years as a reminder of the fate that awaited murderers. It was a message that Mr Winter seems not to have fully absorbed. Four years previously his father and brother had been hanged in Morpeth for the lesser crime of breaking and entering.

Two miles south of Ottercops masts, I skirt past the spot known locally as Wolf's Nick. You won't find it on any OS or road map. You'll find those other places strung along the A696, but not Wolf's Nick. Wolf Crag however, a few hundred yards away, you *will* find on a map. I am not sure where the name 'Wolf's Nick' came from, but *nick* makes sense. As the topography dips south to Knowesgate, from moorland into pasture, the A696 cuts through a shoulder of sandstone; a nick or notch in the landscape.

Wolf's Nick, or Wolf Crag—this vicinity anyway—is reputed to be the site where the last remaining wolf in these bleak and lonely moors met its end in Tudor or early Stuart times.

It is also where Evelyn Foster met hers.

CHAPTER TWO

Newcastle Law School: the present day, 7-14 January
Concerning 6 January-5 February 1931

These are the notes I prepare for my students. They are deliberately brief, thus many details and nuances are lost, but are intended as an introduction; something, if you will, to whet the appetite. Flesh will be put on these bones. Inconsistencies and inadequacies, curiosities and interpretations, truths and omissions, will come later:

CASE STUDY: EVELYN FOSTER OF OTTERBURN

Evelyn Foster, 29 years old, died from shock induced by severe burning on the morning of 7 January 1931. She was a native of Otterburn, living with her father Joseph, her mother Margaret, elder brother Gordon and two younger sisters, Dorothy and Margaret, in a house called The Kennels on the south side of the main road (A696) at the western extremity of the village.

The Fosters were a stable, hard-working family. Joseph, a self-made man, operated a garage, bus and taxi business from premises opposite. One petrol pump stood outside the house. Latterly, besides helping with the books and working as a bus conductress, Evelyn had run the taxi business almost by herself. She had owned a series of American cars, the latest a Hudson Super-Six bought fourteen months previously for £240. She was a sturdy girl, 5 feet tall, comely rather than beautiful, a hair-line marked by an inverted widow's peak (or middle-parted), well-liked in the community and with no known personal or personality problems. Other than casual friendships with village youths, boyfriends had been few (recently a Scot, Ernest Primrose) but locals now expected her to marry a Foster employee, a joiner, George Phillipson.

At 6.30 pm on 6 January, Twelfth Night, the Hexham-Otterburn bus arrived at Foster's Garage; Cecil Johnstone driving and Tommy Rutherford conducting. They had three passengers for onward transit to Rochester and beyond. As was the norm, Evelyn readied her taxi and dropped two of them, both men, at Rochester. She then took the third, Mrs Mary Murray, a little further to Birdhopecraig Hall, a convenient place to turn and head back. Two cars passed them going south, one at Horsley, one at Rochester. There may have been another which drove past as they chatted, but this is unconfirmed.

On her return, Evelyn said she had been flagged down by a man who emerged from a car at Elishaw Road Ends where the A68 meets the A696 two miles north of Otterburn. He was seeking a bus to Newcastle. She knew it would have just left, operated as before by Johnstone and Rutherford. The regular bus services, Otterburn-Hexham-Otterburn-Newcastle-Otterburn, were almost metronomic. There were other routes, but these are germane.

Evelyn Foster's Tale
Evelyn arrived back at The Kennels at 7.00 pm, having arranged with this man that she would take him down the A696 to Ponteland, where he would

find it easier to catch a Newcastle bus. She would charge him £2. There was a thought he may call into the Percy Arms to see if he could hitch a free ride, but according to witnesses later he did not. At a cost of £1.80 in decimal currency, recalculated with her father's help, she met her passenger at the bridge close by the hotel. She gave her brother a description: the man was Gordon's height (5'6") but slimmer, well-spoken (not exactly 'Geordie' but close), dressed in a dark overcoat and bowler hat; a bit of a *knut* (toff). Her mother suggested she pick up George Phillipson opposite the Memorial Hall at the bothy (his lodgings) to accompany her. This did not happen. Having filled her tank with petrol, she set out from The Kennels at around 7.15 pm, and there was a confirmed sighting of her car (by another Foster bus driver, John Robson) at 7.22 pm at Raylees, 2.5 miles from the Otter Burn bridge.

Evelyn was to say she drove through Belsay (15 miles from Raylees), her fare smoking 'a lot of cigarettes.' There, he changed his mind, told her to return to Otterburn, would not say why, said he would take over the driving, and struck her. She was confused about what happened next.

Approaching 10.00 pm Johnstone and Rutherford, on their return leg from Newcastle to Otterburn, saw a car burning at Wolf's Nick (11 miles from Belsay), stopped their empty bus to investigate, and identified it as one of their employer's. They heard moaning and found Evelyn lying several yards from the car, licking grass. The night was bitter, frosty. She was badly burned, most of her clothing below the waist gone and the stench of burned flesh made the men gag. They carried her to the bus and headed for Otterburn, stopping at a farm to get her a drink of water and arriving at the garage at 10.30 pm. Thomas Vasey, another Foster employee, carried her up to her room while her mother prepared her bed. A neighbour, doctor and nurse were called to help, and then the village constable, P.C. Fergusson. When asked by her mother what had happened, Evelyn kept saying 'that awful man', had struck her, pinched her, forced her into the back, thrown liquid over her and set it alight. She was not clear whether this burning began on the road or when the car had come to rest on the moor. Her burns went deep, the skin of her thighs split down to muscle; the edges of the open wounds weeping and crusted.

A local shepherd, apparently a reliable witness who was walking along the Harwood road, roughly parallel to the A696, had seen what he believed was a car ablaze on the main road, across two miles of moorland, at 8.45 pm. By 9.00, at his destination, the fire had diminished.

Fergusson, along with Sergeant Shanks from Bellingham, interviewed Evelyn Foster in her bed for about twenty minutes soon after midnight. Also present were Mrs Foster, Dorothy Foster, two doctors (another had been called), and the district nurse. The questions were addressed to Evelyn by her mother, Fergusson taking notes. According to Dr McEachran his patient, for whom his prognosis was dire from the outset but for whom he did his best with ointments and drugs, was lucid and sensible throughout.

Of the car she had met at Elishaw, she said a woman was driving and there were two men in it (Fergusson's notes suggest this included the man who hailed her). The car was dark-coloured and closed. Later, on their journey to Belsay, her passenger had mentioned that he owned a car and lived in the Midlands. Evelyn confirmed she had driven to the far side of Belsay and met two cars heading north, one of which she knew as Mr William Kirsopp-

Reid's, a farmer at Old Town, near Otterburn Mill. She repeated her earlier answers to her mother, adding that the man had struck her over the eye, which left it feeling as if it was 'full of sand.' He had stopped the car at Wolf's Nick and offered her a cigarette, which she declined. He commented that she must be 'an independent young woman' then attacked her again, bundling her into the back of the car. Her mother asked if the man had 'interfered' with her. She replied 'Yes' and at her mother's exclamation of horror added, 'Oh, mother, I couldn't help it. I fought for my life.'

She said her assailant then 'took something out of his pocket and threw it over me. I don't know if it was a bottle or a tin. It went up in a blaze.' She remembered a bump, as though the car was travelling over rough ground, and finally managed to get out and crawl away. She said she heard a car pull up on the road and a whistle; also an explosion (she thought the petrol tank). She lay on the fell 'for a long, long time. I was so thirsty I lay and sucked the grass.'

The interview was over by 12.30 am. It was not resumed. An hour later Evelyn lapsed into unconsciousness, waking only once when her mother spoke to her before she died. 'Mother…I have been murdered,' she said.

According to the Police Officer's Report, she died at 8.00 am.

The Policemen's Tale

At first the police believed they were investigating a murder. Given the time of night and their shortage of transport it took them some time to muster. First on the scene was Fergusson at 11.00 pm. Having phoned Sergeant Shanks in Bellingham (nine miles southwest), he spoke in their garage with Joseph and Gordon Foster. Shanks arrived at 11.30, shortly followed by P.C. Proud, also from Bellingham, who had driven the second doctor, Miller, over in the latter's car. At 11.45 Fergusson and Shanks walked to the Otterburn police house to call Superintendent Shell in Hexham. They were joined by Proud.

This done, Fergusson and Shanks entered The Kennels at about 12.10 am and began their interview with Evelyn Foster. Proud 'kept a watch' in the street. Twenty minutes later the two interviewers left the house, whereupon all three policemen made their way to Wolf's Nick in a Foster car driven by Vasey and accompanied by Johnstone. They arrived at 1.00 am, examined the scene, the burned car and its semicircular route from the road, noted a 3-gill bottle which seemed to have contained lime juice; a Shell petrol can (its cap missing) on the burned-out carrier platform; and a charred purse holding two 10/- notes (50p each), 9/6 in silver (45p)—c. £90 in today's money—and Evelyn's driving licences (one expired, one current).

Fergusson and Shanks left Proud on guard with Johnstone and departed in the car with Vasey; first to Kirkwhelpington police house (to inform the village constable, Francis Sinton) then back to Raechester Farm, just south of Wolf's Nick, to search the outhouses and speak to the farmer. They then returned to the crime scene, picked up Proud and Johnstone, and headed back north, stopping at Ottercops and Raylees Farms for the same purposes. They neither saw nor heard of any strangers, and were back in Otterburn at 4.00 am.

Inspector Russell, stationed at Prudhoe south of the River Tyne, arrived at the Foster garage shortly after six, having called at Ridsdale police house (seven miles south of Otterburn) to instruct P.C. Turnbull to proceed to Wolf's Nick and take charge of the burned car. Turnbull had a motor-cycle and took up his post at 6.30 am. He later testified that several people arrived during the morning, mostly reporters, and he was joined at 1.00 pm by P.C. Fergusson. They took some measurements of distances between the car and road before Turnbull was relieved at 2.00 pm by Sinton from Kirkwhelpington. Russell meanwhile, on finding Evelyn Foster unconscious, headed north beyond Elishaw to the Horsley area to 'conduct some enquiries' and when he returned to Otterburn at 9.15 am was told Evelyn had died. He 'made further enquiries in the district' and at about 3.30 pm proceeded to Wolf's Nick.

Russell applied himself to taking careful measurements and inspecting the car and the ground around it. He found the petrol can's screw cap ten inches from it, spots he believed to be blood in six areas, part of a brown tweed coat, some dress material, a short brown and yellow scarf, bits of linen and corset material, suspender buckles, and a piece of white wadding. (A dark brown felt hat which Evelyn had been wearing was never found). Among his conclusions on 7 January was that the car had burned where it stood. It was taken to Foster's Garage for detailed examination by two motor mechanics later that day. At the garage on 9 January Russell found the remains of a pocket flashlight, a cone-shaped piece of burned material (later identified as a rubber tyre-hammer) and the burned remains of Evelyn's account book in which she had recorded her fares and expenses. He took the items he had found into his safe keeping and handed them to Professor Stuart McDonald, pathologist, in Newcastle on 15 January. Returning to Wolf's Nick that day with the Professor and others, he found two pieces of skin. On the following day, Friday 16, a heavy police contingent descended on the site including no less than the Chief Constable. A rectangle of turf where the car had rested, 10 feet by 8 feet, was dug up by Russell and Superintendent Spratt of Alnwick. Individual turves were numbered, bagged and carried away in a lorry. After washing and sieving, a hairpin and bit of car fabric were discovered.

No fingerprints were recorded; one cast was made of a footprint (which turned out to be innocuous); the scene had been left unattended for several hours during the night; the ground was churned up by a variety of visiting feet; and although few policemen had been in evidence earlier, by mid-morning they were on duty near all main cross roads in the area, twelve hours after the car had burned. It was all to no avail. Evelyn's assailant had vanished. The police issued a statement saying she had been found three miles south (*sic:* northwest) of Kirkwhelpington and asking (a) for anyone travelling the A696 between 7.30 and 10.00 pm to come forward, and (b) for anyone travelling south from Scotland by car at about 6.30 pm (it was 7.00 pm when Evelyn was hailed) to do likewise. A driver of a car did contact police in Doncaster; he had been in the Redesdale Arms at Horsley with two male friends from County Durham around that time (a visit which Ben Prior, the landlord, had already told Russell about) and was able to satisfy police they had no link with the Foster case. The initial police statement carried no description, as provided by Evelyn Forster, of the man they were seeking.

The Immediate Aftermath

It was not long before the police transferred their attention to the possibility that Evelyn had set herself, and her car, alight—most likely as an insurance fraud. This theory was to be the elephant in the room at the inquest. It began on 8 January, a session held to confirm the deceased's identity by her father, but was then adjourned by the coroner until 2 February, when it would span four days. Stuart McDonald, Professor of Pathology at Newcastle University, assisted by his son and Dr McEachran, also carried out his post mortem in the Foster Garage on 8 January. He subsequently visited the site at Wolf's Nick.

The case study will explore how and why the police theory came about.

With the permission of the owner, Mrs Marna Pease, the police made Otterburn Tower the headquarters of their continuing investigation.

Evelyn Foster's funeral service and interment took place in mist and rain at St John the Evangelist's Church on Sunday 11 January 1931. Several hundred attended, many from outside the village. Among them was the Dowager Lady Redesdale, Lady Clementine Ogilvy, who had married the 1st Baron Redesdale, Algernon Freeman-Mitford (*those* Mitfords, yes) in 1874.

By then, and certainly by the inquest, a chasm had opened up between the perceptions and attitudes of the community and of the police. The press were a constant presence, and a measure of concern, if not panic, spread through the area as days and nights passed with no killer being apprehended.

In the first week of February the inquest jury, nine good men and true (all local) returned a verdict of 'wilful murder by person or persons unknown.' Through their Chief Constable, the Northumberland County Constabulary dismissed the jury's verdict as being contrary to the weight of evidence.

Twenty-seven witnesses were called. The case study will consider their evidence, but witnesses aside the main personnel were:

Philip Mark Dodds, H.M. Coroner for South Northumberland;

Thomas Hedley Smirk, a Newcastle solicitor representing the police;

Ernest Bates, a Newcastle solicitor representing the Foster family; and

The Jury: George MacDougall, head gardener at the Tower, foreman
Reverend Joseph Philip Basil Brierley, Vicar of Otterburn
Robert Brown, an employee at Otterburn Mill
John Geddes, an employee at Otterburn Mill
John Hodgson, landlord of the Percy Arms
Stanley Potts, Otterburn sub-postmaster
George Sinclair, manager, the Co-op, Otterburn
George Waddell, managing director, Otterburn Mill
Arthur Wallace, a local farmer.

Selected Further Reading

*   *The Burning of Evelyn Foster* by Jonathan Goodman;
*   *A Reasonable Doubt* by Julian Symons: a collection of essays;
*   *Murder Casebook (Issue 84),* ditto;
**   *Murder Most Mysterious* by Hargave Lee Adams, ditto;
*** *Murder or Fraud on the Northumberland Moors* by Robert Dixon;
*   *The NARPO magazine (Summer 2012 issue).* Article by Robert Dixon;
*   *The NARPO magazine (Winter 2011 issue).* Article by Paul Heslop.

*   Individual copies purchased and distributed with these notes
** Uploaded from the internet, also distributed
*** On computer: Kindle (Dixon has a somewhat alternative view to Goodman)
    Note: ITV also showed a programme in 1994, *The Man Who Melted Away*

I write these notes in the second week of January in my flat in Jesmond, the week in which the new Spring term gets underway. I wish it looked like Spring, but there is not yet so much as a snowdrop poking its head above ground. Perhaps it should settle for being called 'Lent' term.

Once or twice during the week I have been tempted to return north, to check some of the things I was writing about, but realise they can wait. I do not want to rush things unduly and the weather, a mixture of snow and sleet and hail all accompanied by what meteorologists call fresh to strong gales, occasionally storm force, has not encouraged travel.

So I have contented myself with being as objective as I'm able in between drinking too many cups of coffee and tidying my flat which, being within easy walking distance of Newcastle Law School, I have never for a moment regretted buying. It has to be said it needed the attention, but its state of disarray was not one-thousandth as incurable as that of the Percy Arms. It occupies the upper floor of an old red-brick building and, bathroom apart, is open-plan. The fixtures, fittings and furnishings are Scandinavian-style, crisp and smooth and geometric (pieces by Hans Wegner and Børge Mogensen among them, if you like things Danish) so tidiness and cleanliness are easily achieved even for people who are easily distracted (which I am) or lazy (which I'm not).

I have enjoyed previous sessions with my four volunteers on this case study and wonder where it will lead us. There is perhaps a month of work on it, perhaps longer, meeting two or three times each week. They will have other things to do, as will I, but I hope this one will grab them.

Two stark truths that will surely be rammed home are that the bad guys are not always found where you expect them, and that damage invariably outweighs punishment. If there is any punishment, save guilt.

I add the following note as an afterthought, to put things better into context. My students will, after all, need to take themselves back in time:

The Donkey Stone

I am taking some poetic license here as 'donkey stones' were more prevalent during the first half of the twentieth century in Yorkshire and Lancashire. Nevertheless, they appeared in Northumberland and serve to illustrate a point. They were composite stones, about double a bar of soap in size, made of a mix of ground sandstone or limestone, water, cement and a bleaching agent. Often carried by rag and bone men as a means of barter (*Rag bone! Donkey stone!*), they were used when wetted to scour doorsteps, windowsills and frontage pavements. Their name derived from a donkey logo used on the stones by one of their big manufacturers, Reads of Manchester.

What relevance has this? I hear you asking. Simply to point out that before the days of 'all mod cons' (fridges, freezers, washing machines, TV sets, food mixers, dishwashers, vacuums, electric/gas ovens, microwaves, toasters, coffee-makers, spin dryers *et al*—some of which could be owned in 1931 by the well-off) a diligent northern housewife never neglected this part of her weekly duties. If she had, she would have been classed as a sloven. And she would have missed out on socialising and on friendly competition, for her neighbours would have been out 'doing their steps'.

We are journeying backwards into a different time-zone, a different mind-set, a different way of life. We are journeying back to a time pre-Mars Bar, Kit Kat, Aero (there were Jaffa Cakes from 1927 and Crunchies from 1929); to a time before driving tests and cat's eyes (both 1934); to a time when radio broadcasting was ten years old and a bespectacled Scot called John Logie Baird, after years of experimentation, had just made the first TV programme for the BBC (1928); to a time when unemployment ran at 20 percent and it cost 2/6d to see a doctor (£7 in today's money, medicines being extra—and this in an age when many children would have been grateful for a threepenny bit in their Christmas stocking), to a time when recycling, 'make do and mend', was the norm.

We are journeying backwards to an age when a woman's place was in the home, and she worked in it or for it (I include daily trips to the local shops—butchers, greengrocers, fruiterers, Post Office, ironmongers, bakers—no supermarkets then) sixteen hours a day. And it was hard work, unrelenting work. Chore piled upon chore, all for the benefit of the 'bread-winner', their children and pure house-pride. There was washing-up, dusting, tidying, cleaning grates, making beds, hand-washing and 'possing' clothes, putting them through the mangle, hanging them to dry on clothes-horse or washing-line, ironing (a flat iron), baking (a coal range), preparing meals, fixing sandwiches, filling bait boxes, sewing, mending, beating carpets, sweeping stairs, disinfecting, boiling dishcloths and towels, making jams—and scouring the front doorstep. (I am talking of the 'working class' throughout, not those blessed with servants.)

Some rebelled of course, some let things slip, many complained. Most got on with it and felt righteous (it is questionable how many felt fulfilled) doing it. This was their contribution to a partnership, and there was always a cup of tea and biscuits at eleven, and maybe a dance or the cinema to look forward to on Saturday night (it was the great pre-TV age of cinema-going). Or maybe there was an illness in the house, one of the kids, or a work accident, to complicate things further...

...a day in the life of Mrs Margaret Foster, husband to Joseph and mother to four children.

And *then* there were the various elements of the garage business.

CHAPTER THREE

Newcastle Law School
The present day, 15 January

I have commandeered one of our seminar rooms for an hour or so this morning and we have plenty of space. The Law School occupies part of a mellow brick terrace of former Victorian houses off Jesmond Road in this great northern city, a ten-minute walk south-westwards to the city centre shops, rather less than that to the beautiful neo-Jacobean Student's Union building and the not-so-beautiful Haymarket bus station.

In the last few years the School has regularly occupied a Top Ten spot in a variety of Good University Guides (*The Sunday Times* gave it top rating in 2012)—a good deal better than the local football team, the famous Magpies, has achieved in the English Football League. Newcastle University as a whole has a reputation for excellent research-based learning, and is an altogether pleasant environment in which to teach, study and learn. I have spent three happy years here after ten not-so-happy years in London and five in Manchester. It continues to seem precisely what it was at the time; a homecoming.

The thought sometimes crosses my mind that it may actually be *too* pleasant an environment, and to keep them sharp and fully engaged with society my postgraduates need an occasional rude ducking in the outside world (something our average MP would do well to emulate, which is another change that has occurred since the mid-twentieth century). This is what I hope I'm about to give them, not for the first time. It should teach me a thing or two as well; I am a great believer in lifelong learning.

"A case study for you," I tell the four in front of me, dishing out my carefully-worded, pre-cooked offering to each. "A little something to stretch your minds. Fifteen minutes to read and absorb."

I watch them as they read. Come what may, they have volunteered for this project and I could not, in truth, have done better had I hand-picked them. Warts and all, they are a promising bunch, not least because they have different backgrounds and interests.

Ladies first.

Frances Wentworth is a lissom beauty from somewhere near Sandy in Bedfordshire. Long dark hair, full lips, nice teeth, high cheekbones. Fran has made her way into the Law School via an under-graduate course in Politics and a doctoral scholarship in criminology. She is in her late twenties, as personable a young woman as you could wish to meet, and I believe everything she has ever touched—academically speaking of course—has turned to gold. She is smart in all respects, and very sharp. If she has a failing in this world, it has to do with tenderheartedness.

Which, my friends, is a sad reflection on the world.

Bradon Young, an American from Salt Lake City, is an honors (*sic*) graduate of Brigham Young University (no relation of the founder, he assures me, or if so too obscure to brag about) in Provo, Utah. He is a Mormon, but doesn't make an issue of it. The designation 'University Honors' is the highest accolade BYU can award its graduates, and less than 4,500 have achieved it in the last half-century. Its students are obliged to follow a strict code that governs behaviour in line with the teachings of the Church of Jesus Christ of Latter-day Saints: academic honesty, grooming and dress standards; abstinence from drugs, alcohol and extramarital sex. (I am not sure all of them succeed all the time in all these goals, in fact would bet against it, but hasn't that always been the way of the world, in the mid-twentieth century and now?) Before coming to Newcastle, Bradon had taken a sabbatical to serve in France as a Mormon missionary, following in the footsteps of one Willard Mitt Romney. There the resemblance ends; Bradon is a short, muscular, blond-haired, blue-eyed all-American boy.

Peter Maxwell, a Reiver name of the Scottish West March, is from Jedburgh in the Borders. He is the youngest of the group, twenty-five years old, dark, lanky, narrow-eyed and altogether rather sombre-looking, but the last is misleading. He has a caustic wit and a mind like a scalpel, and is among past winners of the Law School's 'mooting' competition aimed at helping students gain experience in the art of legal argument and analysis. Peter, in my opinion, is heading for a star-spangled career as a barrister. Also, if he engages with this case study (he can be unpredictable in his likes and dislikes), he will have local knowledge of Evelyn Foster's homeland. He will have travelled the A68-A696 from Jedburgh to Newcastle more times than he can count.

And finally our Norwegian, Sven Carlson, who is an LL.M in Public International Law from the University of Oslo, his selected specialism having been international criminal and humanitarian law. I can expect him to disappear from time to time skiing, in which he is expert, but I'm glad to see him here because of all of us, me included, he is the most enthusiastic naturalist and historian. He is twenty-six, brown-haired, lightly bearded, loose-limbed, has a crookedly engaging smile and speaks better English than any of us. He tells me he learned to ski, strapped between his father's legs, before he could walk.

Ah, yes...and as for me? Well, I am Dr Matthew Armstrong (another Reiver name), tutor and would-be scratch golfer. I was born in Hexham, went to school there, graduated in law at the University of Newcastle upon Tyne (as it used to be known), and have held various teaching posts since. I am neither English nor Scots, but a Northumbrian—and can be exasperatingly proud of the distinction. I am forty-three years old, 5'11", passably slim, unmarried (one youthful aberration), but with a—what shall I say?—a relationship with a beautiful female professor in Durham. We are both too busy to make our relationship more than it is. We are comfortable the way we are, weekends especially.

Sven Carlson is the first to speak. "We will need a familiarisation trip to the Northumberland moors. The land of the Border Reivers, I believe."

"Of course," I tell him. "And perhaps more than one trip."

"Why have you chosen this very cold case?" Peter Maxwell asks. "What is to be gained now? Everyone will be dead, unless they were infants at the time. What good can we do, eighty-odd years on?"

I take a breath. "I believe we can do some good, for ourselves and for the good people of Otterburn. For ourselves is easier; we can learn something of how the law and policing has moved on, of the institutions at the time and their culture, of how and why regimes and methods of inquiry and investigation have changed, of the social context in which this case took place and all its ramifications. So for us, this is a practical exercise which ticks a number of boxes. For Otterburn, I am on shakier ground. I do not imagine that we can 'solve' this case or put it to bed once and for all. I do not expect we can reach a radical conclusion no one else has dreamt of, a blinding flash of understanding as it were. I do, however, imagine that we can stimulate some conversation, explain some things that have not been properly explained before, shed some light in dark corners, put our collective intellects to work in a way that will be careful and objective and transparent, and not least provide this unfortunate girl with a history and a legacy that is well-considered and robust."

"You believe she was murdered," Peter says.

He really is the limit. What did I just say that was not eminently reasonable and measured?

"I believe she is innocent until proven guilty beyond a reasonable doubt," I reply. "Isn't that what we're all here for? The jury at the time concluded she was murdered by a person or persons unknown. Nothing further was done following that verdict. The police believed she was guilty of an insurance scam, either that or she had somehow gone loopy, which seems to have inspired a lack of activity. In effect, the young woman was posthumously placed on trial for fraud, and when she was found not guilty the case was closed. Let us see if we agree."

"Have they ever revisited the case?" Peter asks. "The police, I mean? Reopened the files, taken another look?"

"Not to my knowledge. They have had little incentive to do so, even given new technology. To bounce your earlier question back at you, what would *they* have gained? The Chief Constable of the Northumberland Constabulary, whose acquaintance awaits you, remained in post for almost five years afterwards, and would certainly have gained nothing. Conceivably, quite the reverse."

Bradon Young has been looking thoughtful. "I'm not sure," he says. "What could I contribute? I mean, this is an ocean and a century and a whole context removed from me. You guys will enjoy picking through the history and the area and the people. I may as well be from Mars."

"But is that so?" I ask him. "You came here to learn about those very same unknown quantities. You are an upright, law-abiding citizen who deplores injustice, aren't you? Who dislikes secrets and I imagine enjoys the challenge of a mystery? Consider it another mission, Bradon, if you will. We need as many perspectives as we can muster. I think you may pick up on things that others of us might take for granted."

"Hmm," Bradon says, and smiles. "The jury's out on that one."

"Will anyone in Otterburn still be interested?" Sven asks. "Or will anything we do be seen as interference? An intrusion? Isn't there an English phrase about letting sleeping dogs lie?"

"There is," I tell him. "Only I suspect this dog has never truly fallen asleep. Maybe it never will. I don't know how the villagers of Otterburn will view it, and of course we will need to be circumspect and treat people considerately. But I do believe there is a hangover of distrust in that community about the law and the police, mitigated somewhat by the work of Joe Carroll, a village 'bobby' who came along after the event and to whom I noticed a memorial seat has since been erected, but old grievances and perceptions die hard. And there is still the sight, for parishioners, of Evelyn Foster's headstone, and her family's plot, as one of the first things they see on climbing the steps of the lych-gate each Sunday." I direct a smile to Bradon. "There are other churches, but I guess this is the main one, although it's far from Latter-Day Saints."

"I'm intrigued," Frances Wentworth says finally. "Like Peter, I'm intrigued as to why you've selected this old case, but I must say I'm more intrigued by the case itself. I'm trying hard to be objective, but feel very sorry for this poor girl. Whatever happened out on those moors, and why, it must have been a dreadful way to die." She shivers. "To burn to death, and take all night to do it."

"I have to confess a personal interest," I tell her, deciding to come clean, "although not a very strong one. Of the dormant variety." I briefly take them through my recent visit to Otterburn and of my father's retelling of the Evelyn Foster story all those years ago in the hotel bar.

"Nevertheless," I add, "I believe the case has a number of interesting aspects—legal, criminological, cultural, historical and social, to name a few, and maybe psychological too—and I would not have suggested it had I felt it would be sterile ground." I look at each of them in turn. "Do you need more time to think it over?"

There is a pause.

"Let's give it a go," Sven says. "I'm sold. I'd like to see this village, the hotel you stood outside."

The others nod their heads, Bradon not altogether enthusiastically.

"To start with, we need to read the background documents you've got listed here," Peter says. "Will we have the weekend to do it?"

"Yes," I tell them, looking at my notes. "I should explain, lest you think I was being lavish, the background material, with one exception, was not expensive to acquire. The exception was an unlisted item, the Inquest Report, which will be available to you also. It *was* quite expensive so, like the Kindle document, unless you're inclined to piracy, you will need to take turns in reading it. Your personal copies of the rest are here."

"What is NARPO?" Sven does not like acronyms.

"The National Association of Retired Police Officers," I reply.

Frances snorts delicately. "Which may begin to explain Mr Dixon's alternative view."

You see what I meant about sharp?

"Now, Frances," I admonish her. "Let's not make any premature assumptions, please. For all we know at this stage, any of these learned writers could be correct. All they have been able to do is hypothesise. None were present in Otterburn at the time. Only Mr Dixon has had access to the same material as us. Goodman, Symons and others did not survive the 75-year disclosure rule. Goodman's book, written in the mid-1970s, is based around interviews he was able to conduct with people who knew something and were still alive. As such, he may arguably have had an advantage over everyone, as I think you will find that the Inquest Report is precisely as limited as the inquest itself."

She will not let go. "But apparently one or two of the sources have been paid by the police, or one of their mouthpieces, to write about it."

"That is an assumption," I repeat. "And this is a community which has had its fair share of violent crime in recent times. Enough to occupy any crime writer seeking to make an honest living for a year or two."

"In what way?" Peter asks. "There's been more? Are we to spend this whole term—sorry, Bradon, *semester*—physically and metaphorically in the wild and lonely moors of north Northumberland?"

"No, you are not. I'm thinking of another case, a couple of years before Goodman's book first hit the shelves. This one isn't cold, far from it; the culprits were brought to justice. But it demonstrates that while Otterburn is a small, relatively remote community, it has never been cut off from the outside world and its accoutrements; in this case, the large military establishment on its doorstep. It also serves to illustrate, if we needed it, that not everything is always as it seems."

I pause to collect my thoughts. "In 1974 the Percy Arms had a porter, a Walter Mitty character who called himself Sean O'Conaill. His real name was Pepperdine, later changed to Burton. He claimed IRA links; that he'd ascended to the rank of captain in that organisation. He enjoyed provoking the squaddies at Otterburn Army Camp, who in those days treated the hotel as a local, by broadcasting Irish rebel songs over the PA system and generally sneering at them. Then things got out of hand. In the early hours of April 8, 1974 he and a couple of accomplices — a fellow worker at the hotel, Charles Kane, and a Camp employee, Barry Reid — paid a visit to the Camp and knocked on the door of Lt Col John Stevenson's house. They had been heard earlier in the hotel conspiring to commit murder. The commandant, who had been asleep with his wife, answered the door and was met by three bullets, one of them through his heart. He died almost instantly. O'Conaill returned to his room at the hotel, liberally decorated with IRA posters and anti-British slogans, reloaded his Webley pistol and sat back to await the arrival of the law. When it appeared, he began blazing away and succeeded in wounding two unarmed police officers before they overpowered him."

"So these men were known to everyone and caught," Frances says. "And presumably also tried and sentenced? And this was the mid-1970s, so no capital punishment."

"No; they must have been relieved to have escaped death by hanging, if only by a few years. Not that it did O'Conaill much good. He protested that the shooting had been an accident and he hadn't intended to kill the colonel. Kane claimed the plan had been only to kidnap him. Both were found guilty of murder and were jailed for life. Reid, who had knocked back a dozen pints of beer and several brandies that evening, protested he had only gone along for the ride. He was found guilty of manslaughter and jailed for five years. But as things turned out, O'Conaill served only three years of his sentence. In October 1977 he died of cancer in Parkhurst prison on the Isle of Wight. All of which, apart from anything else, serves to demonstrate that there will always be those who take their prejudices and half-baked beliefs way beyond the limits that society finds acceptable."

"That makes me feel a whole lot better," Bradon says.

"How?" I must be losing my touch. It shouldn't have been a story to make anyone feel good.

"Well, it's not unlike the Wild West, is it? Home from home."

"But it would have been traumatic for the colonel's wife," Frances points out after the chortles have subsided. "Not to mention people in the hotel. As it would have been years before," she adds, "for the Fosters and their friends."

I nod. "The commandant's wife had the small comfort of seeing her husband's killers receive a just sentence. She may have wished the law hadn't been changed, but at least O'Conaill and Kane were put away. And even that small comfort escaped the Fosters."

"Umm…we still have it in Utah, you know," Bradon says. "The death penalty, I mean. By firing squad, too."

"Barbaric," Frances tells him.

"Arguably effective," Bradon replies. "Even with liberal gun laws. No chance of changing them, the NRA being what it is. But bad as they are, how much worse could things get without the death penalty?"

"I think you can all discuss that at your leisure," I interject. "In the meantime, enjoy reading this stuff and we'll pick it up from here next week. I'll check your timetables and choose a day we can head north."

"Not in the dodgy TR6, please," Peter says. "It couldn't cope."

Cheeky blighter. I saw him surreptitiously admiring it a month ago. He was actually running his hands over the wings, like some sort of aspiring lover.

"I'll do my best to find something more reliable and comfortable," I tell him.

"The police in this Foster case seem not to have reached a standard of mediocrity, let alone excellence," he comments.

Of course, he wants to get straight into it. Patience is not among Peter's strong points. Authority is there to be shot at; eye-witnesses are there to be doubted; witnesses of all descriptions are there to be put through the wringer. I don't intend this case study should divert them from other work between our sessions, but Peter is liable to behave like a shock trooper and will want it solved tomorrow.

"I'd prefer it if we all read the stuff thoroughly before we have any fuller discussion," I tell him. "Let's leave our assessment of the police, and indeed everyone else, until we have read the various documents."

"Do you think any usable items of evidence will still be held in cold storage?" Peter also has an irrepressible tendency towards persistence. No doubt it will pay him many dividends.

"Perhaps, but we'll need to check. There are several points to consider. First, we have a time constraint on this study. Second, there may exist boxes or files of bits and pieces, including notes, somewhere in police archives, but their usability remains to be seen. The care taken today would not have been practiced to the same extent then, and it's possible, given the way in which the crime scene was managed, that any such articles would have been compromised eighty hours after the event, let alone eighty years. Third, the Chief Constable was very clear that he could not accept the inquest jury's verdict; you will have this view confirmed the more you read. In that sense, the police may not even have classed the case as 'cold' or 'unsolved'. Fourth, if any items still exist, they'll be those found at the scene and listed in what you've read, plus notes of police interviews. The former will comprise parts of Evelyn's clothing or car accessories; the car itself is long gone. Nothing was found that may have belonged to a third party, no fingerprints were lifted, DNA profiling was five decades away. But with all that said, we will become acquainted during this study with another case from long ago; the case of Alfred Rouse. He was hanged in 1931, two months after Evelyn died, for an arson murder in Northants, having been arrested on 7 November 1930, a day after the killing. Given the similarity of the crimes, there have been suggestions that his methodology may have indirectly impinged on Evelyn's death; we shall see. Rouse's victim in this so-called 'Blazing Car Murder' remains unknown, but mitochondrial DNA from a microscope slide over 80 years old was used in 2014 to prove it could *not* have been a man called William Briggs, whose family had asked for help as part of their ancestry research. They were disappointed, but my point is that in *Rouse* small tissue samples were taken at the time by Bernard Spilsbury, an eminent pathologist, and later stored in London Royal Hospital's museum. Whilst the same care may not have been taken in the Foster case, it serves to illustrate the strides science has taken, and I understand the scientific team is hopeful that the Rouse victim's real family can still be found through missing person records. For mtDNA to work, an unbroken maternal line of ancestors is needed, but the case shows what can now be achieved given the availability of uncontaminated samples."

Peter begins to speak again; another thought, another probe.

I interject quickly: "I think we should leave it there for today. I'm sure there will be a great deal more to talk over when we have read what's in front of us and thought it through."

He grins. "Your wish is our command, Master." He looks over at Frances. "Unless Fran wants first bite at it, could I have a look at the Kindle piece?"

He can be a gentleman too, when the mood takes him.

CHAPTER FOUR

The road to Otterburn
The present day, 22 January

For an outlay of a bottle of Jack Daniel's, I have been able to acquire a Vauxhall Zafira from a colleague for the day, provided it is returned washed and vacuumed. Which is to say, in better condition than now.

The Newcastle outer suburbs and Ponteland receding behind us, we are approaching a stage of practical research. And we are lucky; it is nine o'clock on a beautiful clear morning. Bradon, Sven and Peter are in the back, chatting back and forth; Frances is in the front passenger seat, an OS Explorer Map spread on her lap, which for me carries the advantage of being able to admire her knees. We are travelling through gently-treed pasture and arable land, and she tells me we are two miles from Belsay.

"I found the Dixon book tough going," I overhear Sven say. "Even allowing for Kindle's eccentricities, he has an uneasy relationship with punctuation. My English teacher would…well, it was as hard as reading Kerouac's *On the Road*, and Kerouac's style was his own. Still, Dixon had an argument which may or may not stand up to scrutiny. What I would say, from reading all the material, is that calculations of times and distances are crucial, and even in this basic respect the police can't be trusted. Unless I'm reading it wrong, our good Inspector Russell had a distance of one mile 1503 yards from Foster's Garage to Elishaw, and I measured it on a map at over two miles. Has the road shrunk since 1931?"

Peter laughs. "I noticed that. You're right about times and distances, though. We have to do our own, and accurately."

I slow down to forty, to the annoyance of a Mercedes-Benz SLK behind me, and say to everyone, "We can be accurate within tolerances. For example, and for understandable reasons, Evelyn was not precise as to how far through Belsay she got before she decided, or was asked or forced, to turn around. As the police were not at all interested, we'll have to assume the southern edge of the village. Does anyone have any theories about why this man, assuming there was a man, may have decided at this point he wanted to turn back?"

"Let's call him Bowler," Frances suggests. "It's easier than to keep saying 'this man' or 'the stranger.' He did apparently wear a bowler."

"He saw the bright lights of the city ahead," Sven says. "Or at least a glow on the horizon. What would the city have looked like from twelve miles away in those days? Would there have been much of a glow?"

"Probably a lightening of the sky," Frances says. "Not as much as today, given urban expansion and less street-lighting. But here's a fact I looked up: starting as far back as 1879 in Mosley Street, Newcastle was one of the first cities in the world to be fully lit up."

"You don't say?" Bradon's surprise is evident. "Well, in that case we can certainly assume some visible glow, especially on a clear, hard, frosty evening. And we've come how far, Sven? You said twelve miles?"

"Sex or money," Peter says, musing on my original question. "Or Evelyn poked her nose in where it wasn't welcome. I wonder if the fellow couldn't cough up the fare…no, that doesn't make sense. He'd just have battered her and got out, preferably somewhere he could quickly get lost. In which case he'd have journeyed on to Ponteland or into the city, wouldn't he? And she had money in her purse when she was found, although not enough to suggest he'd already paid up. 35p short I made it, near enough twenty quid in today's money. And why was the purse lying a yard behind the car? Hmm…not money then; sex. Not to get too far ahead of the game, but he'd have seen enough secluded spots coming down this road. He may even have *known* the road. By the time they reached Belsay, he may have realised he was running out of them."

"Maybe that's why all of a sudden he wanted to drive," Frances says "and he'd have been in a small minority in those days with that particular skill. Do you think the continual smoking was a symptom of anxiety? Gearing himself up? Chatting her up about where he lived and owning a car? Or would that just have been normal conversation?"

"It could have been either," Bradon says. "Is this the township?"

"Yes," I reply. I pull into a junction, a road leading off left to Belsay Hall and Castle, and flick the trip metre to zero. "We could be hundreds of yards out either way, certainly back the way we've come, but this is as good a place to start as any. If she reached Belsay as she said, she would need to find somewhere to turn around. This could have been it."

"Good thinking, Kemo Sabe," Peter says.

"Aw, you're just too good, you guys," Bradon says in a Texan drawl. "Tryin' to make me feel at home again. Shucks."

He is rewarded again by unanimous laughter.

"How would this road have been in those days?" Sven asks as I wait for a gap in traffic and pull back onto it.

"Not too different," I tell him, trundling along at a steady 25 mph. "A few bumps and bends straightened out, not too smooth, wider here and there, but basically the same route. That will apply to everywhere we go today. No dual carriageways in these parts, not then, not now. And no cat's eyes then either, not even intermittently."

As we are going, I explain that without making a complete nuisance of myself to other road users I will try to maintain this pace to Wolf's

Nick. If I have to pull in occasionally, so be it; this will reduce our average speed but our intention is to match as nearly as possible Evelyn Foster's journey those decades ago, and not go much faster than she may have done. That said, she was no timid learner driver and the Hudson Super-Six was no jalopy. It was the latest pride and joy of its designer and manufacturer, a 1928 model (a precious few still get wheeled out today), a big, powerful car with a rating of 29.4 horsepower. It had a top speed of 65 mph and strong headlight beams. She would not have been travelling at anything like top speed in conditions close to freezing, but she would not have needed to chug along at 10 mph either.

As Peter has pointed out, our first task is no more or less than a time and distance study. The police and others have questioned whether Evelyn Foster could have made the journey she described; it is the first thing we need to take a view on.

We chat about this and that as we go, the students' attention focussed at this stage on the Hudson Super-Six and its driver. By now, of course, they have all read the background documents.

The Hudson's advertising puffs at the time (okay, we know about advertising people) claimed *a brilliancy of performance, an ability beyond anything heretofore known.* You, the lucky driver, will *pick up faster and level hills with ease.* You will *scarcely encounter a situation to tax its limit of power.*

While Henry Ford is credited with giving the world the affordable (black) car, it was the Essex company which brought the enclosed sedan within reach of the populace. The Super-Six was a natural progression; Essex, dissolved in 1922, was in fact a wholly-owned entity of the Hudson Motor Company of Detroit. By 1929 Hudson had been making cars for two decades, had factories in England and Belgium, and occupied third place in U.S. sales behind Ford and Chevrolet. They weren't novices in the game.

And neither was Evelyn. An experienced driver (at that point she had driven half her life), she was much in demand. She had her own regular customers. She took local ministers to and from their churches on Sundays (those that had them: the Revivalists made do with open fields). She transported soldiers who detrained at Knowesgate north to Otterburn Camp and vice versa. She introduced a 'share-a-fare' principle, taking people to and from the Memorial Hall for village hops and jumble sales and whist drives, and to and from Newcastle for shopping or 'the flicks', or shows at the Theatre Royal. She took local children onto the moors for summer picnics free of charge, played games with them and plied them with 'pop' and biscuits. A popular girl, fair- or mousy-haired, inclined to plumpness and with a quiet smile, she worked a seven-day week and — without exaggeration — loved her cars, and especially American cars. She could happily talk for hours about them. Since her father's present of a 'tin Lizzie' Ford about eight years earlier, when Dr Miller of Bellingham, her local GP, had advised her to get more fresh air after a spell of anaemia after a dental operation, she had owned a Buick, a Dodge, an Overland and an Essex. She was a progressive young lady, as young ladies of her day were increasingly tending to become. The world, as ever, was changing and after the Great War, through the Roaring Twenties and women's enfranchisement, the changes seemed to be coming thick and fast. Not always, it must be said, to the liking of their elders and betters. Or, come to that, the opposite sex.

At 25 mph it feels as if we are crawling, and it is not long before a truck appears in the rear mirror. I pull into a lay-by near Ferney Chesters.

"I've really taken to this girl," Frances says. "I'm trying hard to keep an open mind, but every instinct I've got says she is genuine and likeable. It's already becoming difficult to imagine her deciding on a whim to destroy one of the vehicles she took so much pleasure in, to become a fraudster. *Why* would she do such a thing?"

"People can get driven into situations," Peter says. "They can let pressure get to them, step out of character. Go temporarily crazy and do unaccountable things."

"There is nothing in her character or recent history to suggest it," Frances says. "I realise it can happen, but surely her family, the passengers she picked up from the bus, would have noticed a change in her behaviour. She spent some time chatting to Mrs Mary Murray at Birdhopecraig, a minute or two anyway. In all we've read, she was behaving perfectly normally that evening."

"It's going to get difficult if we begin to hop about from place to place," Sven says. He taps me on the shoulder. "How do you intend we structure this study, Matthew?"

It's a good question and I'm glad someone has asked it.

We are now showing 8.3 miles from Belsay and I pull in to a turn-off near Kirkwhelpington and switch off.

"I think you're right," I tell him. "We have to try to be as logical and sequential as we can. I'm aiming first, today, to get our geography right and get to know the area a little, so we all know where key points like the garage and house, Elishaw, Raylees, Wolf's Nick and so on lie. I thought we could concentrate on two aspects: the village itself and the first part of Evelyn's journeyings that evening, the part between the Foster garage and where she dropped Mrs Murray off and her drive back to Otterburn. As the next stage, Stage Two if you will, apart from measuring distances today, we could look at the rest of her final journey; the drive from Otterburn to Belsay, and back to Wolf's Nick. See how her story stacks up there. In each case, for each leg, we would pick up on the statements made by witnesses and see how *they* stack up. We would then, in Stage Three, move on to the police's involvement, including their interview with her, what they did or did not do at the scene, their canvassing of witnesses and how their assessment of the case developed. Then, in Stage Four, we'll review the inquest proceedings and what we can learn from them, including the *dramatis personae*. Finally, in Stage Five, we come to our own thoughts, theories, hypotheses and so on. Our conclusions."

Peter says, "It sounds okay, nice and tidy, but it might be difficult to achieve in practice."

"Discipline, dear boy, discipline," Bradon says in his best BBC.

We have a chuckle at him, and I start the car again and turn.

"About three miles to Wolf's Nick," I tell them, moving onto a temporarily traffic-free A696. "It should be our next stop, but please register the hamlet of Knowesgate as we pass. With luck, there'll be some kind of lay-by we can use nearer the site."

"I'm pretty sure there is," Peter says. "There's a turn-off just short, up to a farm called Catcherside, and another track leading towards Wolf Crag and overlooking Wolf's Nick. Gated, I think. Both on the right as we go. Local knowledge," he adds modestly.

"I see them both on here," Frances says, spreading out a second Explorer Map, half on her lap, half spreading up the door. "How on earth do people manage these things, hiking, in rain or a gale?"

"They bring them pre-folded, dear," Peter says. "In designed plastic sleeves. Practice and preparation make perfect."

"Huh."

"This is Knowesgate," I tell them, as Frances seems to have lost her battle with the map and with Peter.

I improvise and pull into a lay-by opposite the Inn to let half-a-dozen vehicles, which seem to have been lying in wait, to overtake. There is still pastureland to east and west, a few sheep grazing, one or two arable fields, the land rising to our right. "You called Belsay a township, Bradon," I add. "What would you call this?"

"Umm…a motel?"

"A recently refurbished English roadside inn," I tell him. "And one which has been variously rated in the past by its clientele."

"Very nice," he says. "It has character." He's a true gent.

"We're talking British tourism here," Peter says. "God forbid we should aspire to anything like excellence. It would cause us work, bring floods of tourists and embarrass the competition."

"Have you been inside the place?" I ask him.

"No."

"Then I'd say you aren't qualified to comment."

This shooting off at the mouth, tweeting, twittering, blogging, call it what you will, friends, is not entirely a twenty-first century invention, but it has indisputably become an ego-driven rash, and is unpleasantly short on depth or dignity. It joins 'selfies' in my personal dustbin, and I will do my best not to stand for it with this bunch.

I wait for a gap and pull out again. Now, as the road rises, we can see the pasture segueing into the browns and ochres of moorland. We pass Raechester Farm on our right and the track to Catcherside running alongside a mature belt of conifers.

"Keep going." Frances is map-reading. "Not far now."

And there, on either side, are the low sandstone bluffs I recall seeing before, the grass verges at one time strewn with boulders that the motor mechanic who examined Evelyn's car said had scratched the underside of its running board. But I'm getting ahead of myself…

"There," Peter says, pointing. "Pull in across the road, to that gate."

I check in the mirror and pull over, facing the moors. Or more accurately, in the Northumbrian and southern Scots tongue, the *moss* or peat bog. There is an expansive area in front of us, shaped vaguely like a shallow saucer; some woodland added, but much as old photographs seem to suggest. It looks spongy rather than waterlogged, a few gullies cutting across, a long rectangular plantation of conifers snaking its way up a rise in the land northwards. More greenery, rough grazing, is visible in the distance where Ottercops Farm sits on a hillside protected by more belts of trees. Ottercops masts poke skywards above and beyond them.

There is nothing now to suggest, even to hint, at wrongdoing or tragedy or menace in this barren land. How could there be, after so long?

"Wolf's Nick," I say. "There's the bend in the road, although there are scrub hawthorn bushes obscuring it now, and right over there ahead of us is where the Hudson came to rest. Wolf Crag is to our right."

Wolf Crag is certainly visible up the curving dirt track beyond the gate and some stunted silver birches; a stark low escarpment, with rocks that look as if they haven't changed for millennia, and topped with heather. The effect is like a sleeping dinosaur, made more so as the rocks are glistening in the sunlight as though wet. Maybe there has been a recent shower; in this part of the world, they've been known to appear out of a cloudless sky.

We all pile out. There is just a trace of mist over the trees, a score of cattle grazing in the distance, rooks in erratic flight above them.

"Well," Frances says, "this brings it all to life. Into 3D anyway. So, this is where she was burned. Left to die like a diseased *animal* or worse." Between her and Peter, I think the authorities are in for a savaging.

"How far on the trip meter?" Sven asks me. "Did you notice?"

"Just over 11 miles from the south end of Belsay," I tell him.

"In less than half-an-hour," he says. "Average 20 to 25 mph with stops. On a more or less flat, quite straight road, a gentle curve here and there, probably not greatly changed in its alignment from then until now. A few rough edges taken off, a better surface, cat's eyes installed." He takes a beat. "So at about the same speed, to be here at quarter to nine in the evening, manoeuvre off the road, set the car alight as the Harwood shepherd saw, they would have needed to leave Belsay at 8.05 or 8.10 pm. How is my maths? Sorry, Bradon, *math*."

"They're fine," Bradon tells him. "But that's for another day, right?"

"Yes," I say, "but notice the land dips down from the road. It did then by all accounts, but the fencing is more recent."

I give them five minutes to take it all in, Peter and Frances walking with me down the road a little way, Sven and Bradon plunging over the moss. I've been told that the area around Wolf Crag holds a nice array of rock art; rings, concentric circles and cups that would have been carved on a prehistoric route in Neolithic or Bronze Age times, maybe 5000 years ago, give or take, with ancient burial sites nearby. Sven mentions them when he and Bradon return, but is dissuaded by the others from pursuing it. The carvings have been there a long time and will keep for another day. I wonder how many enthusiasts of the old rock carvings realise there used to be a crime scene a few hundred yards away. Certainly, nothing seems to mark that particular site.

But then I suppose all of us walk within a few hundred yards of old crime scenes most days of our lives and don't realise it. Rather like that old story featuring the proximity of rats (which I suppose may be true).

"Difficult walking," Bradon says. "It looks flat enough from here, quite easy going, but there are ditches and mounds and hollows all over. Ten times worse if it's wet, I guess."

Then we drive on, another quite flat stretch of road, through rough pasture and moorland punctuated by geometric conifer plantations, to Ottercops masts. I tell them as we pass that the two large masts (if not a smaller third one) were part of the Chain Home radar air defence system developed in the Second World War. It was this station that first detected Rudolf Hess's Messerschmitt as he flew solo on his peace-broking mission over the Northumbrian coast to crash-land on Eaglesham moor near Glasgow. Today, the masts are used for telecommunications, which carries with it the sobering thought that potentially this may be their least benign purpose yet.

We descend the hill, a dark and deathly conifer wood to our left, rough grazing to our right, through an 'S' bend, to Ravenscleugh and

Raylees. I pull into a junction leading north to Elsdon and cut the engine. Temporarily, the flow of traffic has eased. Outside the car the only sounds are the chirping of birds. A cock robin in particular is making a racket, no doubt a territorial matter.

"15 miles from just south of Belsay," I tell them. "Excluding stops, we've done it in thirty-six minutes, an average of 25 mph. I think this is key. Evelyn's round trip from here to Belsay and back to Wolf's Nick would have been twenty-six miles or so, if we were right with our starting point. She was seen by a bus driver right here at 7.22 pm, and her burning car by our Harwood shepherd at 8.45 pm. Eighty-three minutes, less time for stops and manoeuvring. The only problem section, especially at zero degrees, would have been the bends and climb from here to Ottercops. But that would have been only two of the twenty-six miles."

"And being knocked about and set on fire by Bowler," Frances adds. "That would have occupied several minutes."

"Quite," I tell her. "But these are two timings in all we have read which seem to have been accepted by everyone. Let's move on."

I put the Zafira in first and we head for Otterburn, occasional haunt of at least one of my forefathers.

CHAPTER FIVE

Otterburn village
The present day, 22 January

Five minutes and 2.5 miles later we are parked in the forecourt of the
Percy Arms, having negotiated the severest bend on our journey at
Monkridge Hall. Sven, who may well be correct, has pointed out it would
probably have been much the same eight decades ago, simply because of
the existence (short of a compulsory purchase order) of an immoveable
object, the gable end of the house, up against the roadside.

It is time to stretch our legs.

The village of Otterburn is two-thirds of a mile from east to west—
excluding its First School (*Be Happy, aim high and achieve your full potential*),
another two-thirds of a mile on towards Elishaw. But this detachment, I
believe, is a historical accident rather than a local authority attempt to
make life difficult. The property in which the school buildings now sit
was owned in the mid-nineteenth century by a man who reputedly began
to offer impromptu lessons to the children of the village. With the advent
of compulsory primary schooling, the choice of a school site seems to
have been a no-brainer. Otterburn First School officially dates from 1872.

The main road through the village, the A696, would have existed in
Evelyn Foster's time and long before. The Percy Arms itself was a
staging-post for the 'Chevy Chase' coach and others rattling along the
Newcastle-Jedburgh road. But many buildings by the roadside have
changed or gone. What would *not* have existed in Evelyn Foster's time is
Brierley Gardens, a group of post-war houses on the north side of the
main road next to St John's Church, once an important part of Reverend
Brierley's ministry. Neither would a newer and bigger estate which has
developed as an extension of Brierley Gardens off the road leading up to
Otterburn Hall, a neo-Elizabethan building built in 1870 as a country
retreat for Lord James Douglas and due to go under the auctioneer's
hammer. (By the bye, it sold during our case study for £300,000).

In the 1930s the great majority of Otterburn's residents would have
lived on both sides of the main road. Today, the great majority live in the
newer estates, but we are talking only of 450 or so in the whole village.

I explain this to my four colleagues as we stand outside the Percy
Arms and tell them we need to focus on the main road frontage only. Not
even the Hall, a half mile north and detached from the village, had any
part to play in the events of January-February 1931. And Otterburn Mill,
just south of the village beside the River Rede, had no part either, save the

provision of three jurors and some items of Evelyn's clothing, which if nothing else suggests she was a young woman of sensible tastes.

Bradon's attention has got no further than the hotel; he is looking at it in bemusement and shaking his head. I'm sure there are buildings as bad or worse in the States, but maybe he is surprised to see one here.

"Yes," I say to him. "This was once a fine hotel, but much changed since the Foster family lived here. Then, it was a hotel and village pub alongside a row of three cottages with a low curved wall in front. The cottages were later absorbed into the one structure. And now…"

"A demolition job?" He seems almost worried about it.

"With luck, not quite as bad as that, not yet. There may be a white knight in the offing, you never know."

"He will need to be a very wealthy white knight," Bradon says. "A major lottery winner. Or a local Donald Trump." He grimaces.

Sven meanwhile is peering at a small plaque on the wall, halfway up window height near the original front door. The Otter Burn is a small stream, its headwaters in the bleak uplands of Greymare Rigg five miles north, but from time to time it has made its presence felt.

"My word," he says. "Half the houses in the village must have been under water. That little stream caused *this*?"

He is pointing at the Otter Burn. The plaque reads '*High Water Mark of the Great Flood in Otterburn on Sunday night 9 June 1907.*'

"Nearly as far as the Butterchurn Guest House," I nod up the street, where the road rises. "It's another new arrival since Evelyn's day. The Co-op, which has gone but features quite heavily in her story, used to be about there, opposite the churchyard. But before we walk up, note the bridge over the Otter. It does feature in Evelyn's story as the place where she said she picked up Bowler the second time, bound as she thought to Ponteland. Some trees have grown and some have gone, but you will find them referred to as their possible meeting-point."

We wander onto the bridge, which is no more than a few yards wide. Further down, back the way we have come, the Border Reiver Store sits on the roadside—another much changed property since Evelyn's day, and one no doubt given a boost by the closure of the Co-op. Indeed, it may have helped precipitate that closure, but long live competition.

"And that, one assumes, was Northumbrian police headquarters, pro temps?" Peter asks, indicating the Tower/Castle sitting splendidly in its tree-lined grounds. He sniffs. There is a scent of rotten leaves in the air.

"Yes," I reply. "The incident room, or rooms. There are tales that some policemen used to get literally lost in the place and the head gardener, our jury foreman George MacDougall, had to search them out."

"There's a well-known American phrase that seems to cover it,"

Bradon says. "It begins, 'they couldn't find' and then goes on to feature a part of the anatomy and 'both hands.' But as there's a lady present…"

Frances laughs with the rest of us. "Lady, maybe," she says, "but not a shrinking violet."

We turn back and walk the length of the Percy Arms forecourt. Across a gap which leads through to a yard and the defunct care home (with which I don't intend to bother them or depress myself further) there sits the Village Memorial Hall, first built in 1923 (and now tastelessly extended) to commemorate the lives of the nine local servicemen who lost their lives in the Great War—and those who served and survived. A tenth name, a fatality of World War II, has been added alongside. But it is also a Hall which in early 1931 held an irresistible allure for the world's press.

"Ah," Peter says. "The scene of the second crime."

"Hear, hear," Frances says. "And the third."

I truly believe that if Chief Constable Fullarton James and his troops were alive and present today, they would stand in grave danger of becoming the objects of citizens' arrests from these two. I need to try to get them back on level ground, metaphorically, or this case study will be seriously compromised before it properly gets under way. I assume they are talking of criminal negligence and perverting the course of justice, but I simply cannot allow that to happen.

I turn to face them, and wait for a truck to thunder by. "No, Peter. Please do *not* go there. You will both need to approach this task more responsibly. Please remember what I said at our first meeting about the need for fairness, circumspection and transparency. If you persist in jumping to conclusions before we have sifted thoroughly through all we need to sift, I will withdraw your participation. I would regret that, but not nearly as much as you might."

Peter smacks his hand. "My apologies, Lord and Master," he says.

"No," Frances says. "You are right, Matthew. Not good enough. We apologise sincerely."

Somewhat mollified, I relent. "I cannot stop you talking about this case in your own time, in fact I welcome it. But you will diminish any effectiveness it has for you and the people of this village—to *history*, if that is not too high-flown—if you do not properly analyse it, warts and all. Remember Poirot, and please use the little grey cells."

"Who ees theese Poirot, s'il vous plait?" asks Bradon innocently.

I am beginning to appreciate Bradon Young.

Peter tries not to laugh. Frances cracks up. We start walking again. I'm intrigued to see that Bradon has donned a tweed cap, of a type that could well have come from Otterburn Mill, and is doffing it to the few people, especially the ladies, we meet. They clearly enjoy it (from which you can assume that feminism hasn't yet reached absurd lengths in this part of the world), and I'm delighted he has taken on board my words about courtesy. No doubt it's his usual standard of behaviour, only I haven't seen the cap before. I think it's quite fetching.

"The houses on our opposite side," I tell them, "must be much as they were, some pebbledash aside, but they aren't of great importance to us; that is, until we reach the church. We are passing what used to be the Post Office and Lloyd's Bank, where Stanley Potts, a jury member and the sub-postmaster, was based. Unfortunately, Otterburn seems to have escaped the latest government edict that the last bank in a village should remain. As far as I know, the nearest banks are in Bellingham and Rothbury, nine and fifteen miles away. And there opposite us is the site of the bothy where Evelyn's boyfriend George Phillipson lived."

"There have been a lot of changes," Peter says. "And one wonders how many have been beneficial." He is still talking to me, thankfully, and I know there is no shortage of grey cells under that sleek black hair.

"There have," I tell him, "but maybe the most important buildings are still here. You've seen Otterburn Tower-cum-Castle, the Percy Arms and the Memorial Hall." I wave up the street. "We'll get to the others, but meantime here is another missing link. The Co-op used to stand here, George Sinclair's place of work."

"Ah, yes" Peter says. "Our jury member who should have been a witness but couldn't. Oh, to have been a fly in that jury room."

Frances gives me a quick smile and says, "Careful, Peter."

"But it's true, isn't it? As far as the inquest jury were concerned, they would have been privy to evidence in that room which would have far outweighed anything they heard in the formal proceedings. Here was a man who might actually have seen Bowler, as you call him, that night, one of three or four people excluding Evelyn herself. And only one of them, an indeterminate one at that, was called to give evidence."

"You are right, Peter," I tell him. "And I have no quarrel with that contribution except that it is premature. It belongs to Stage Two."

He grins. "You'll remember what I said about things being difficult to achieve in practice."

"To paraphrase Bradon, only if we are undisciplined."

"Touché," he says, and grins again. "Seriously, I will do my best."

I look right and left in the time-honoured way and lead them across the street. We walk through the gate and up the short flight of stone steps to the church, which in more ways than one has a central position in the village. On our right is a smart black-marble headstone with the name 'Foster' on its back. We walk around it to see an inscription to *Evelyn* and *Margaret Elizabeth* (who died much later, in 1979), *dear sisters of Dorothy.*

Then, in front of it, is a matching headstone to the Foster parents, Margaret (died 1951) and Joseph (died 1953). From which I assume that Dorothy herself may have gone on to make her own family and will be buried elsewhere. The rectangles of kerbing stones around both graves, visible in old photos, have been removed to facilitate grass-cutting and maintenance (or when Margaret was interred), but the headstones are as they were. Gordon's grave is beside his parents', along with his first wife.

We all stand in silence for a minute or so until Peter, to my astonishment, produces a single red rose from an inside coat pocket and lays it reverently on the base of the first headstone.

No one can follow that. No one attempts to.

I take them briefly inside the church, which is of a lofty arced design and I think is simply beautiful. Built of ashlar with a Lakeland slate roof, it is a creation of John Dobson, the architect who, among other splendid buildings, gave Newcastle Central Station, Beaufront Castle and Elsdon Square (destroyed in the 1960s) to posterity. The church's foundation stone was laid in 1855, it was dedicated in 1857 by the Lord Bishop of Durham and, like the Otter Burn bridge, is now a Grade II listed building. Before we leave I point out three internal features: the stained-glass windows of the sanctuary at its south end; the altar frontal with its high-relief wood carving of Leonardo da Vinci's Last Supper; and the original cross head of the Percy Cross in the porch. I tell them we may see more of the Cross during our travels, and hope Sven may be interested.

We stop in the graveyard to view the headstones of Howard Pease and his wife Marna, and also George Waddell of Otterburn Mill and some of his family members. Back down the steps we resume our walk up the road past the 'Millennium Green', with Brierley Gardens behind. On the way, I tell them that the Green is a small example of the way direct action can ruffle feathers; several years ago some residents descended on it with chainsaws and axes, making short work of clearing unkempt shrubbery that had been allowed to grow unchecked. This upset the Parish Council, not so much because the work had been done, but had been done without proper consultation with them.

Sven laughs. "Maybe it goes to show that a lot can be achieved if people ignore the sensitivities of government, big and small. Without breaking the law, of course," he adds.

"You are a closet revolutionary, Sven," I tell him.

"Oh, I wouldn't say closet exactly," he winks and smiles.

We have reached a road junction. The route to our right leads up the hill to the new housing estate and to Otterburn Hall. But in front of us is what used to be Foster's Garage, a diesel pump against its long side wall, and behind the main shed a host of Howard Snaith coaches.

"You will recall photos of this building in the background papers," I say. "One of an infant Evelyn and her parents and some employees, with two of what Joseph Foster, or rather his passengers, christened his 'blacking boxes.' What do you think?"

Joseph Foster's earlier vehicles, his blacking boxes, were so called because they were open-topped and habitually baptised their human cargo with dust and grime and fumes along the way. But by 1931 he had developed a much more sophisticated business. The garage, his buses and taxis and petrol sales, had made him, bar Otterburn Mill, the village's biggest employer. Both Mill and garage exist today, one at each end of the village, but both are under different ownership. Some of Snaith's services are recognisably those that were operated by Foster's, but the Mill is now more retail than manufacturing.

An entrepreneur from an early age, Joseph was born in 1874 in Haltwhistle, just south of Hadrian's Wall in the Tyne Valley. At age eleven he began selling bicycles before leaving to train as a mechanic at the Daimler factory in the Midlands. On his return north he worked as a groom in Hartley, near Whitley Bay, and married Margaret Gordon of New Hartley in 1899. Shortly afterwards, with their first child Gordon imminent, the young couple moved to High Rochester, five miles north of Otterburn, and then to Otterburn itself. At this point they joined the 25 percent of English families who then owned their own homes.

In 1904 Joseph embarked on his mission 'to bring the country to the town and the town to the country.' The blacking boxes were followed by other vehicles: by other cars, by buses (he had ten by the late 1920s), by wagons to transport agricultural machinery to farms and artillery to the Camp, and by taxis. The motor-repair side of his business grew, petrol sales were added. His growing workforce, including Ernest Primrose of Leith until his parting of the ways with Evelyn, was being drawn from a far wider area than Otterburn itself. The antiquarian Howard Pease of Otterburn Tower, a motor enthusiast and avid conversationalist, became a frequent visitor to the garage. In the late 1920s Foster's was an established and thriving motor business, a turntable operation, about to hit a pothole that would severely shake its equilibrium.

In all these endeavours Joseph had Margaret by his side, chivvying him along, encouraging him, doing the paperwork, dragging him when necessary from his hobby of breeding collies ('The Kennels' was appropriately named, although by a previous owner), and bringing up their growing family. All the children began to engage with the business before they left school. By 1931 Gordon was effectively the garage foreman and in charge of the buses, Evelyn was making the taxi business her own, Dorothy and young Margaret were working as conductresses.

And when it came to intermediaries or a need for mediation in this close-knit family—as when Gordon let rip at Foster employees (he had a tendency towards irascibility not shared with his father)—it was Evelyn in the workplace or her mother in the home who stepped into the breach. People appreciated this trait in 'Evie'. They called her friendly, pleasant, happy. They also knew her as an expert driver (she had learned to drive before she left school), a hard worker (she worked a seven-day week and filled in as a conductress, petrol pump attendant and office secretary when needed), and altogether as a quiet, generous but determined young woman. And her taxi clientele was catholic; soldiers, farmers, ministers, the local aristocracy, housewives, youngsters and working men.

"It's still recognisable," Frances says in some surprise. "Expanded, and without the original signage, but in much better condition than the Percy Arms. The basic shape and forecourt are still there."

"Yes, so we have at least one fixed point, two if we include the Percy Arms and bridge," I tell her. "And there, across the street, is the third."

I hear Bradon's intake of breath. "Oh, no. That's worse again."

We view The Kennels, the Foster family's old home set back from the road, two houses at right angles knocked into one by Joseph Foster. I think it comes as much of a shock to them as it did to me two weeks ago. There is a stillness here. Half the building is minus a roof; another section is patched with tarpaper. The windows are blocked up with plywood or hung with curtains, including what was Evelyn's bedroom, upper left as we look. They appear not to have been drawn or cleaned in decades. Another panel of raw plywood has been hammered over the top half of the front door. Ferns have colonised what used to be flower beds along the frontage, autumn's leaf-fall is still strewn over the front path and garden, the property's stone wall is festooned with moss and lichen. The wrought iron gate is rusted and, as we cross the road, we make out under a beech tree a lead-coloured plate over what must have been the intake of a fuel storage tank. Finches and coal tits and blue tits flit to and fro, clearly undisturbed by our presence as they forage for larvae and insects.

I understand none of us wants to walk down that short path. It would somehow feel like an invasion of privacy, and we would be able to see nothing anyway within those shrouded cobwebbed rooms.

The smell of wormy soil and mildew assails our nostrils, and then something more pleasant drifts to us from neighbouring houses down the street. Woodsmoke. A smell that conveys habitation, warmth.

"Of course," I say, "it's only speculation, but it looks very much like a house in which calamity has struck and no one is interested any longer in what happens to it or in taking it on as a dwelling. It looks positively haunted by its past, yet it must have been occupied, or at least in the

Foster's ownership, for many years after Evelyn died."

"It looks totally abandoned," Frances says. "Joyless." She purses her lips. "It goes to show how tragedy builds walls around families. Looking at it now, you have to hope there may have been some more prosaic reason for its dereliction. It's hard to believe how Goodman in his book describes Evelyn's room as neat and cheerful, with bric-a-brac, holiday souvenirs and ornaments set out on the mantelpiece and dressing-table and window-sill. And the climbing roses have gone. It looks like no one could have lived or loved or been happy in it at all. It's just so *bereft*."

"The walls, the basic structure," Peter says, "look sturdy enough. But open to the elements as it is, it would be a brave man who took it on."

"We don't know what harm has been done inside, with damp or dry rot," Sven says. "The lower stones and the course between the houses look very bad. It can only be its history that has caused this neglect."

"Or intestacy," Peter says. "Or the family want it left this way."

"Either is possible," I say. "But it is what it is, and what we are more concerned with is its past. It is the last of our markers in the village, so I think we should return to the car and take a drive further up the road to Elishaw and beyond, and then have some lunch."

"Please," Frances says. "This has been an eye-opener."

On the walk back, Sven asks if I will point out the site of the 1388 Battle of Otterburn, the second bloodiest of Northumbria's battles after Flodden Field, which occurred over a century later. I tell him there is debate among historians about the exact site, but I will show him the rest of the Percy 'Cross' (a dirk-shaped stone obelisk) which marks it. He tells me he has been fascinated by the Percy family, especially Henry 'Hotspur' Percy, son of the 1st Earl of Northumberland ('a compelling name for a young scholar,' he says) since reading Shakespeare. He clearly knows the main protagonists: the Scottish army under the command of the 2nd Earl of Douglas, and the English army under the command of Harry Hotspur assisted by his brother Sir Ralph, and he knows the battle was fought by moonlight. Although outnumbered, the Scots prevailed (with a loss of life of around 1:5) but lost their leader. It was an English defeat which in part has been put down to Henry Percy's rashness and volatility, traits which earned him his nickname. Despite being captured (he was to die leading the rebel army at the Battle of Shrewsbury in 1403) his ransom was paid largely out of the public purse and his reputation as a heroic warrior, with a little Shakespearian help, assured.

"It's an interesting thought," Sven says, "that in an area which has had more than its fair share of bloodshed, with maybe 2,000 killed in this battle alone, we should be looking at the death of one young woman."

"It's personal," Frances Wentworth says. "Or it's becoming so."

CHAPTER SIX

Elishaw and Birdhopecraig
The present day, 22 January

I worry a little about Frances's last comment, but let it pass. These students have been told ad nauseam that they must step back, assess their cases dispassionately, try not to become entangled. But this case study is about trying to find a pathway towards truth. It is not an occasion for strategy or witness grooming or the finer points of presentation, certainly not of 'spin.' And if Frances, for whatever reason, feels sufficiently fired up to probe to her analytical and emotional limits, then so be it.

Halfway to Elishaw (at Forster's Garage I have again turned the trip meter to zero) I point out to Sven the access path to the Percy Cross and tell him we will take a look on the way back.

"But here is the school," I say, "which is of interest because it has a connection with three characters in this story. One: George Maughan, a witness at the inquest, who apart from being assistant at the Co-op had a second job as a cleaner here and stoked the boilers on winter nights. Two: Miss Mary Ferry, the second teacher here, who might have been called as a witness as she allegedly saw Bowler at the Otter Burn bridge but, as Peter implied earlier, was not. Three: the headmaster, William Blackham, who also escaped the witness stand but who had some interesting if rather gossipy things to say about the car from which Bowler may have emerged at Elishaw; a junction which, incidentally, had a history as a gathering place for tinkers. Another connection was that Blackham's wife was the sister of George Sinclair, the Co-op manager, who as Peter also pointed out was not only a juror but an unused witness."

"At what point in these proceedings was the jury picked?" Frances asks. "Would it be before or after the police, or *prosecution*, produced their list of witnesses to the coroner?"

"I don't know," I reply. "It could be worthwhile to find out."

"You bet it would," she says.

"Even by 1931," Peter says, "coroner's juries were becoming rare animals. I believe the Coroner's Office would convene the jury and the police would provide a list of witnesses. The documents we've read refer to P.C. Fergusson acting as officer of the court, calling out the jurymen unaided because he knew them all. As the inquest first opened the day after Evelyn died, jury members would have been invited by, and sworn in, then. However, because the proceedings on that first day were limited in scope, the police would have the next month to draw up their list of witnesses. George Sinclair gave them his statement the day before he was sworn in. In fact, he gave it to the press, and made very sure everyone knew he was in no doubt as to what he had seen, and what he had seen was a stranger in shadow near the Post Office-cum-Lloyd's Bank shortly after 7.00 pm. *No one will shake me in that opinion*, he said, and we have to assume that strangers did not descend on Otterburn in battalions, then or now. He would either not at that stage have understood his evidence could not be taken, or his name did not register with the police. Or worse, they were happy to have him sidelined. And although by the time the main part of the inquest took place they had formed their own theory on how Evelyn had died—so *would* have been happy to have him sidelined if they hadn't thought of the damage he could do in the jury room—they had not done so on 8 January."

And there, if proof were needed, is proof of the quality of Peter Maxwell's mind. When he applies it constructively. "It is rather ironic, is it not," Peter continues, "that one of the main arguments against a coroner's jury system has always been that lay jury members would not be able to grasp the substance of the evidence, especially the medical evidence, they were hearing? That they would simply roll over and rubber-stamp whatever the coroner said?" He gives a wolfish smile. "I don't think Mr Coroner Dodds would have agreed with that argument, however much he'd have liked it to be true."

While Peter has been talking, I have pulled up on the verge just off Elishaw (*Ill-e-shaa*) Road Ends, an exposed and solitary place even today.

I tell him I'm delighted he is now properly refocused and address them all. I say we have travelled 2.1 miles from The Kennels. A bank of mist is forming over the River Rede valley to our left, and I'm beginning to fear the good visibility we've enjoyed so far may not last. We have travelled roughly parallel to the river's winding course since leaving the village and can now see it flowing under the Elishaw Bridge below us. The bridge is a few hundred yards down Dere Street, the Roman road known colloquially and for good reason as 'the switchback.'

The River Rede swings south at Otterburn, running through West Woodburn to Redesmouth where it flows into the North Tyne. Here, it snakes its way through a green valley between areas of rolling high moorland and blanket bog. The ranges of Otterburn Training Area, 60,000 acres where 30,000 British and NATO soldiers are trained each year to kill (and avoid being killed), lie to our right. We have reached the edge of the Northumberland National Park, which covers a quarter of the county and stretches from north of the Tyne Valley almost to the River Tweed. The area to our south and west is still called the Cheviot Hills, although here they are low-lying and will merge in a few miles into the dark expanse of

Kielder Forest. The Cheviot itself, and the main range of hills, is well to our north, invisible beyond the rising moorland even on a fine day.

"This, then," I say, "is where Evelyn, returning to Otterburn the way we have just come, said she first picked up Bowler as he emerged from a car and flagged her down. It could have been opportunism on his part, as there used to be an AA sentry box here which he claimed he intended to use. That aside, it's important to remember that this was a midwinter night, dark and cold but clear. There was no street-lighting in Otterburn in those days, let alone at Elishaw, and certainly no CCTV. Inevitably, this would have caused more than the usual problems for the police and eyewitnesses at various stages." I point across Frances. "Now, the road leading down to our left, the A68 from Edinburgh to Corbridge and the south, is where the car which dropped Bowler off continued its journey. Unless anyone can add to them, I think there are three main questions for us: first, why was he dropped off here? Second, where did the car from which he came then go? And third, who might have seen this exchange?"

"You can add the type of car and who was in it," Sven says.

"And exactly what time this exchange took place," adds Bradon.

"Excellent," I tell them. "And while we mull those questions over, I suggest we go on to the site of Birdhopecraig Hall, measure that distance, and enjoy some lunch in the Redesdale Arms on the way back."

"You have some real unwieldy names in this country," Bradon says. "Cottonshopeburnfoot, Mrs Murray's final destination, for instance."

"It's technically classed as two words," I tell him. "The 'Foot' is separate. Still, the longest single-word place name in England is not too far away in Kielder Forest. I give you 'Blakehopeburnhaugh.' Mind you, it's still a long way short of the one in Anglesey."

"Which is?" Peter asks, a glint in his eye.

"Pass." I start the engine again.

"Very wise," he says.

"To get back to the point," Frances says sharply, "there is only one reason why Birdhopecraig and Cottonshopeburnfoot should concern us here, and Blakehopeburnhaugh does not concern us at all. Evelyn met the bus from Hexham at 6.30 pm. Allow her a few minutes to transfer three passengers to her taxi. Allow her a few minutes, maybe only a minute, to disembark her two male passengers, the farmers Glendinning and Wilson, in Rochester; in fact, Mrs Mary Murray seemed to suggest the car also stopped at Horsley. Allow her a few minutes at Birdhopecraig to chat to Mrs M, her final passenger, and turn her car. Finally, allow her a minute or two to stop on seeing Bowler here at Elishaw and allow him on board. Let us err on the conservative side, and say those minutes added up to eight. We know she was back at The Kennels at 7.00 pm or shortly thereafter. So, and this is a best guess, we are dealing with a time of twenty-three minutes, give or take, for her to make this round trip. And if that trip meter of Matthew's shows anything like six miles by the time we reach Birdhopecraig, it will mean that Evelyn was travelling at an average of almost 30 mph. Which makes utter nonsense of the police's claim that she could not, in the conditions, have driven twenty-six miles, just over twice as far, in eighty minutes, over three times more."

Frances, now in full flow, stops to take a breath.

We have just passed the sign to Otterburn Camp, open moorland to our right all the way to the Cheviot Hills, the River Rede still winding its way on our left. I think to myself that vistas such as this, like the A68 south to West Woodburn from Otterburn and the great expanse of moors and hills to our north, are why this wild and sparsely populated shire is called, among other things, 'the land of wide horizons'.

"That is Birdhopecraig's sole relevance to this case," Frances continues. "As I understand it, Mrs M walked the last three miles to her home in Cottonshopeburnfoot. She testified that Evelyn had left her 'near to 7.00 pm', which could clearly have been several minutes before, and she was in her house at 7.45. Her husband looked at the clock, said she was early, and told her the time. Three miles in fifty minutes or so, in the dark. Not bad going on her part."

"Bravo, Fran," Sven says. "You are absolutely correct. I would only say you may have been too conservative, as Mrs Murray also estimated that they left Foster's Garage at around 6.40 pm. So your few minutes may have been as many as ten at that point alone, nearer fifteen in all, and Evelyn's average speed could have been proportionately quicker."

"And let us not forget," Peter adds, "that Mrs Murray testified to being passed by three cars, all heading south towards Otterburn. There may even have been a fourth, which passed them at Birdhopecraig, but this is something which seems to have crept unbidden into Goodman's and Dixon's books; Mrs Murray did not testify to it. Of those she did testify to, the first was at Horsley and the second at Rochester, both when she was in the taxi; the third was near Saughenside, when she was two miles into her walk." He smiles at me in the mirror. "We could go on to Saughenside. It's only a couple of miles beyond Birdhopecraig, just into the forest, only half a mile from your very own Blakehopeburnhaugh."

Frances groans. "Lunch, please."

"I'm thinking about these three cars," Peter says, ploughing on. "The first seems too early to be the car which stopped to let Bowler out; it would have been through Elishaw by ten to seven. We can rule the third out. Mrs Murray says she would have seen it close to 7.30 pm at Saughenside, by which time Evelyn would have been well on the other side of Otterburn, en route to Ponteland with her fare. Or so she thought. It would be nice if there had indeed been a fourth at Birdhopecraig, only a minute or two ahead of Evelyn, but I don't think we can assume so. Of them all, the one they passed at Rochester seems the most likely. Mrs Murray says it had strong headlights and it would have passed them around ten to seven." I see him grimace. "In effect, allowing for Evelyn to turn at Birdhopecraig, it would only have been minutes ahead of her at Elishaw. If we factor in people's difficulties with exact times, watches not being synchronised and so on, I'd plump for that one."

"Thank you, Peter," Frances says. "Like it or not, you've just ruled out Saughenside. I think we can agree it was the car they passed at Rochester that most likely dropped Bowler off at Elishaw. Unless Mrs M, who otherwise seems to have been an observant woman, missed seeing another car altogether. Or forgot to mention a fourth car to the police."

"I don't think we should worry about the Rochester car being five or ten minutes early," Sven says. "It's possible that if it stopped at Elishaw the people in it would have chatted for a while, even argued if Bowler was reluctant to be left high and dry."

I notice in the rear mirror that Bradon has had his head bent and appears to be writing. I believe now that all of them have become fully engaged and I'm glad to see it. I have no doubt the collective intelligence in this vehicle will produce, if not a concrete solution, then something very close to the truth of Evelyn Foster's death.

Since we passed through Rochester, the Rede has been flowing alongside the road on our left; a belt of trees, some of them this time deciduous, has blocked our view to the right. There are Roman camps dotted in the hills behind, including Bremenium Fort at High Rochester. In fact, there are Neolithic, Bronze Age, Iron Age, Roman and mediaeval relics scattered all over these moors, many associated with defence (or offence) and some with religious rites. I pull in to a gateway.

"This is Birdhopecraig," I tell them. "A name which has also often been split into two words, the 'Craig' detached. The grounds enclosed Algernon Bertram Freeman-Mitford's, Lord Redesdale's, shooting lodge, Birdhopecraig Hall. It burned down in 1957. Winston Churchill was one eminent visitor. In fact, it was rumoured that Churchill's wife Clementine may have been a daughter of Barty Mitford's, as he was called. Be that as it may, he was the paternal grandfather of the Mitford sisters."

"You are a fount of knowledge, Matthew," Sven says.

"How many miles from The Kennels to here?" asks Bradon.

"Just over five and a half," I tell him as Frances punches the air.

Bradon makes another note in whatever he is writing.

I turn the Zafira much as Evelyn may have done, and we head back.

The mist has thickened, but not greatly. We have sandwiches in the Redesdale Arms, formerly Horsley Farm, which has the distinction of being the first/last pub in England on this route over the border. The inn was built on the site of a former 'bastle', or fortified farmhouse of the Middle Ages, when these moors, by virtue of the activities of the Border Reivers, were also known as the Debatable Lands. Northumberland's Middle March, present-day Tynedale and Redesdale, had a bent for hostility and brutality at least equal to its counterparts in Scotland. Such uneasy truces that existed from time to time depended more on the stability of relations between the gentry than anything else—and those relations were not always stable even when kith and kin were involved. It's said, and I can well believe it, that the first thing a Marcher did on waking up was to feel his throat to see if it had been cut during the night.

The historian G M Trevelyan described the moorland heights as 'cloudland.' He wrote of the activities of the 'Mosstroopers', light horsemen and raiders who operated across the Northumbrian-Scottish border, either freebooting or with the sanction of the authorities of the time—the Wardens of the Marches—through the sixteenth and into the seventeenth century. The Mosstroopers came towards the end of the Reivers era (*reave = rob*), partly as a counterforce, but were no better behaved.

When we are seated, Bradon places a page of notes on the table.

"Our timeline for this part of Miss Foster's evening, as near as I can get from our discussion earlier, with mileages. Feel free to comment."

Place	Distance	Time	Notes
The Kennels	-	6.37 pm (say)	Departure with 3 pax.
Elishaw	(2.1 miles)	6.41 pm	-
Rochester	(4.7 miles)	6.47 pm (arr.)	Stop at Horsley?
Rochester	"	6.48 pm (dep.)	2 pax. disembark
Birdhopecraig	5.6 miles	6.50 pm (arr.)	-
Birdhopecraig	"	6.52 pm (dep.)	Mrs M. disembarks
Elishaw	(9.1 miles)	7.00 pm (arr.)	-
Elishaw	"	7.01 pm (dep.)	Bowler embarks
The Kennels	11.2 miles	7.05 pm	

Peter is the first to speak. "Superb, Bradon," he says. "You could be a minute out here or there, but who's to say now?" He smiles. "I'd be the last one to quibble. It fits like a glove."

"A round trip of over eleven miles in twenty-eight minutes, twenty-four of them driving," Frances says. "An average of about 28 mph."

"She was no slouch, was she?" Bradon says. "An efficient cabbie and competent driver who knew the road, wouldn't you reckon?"

We stop at Elishaw again on the way back, and at the Percy Cross. Apart from Sven's interest, it seems a good place to resume discussion...

CHAPTER SEVEN

Elishaw-Otterburn: the present day, 22 January
Concerning 6.30-7.15 pm, 6 January 1931

...and this is what we begin to discuss: the statements of witnesses, which I hope I've summarised accurately, to the first part of Evelyn's journeys that evening. I explain that I have referenced them, those who appeared at the inquest, to the day they appeared—ID1 for 2 February 1931; ID2 for 3 February; ID3 for 5 February—and have made some minor adjustments to their actual order of appearance (which particularly applies to Mrs Foster, who was heard first). This way, we will deal with them in more or less chronological sequence from Elishaw onwards:

Albert Beach's Tale (during ID1)

Beach was a steam-roller operator. He lived in a caravan close by his steam-roller at Elishaw Gate, just over the bridge, quarter of a mile down the A68 from Elishaw Road Ends. At 6.25 pm on 6 January 1931, he washed his face, put on his coat, and at 6.45 (estimated) set off with his pal John Oliver to walk to Otterburn for a beer or two in the Percy Arms. As they approached Elishaw Bridge he had 'some recollection' of seeing a car stationary at Elishaw Road Ends, but wasn't sure if this was before or after their next sighting, for as they reached the bridge a second car—a dark blue covered-in two-seater, maybe an AC car or Morris Cowley—came 'tearing down' the A68, heading from Elishaw past them. He could not see who was in it.

Then, after crossing Elishaw Bridge, they cut across a field to get onto the A696. Halfway across the field, 'probably' 200 yards from the bridge, they saw a car heading towards Otterburn on the A696, 'about five minutes, perhaps less' after their first sighting. Beach could not say what kind of car this was or, again, who was in it. He and Oliver made the main road and arrived in Otterburn at 7.30 pm, at the same time as one of Foster's buses arrived with papers from Newcastle. They saw no more cars, only a motor-cyclist and a pedestrian. They left the Percy Arms at 8.30 pm and were 'home' about 9.30.

Beach appeared as a witness at the inquest, Oliver did not. His statement supported Beach's recollection of when they set out: 6.45 pm. (He thought his watch was passably accurate. Between the evenings of 7-9 January it had lost only five minutes, on the first occasion checked with the help of Bellingham Town Hall clock, on the second with the help of 'a mate').

Robert Townes's Tale

Townes was one of some 170 people who gave statements to the police but were *not* selected to appear as witnesses at the inquest. He was a gardener living at Brownrigg Cottages, about quarter of a mile further south down Dere Street than Albert Beach's caravan, or half a mile from Elishaw Bridge. He stated that he was on Dere Street, near his home, at 6.50 pm and saw Beach walking along the road. Within minutes he saw two other things: first, 'a touring car with the hood up' which travelled south past him from Elishaw; and second, a car which stopped 200 yards towards Otterburn from Elishaw and 'restarted a few moments later.' This car appeared to him to be a saloon.

John Thompson's Tale (ID1)

Thompson *was* called as a witness at the inquest. He was a young farmhand living at Garretshields, just off the A68; over a mile from Otterburn as the crow flies. At 'about' seven o'clock on 6 January he walked into the village, crossing a footbridge over the River Rede and joining the A696 at the school. 'About' 100 yards south of the school, at 'about' 7.15 pm, a car headed past him towards the village. It was a saloon with bright headlights.

Reaching Foster's Garage, he saw a saloon standing at the petrol pump, facing towards Newcastle. He believed he heard Evelyn Foster speaking, but did not know whom she was addressing. He thought it would have taken him 'about' 7 minutes to walk there from the school. (His timings appear to have based on previous experience rather than the use of a watch). Walking on in his cap and dark coat, he said that some 10 yards towards Newcastle from the garage he met two 'young men' whom he could not recognise. One of them wore leggings. He then went into a house 'adjoining Tully's the shoemakers.'

He later amended this statement: 'I am satisfied the man I saw was Maughan at the time.' (He made no mention of Mrs Maughan.)

George Maughan's Tale (ID1)

Maughan, another witness who testified, was a 'traveller' for the Otterburn Co-op and lived next door to it on the south side of the A696. On the evening of 6 January—about 7.00 pm, but he could not say before or after—he set off with his wife to tend the fires at Otterburn School, his other job. From a point approximately opposite the church gate, some 40 yards short of Foster's Garage, he saw a car approaching from the west/Elishaw direction. When it pulled up at The Kennels he saw a woman was driving it. Being dazzled by the car's headlights, he was unable to confirm whether this was Evelyn Foster. He wasn't prepared to say if anyone else was in the car; there may have been but he couldn't see. He was sure, however, that the car had not stopped within his view before reaching The Kennels.

On leaving his house he also met Mr Blackham, the school headmaster, and then 'another man' walking into the village on the opposite side of the road some 35-40 yards from Foster's Garage. At that point he 'could not see the car coming from the west but could see the moving headlights.' He left the school at 8.30 and was home by 8.45 pm.

He added that immediately after passing the stationary car at The Kennels he had seen Robert Luke standing at the 'big garage door' opposite. Luke had shouted something to him, he thought about the weather.

He also later added he had been wearing leggings, that he knew John Thompson and was 'satisfied' Thompson was the man walking village-wards.

Robert Luke's Tale (ID1)

Luke was a bus driver employed by Joseph Foster & Son and was Gordon Foster's brother-in-law. He testified that on 6 January he finished work about

7.10-7.12 pm but immediately before had crossed the road to The Kennels to fetch a piece of wire. At this point he saw George Maughan and his wife walking past and remarked to Maughan 'something about sweethearting again.' He also saw the Hudson Super-Six standing at the petrol pump outside The Kennels but had not previously seen the car in motion. He saw no one in the car, or anyone get out of it, or anyone moving between the car and The Kennels' front door. He added that there may have been someone in it, or someone in the neighbourhood, but if so he hadn't noticed; he took no heed, for it was a common thing for cars to draw up there. He succeeded in getting his piece of wire and crossed back over the road to the garage.

"And what do these statements tell us?" I ask as we gather once more in the Zafira, having viewed the Percy Cross to Sven's satisfaction. In truth, it has been a pleasant distraction, a chance to recharge our batteries.

In 1988, five centuries after the battle it commemorates, the 'Cross' became another of the area's Grade II listed buildings. It is a weather-beaten and tapered sandstone memorial dating from 1777 and stands on a five-step square plinth of rough-hewn rock in a coppice of trees. On it there is dated graffiti of the *I Wuz Here* genre. It is not the original monument, but rests in an old socket which may have been part of the first Battle Cross. A recent addition is an interpretive sign describing the action. Sven was fascinated, the others not quite so.

I take the opportunity while we are sitting in the car park to point out that although what we are seeing across the Rede Valley today may look like quiet farmland and moorland, the landscape around us hides a history of other human activity: a tile kiln at Garretshields, a corn mill at Troughend, lime burning at Greenchesters a stone's throw away, and coal mining at Elsdon and Hopefoot behind us. Excluding Sven, they are equally unimpressed and I don't know what I am trying to prove other than that change is constant and—again—they will need to adjust their mental clocks to another time and place. I hear Peter clearing his throat.

"Well?" I repeat. "What do we get from the first of our witnesses?"

Frances stirs beside me. "We get that women weren't allowed to be witnesses. We get that they were second-class citizens. What happened to Mrs Maughan? And later, Mrs Kennedy? And to Annie Carruthers and Mary Ferry? Arguably the people most observant of those around them were ruled out on sexist grounds. Sorry, Matthew, I'm being premature."

"It's a fair point," I tell her. "It's the way things were."

"Also," she says, "police interference is evident in these statements. Look at the addenda to Thompson's and Maughan's. You can picture the scene going something like: 'Now, Mr Maughan, you saw another man 35-40 yards from the garage? *Er, yes.* You know Mr Thompson was there? *Er, no.* Well, he was, and it might have been him, mightn't it? *Er, yes.* In

53

that case, would you care to correct what you said? *Er, okay, if you insist.'* And vice versa for Thompson. Both suggestible, both nicely turned."

"Very good, Frances," Sven says. "Beautifully crafted."

Frances gives him a smile. "Thank you."

Then, with my head turned towards the back, I can sense Peter has been working up to let fly. He does not disappoint.

"I suppose it is rare for people, then and now, and especially now," he says, "to be summarily fired from their posts, but that is what the Foster family's solicitor deserved, and arguably also the—"

"Stop right there, Peter," I say.

He frowns at me. "What is it this time?"

"If you will bear with me, a brief lesson in two of the aspects of this case I mentioned at the outset; social change and psychology. Please remember that Mr Bates was a long-time adviser to Joseph Foster. He was a solicitor, an 'expert' in law, an educated man, and therefore an object of trust. Very well, he was out of his comfort zone here. His dealings for the business had more to do with the licensing of public service vehicles, but Joseph would have felt allegiance to him and would not have condoned ruthlessness. His son Gordon, by all accounts more prickly and forthright, tried to persuade him after the first day of the inquest that Bates' services should be terminated. He had heard enough to know that Bates, by not asking the right questions, or any questions at all, was doing more harm than good. But Joseph demurred; such a thing could ruin Bates, he would be pilloried by the press. Joseph could not bring that down upon him. His conscience would not allow it."

"He comes across as an honourable man," Bradon says. "Grieving, well-meaning, floundering, embarrassed that his family had been placed in such a harsh and unwavering spotlight, but honourable."

"More fool him," Peter says. "The veracity of his daughter was on *trial* here. Long before February, he should have clicked what was coming and prepared better for it."

"Have some sympathy, Peter," I say. "He was doing his very best to protect her reputation, it was the first thing on his mind, but he was also out of his depth. Wouldn't most people have been?"

Peter grimaces. "Maybe. But he should have recognised his, and his solicitor's, limitations. He should have reassessed his priorities. There's not much excuse for not anticipating what an adversary may do."

I have made my point, and have no doubt Peter will stew over it. "But you were about to suggest questions that could and should have been asked, I think? Take Beach. What would you have asked *him*?"

"Oh, Beach," Peter says, "where to start? For example, did Beach see where that first car of his *went*? How sure was he of its type and marque, and whether it was a two-seater? Was he sure it was dark blue, as opposed to black or dark green? Could he hazard an opinion on this, or had he already hazarded enough by venturing it may have been an AC or Morris Cowley? Did he know the differences between them, that AC cars could be two- or four-seater? Did he know Cowleys came in various guises; two-seater, four-seater, coupé, tourer, closed saloon, folding-top saloon? What did he mean by 'perhaps less' than five minutes between seeing the two cars? Two minutes? Three? Four? Did he know Evelyn's Hudson? Could the second car, although he couldn't quite make it out, *conceivably* have been hers? As he was such an expert in marques and models, could it have been a sedan or saloon? *Was* it a closed car? Did he see its headlights, and how would he describe *them*? Had he or Oliver seen it stop? Could his vague 'recollection' that there may at some point have been a car stationary at Elishaw have been this car? When it passed them, was it picking up speed or slowing down? And as Goodman says in his book, if the inquest was at all interested in getting to the truth, why was Beach not taken to Elishaw, asked to repeat his cross-country ramble, identify the points at which he had seen these cars, and *timed*?"

This has all flooded out of him off-the-cuff. He began by ticking the questions off on his fingers, but quickly ran out of fingers. He scans his papers, searching for more, checking if he has missed anything. "*None* of these questions were asked by Bates or the coroner," he says. "And Smirk, the police solicitor, would have run a mile from asking them. The answers might have shaken his paymasters' theory to its roots. At all costs, they couldn't have Evelyn picking up a fare, could they?"

"You are right," I tell him "And you have amply illustrated one of the inadequacies of the inquest. These and a hundred other questions should have been asked of witnesses, but were not. We have to live with that. We can only work with what we have in the way of background documents, some incomplete, others inaccurate, unsatisfactory as that may be. Now: the first thing I would ask you all is whether any of these testimonies cast doubt on Evelyn's story or indeed Bradon's summary of her movements around 7.00 pm that evening?"

"Not at all," Frances says. "Given that people can be vague, or simply a few minutes out, they corroborate them. We calculated that she was back in the village at five past seven. Beach saw what was most likely her Hudson shortly after 7.00 pm, heading to Otterburn. Townes confirms it, and also that he saw it stop and start up again near Elishaw; so Bradon's allowance of a minute holds good. Thompson suggests the car passed him en route to Otterburn at 7.15 pm, but he is the odd man out. Maughan is frankly all over the place, but seems to have seen the Hudson outside The Kennels at shortly after seven, and Robert Luke confirms it was sitting there by ten past seven when he crossed the road."

Sven smiles. "So, if we are correct, she could quite reasonably have replenished her petrol tank, resumed her journey at around 7.15 pm and been at Raylees at 7.22 pm."

"Not so fast, Sven," I say. "We need to look at other pieces in the first part of this jigsaw, not least the other car or cars. Are you with us, Peter? Are we all back on track?"

"Ruthlessness," Peter snorts. "Faced with annihilation, what other sensible response is on offer?" He has the grace to smile, and then regrets it. "What did Joseph Foster's *honour*, or Bates' *reputation*, have to do with it? Mr Foster would have been better employed thinking of all the people this was harming—his daughter's good name, his wife, his children, his friends, their friends—unfairly, undeservedly, manipulatively, and fired that *inadequate* man forthwith. I have sympathy for Evelyn, but none at all for stupidity. Her father had had a month to think about it, but took what seemed the easy solution, the one which needed no thought at all."

"You may be right," Frances says, "but it's a harsh criticism. The poor man would still have been numb with grief."

"And he was about to bring more down on himself in persisting with this mediocrity." Peter will not relent, and it is getting us nowhere.

"Enough, Peter," I tell him. "You've made your point. Now…where might that first car have gone, what sort of car was it, and why would he have been dropped off at Elishaw?"

"We have two sightings of it," Sven says. "First Beach, along with Oliver, and then Townes. And let's not forget that Evelyn herself said, in her so-called interview, it was a dark-coloured, closed car, the 'closed' part of which gels with both Beach and Townes. Thompson should also have seen it, but didn't, or didn't say so. Beach said he thought it was a dark blue closed-top two-seater, an Auto Carriers car or Morris Cowley, both British marques. But as Peter says, they came in different body types. Townes said it was an open touring car, a car designed for four or more people, but with its hood up, so closed. Arguably Beach, being a steam-roller driver, might have been better at cars, but it was night-time and the car, he said, came 'tearing' past them—in itself suggesting a driver who knew the road, a driver not too concerned by the conditions or in a hurry to get away from or towards something."

He pauses to check his notes and my summaries, and then continues, "So we can conclude it was a closed car and there was at least an even chance it may have been a four-seater. It would have to have been, if it was the car that dropped Bowler off, since Evelyn said later a woman was driving and there was another person in it once Bowler got out. She referred to *people* in it when she picked Bowler up and that he had told her he had eaten a meal in Jedburgh with these *people*. P.C. Fergusson's notes refer to a *lady with a man* in the car after Bowler emerged. And the police may not have included Townes in their witness list because, if he persisted in saying it was a four-seater, it would have confirmed part of Evelyn's story."

Sven has plainly been doing some research; either that or he is a vintage car buff. Founded in 1903 by the Weller brothers of Norwood under the somewhat long-winded title of Autocars & Accessories Ltd, the company Auto Carriers came into being in 1911. It was based in Thames Ditton in Surrey and in 1922 shortened its name again to AC Cars. In 1926 one of its employees, the Hon Victor Bruce, won the Monte Carlo Rally in a six-cylinder AC car. A year later, with his wife and J A Joyce, Bruce set a 9-day endurance record at Montlhéry in France driving an AC Six. Although its history has been a fairly complex one and the company has never been a mass producer, AC Cars still exists and is owned today by Acedes Holdings LLC. With some justification the company claims the AC Cobra has become an automotive icon, 'one of the fastest and most brutal sports cars of all times.' Having reached a speed of 183 mph on the unrestricted M1 motorway in 1964, the car was instrumental in having the UK Parliament impose a 70 mph limit on Britain's motorways and main roads. Today's models include the AC Ace, the AC Aceca and the AC 378 GT. Assuming we are dealing here with what at the time was a relatively new car, the company produced two likely models from 1920 into the 1930s; the AC 12hp and the AC Six. Both were available in two- or four-seater format. Both were fast cars.

"Well put, Sven," Frances says. "And thank you for putting a name to 'AC.' As to where the car went, it didn't go to Hexham, did it? I think Bowler was duped on that score. We need to remember yet another two witnesses who were *not* called at this charade which went by the name of an inquest. We need to remember Messrs Bell and Wallace, who set off at 6.50 pm on their bicycles from West Woodburn to Rochester, nine miles northwest. They said they met not one single vehicle along the A68 until they reached the Elishaw Road Ends. And unless they were very fit indeed, Bradley Wiggins standard, they could not have done those six miles, uphill and down dale, in much less than twenty minutes. So the car that Beach and Townes saw either reached a destination before West Woodburn or it turned off the A68."

"You said Bowler may have been duped, Fran," says Peter. "I would suggest he may have been *dumped*. And that figures if we ask ourselves why, as Matthew has implied, he was not taken into Otterburn. I would suggest because someone wanted to be rid of him, at a point where he might still hitch a lift, but also at a point where the driver would not risk being seen further or would not risk divulging a final destination. And after all, as others before us, not least Coroner Dodds, have asked, if the car was indeed going to Hexham, why not take Bowler all the way? He would have stood a much better chance in Hexham of getting a bus onward to Newcastle. Or why not take him just two miles further into Otterburn? Because, I would suggest in all logic, the driver—most likely a local person as Sven has said—did not wish to be recognised or be seen with him. And finally, if this is not going one step too far, our local driver may have clocked Evelyn's car as she took Mrs Murray to Birdhopecraig. Our mystery driver may have assumed Evelyn would be coming back and, being the accommodating person she was, would pick Bowler up."

Bradon, who has been as thoughtful as ever, then speaks up.

"That all fits in well with what Goodman, Dixon and others have suggested before; that our mystery driver was the person Goodman calls Mrs X and Dixon names as Mrs Charlotte Clark. But before Matthew tells me I am jumping the gun, let me throw a thought into the mix. If Bowler was dumped as Peter suggests, if he was even vaguely aware of the geography of this part of the world, if he knew Otterburn was only two miles away and Hexham-Newcastle buses would be an easier option for him anyway, he'd be kinda raging, wouldn't he? I mean, wouldn't any of us be a little upset? In not our friendliest frame of mind?"

He adds: "And isn't it possible that the first car Mrs Murray saw at Horsley could have held the guys who dropped into the Redesdale Arms for a drink, who the cops later ruled out? I know the landlord, Ben Prior, said they were there from about 6.30-7.00 pm, but couldn't he also have been a bit out with his timings? As in six forty-three, rather than six thirty? If they only stopped for a glass of beer on the road, twenty minutes would have been enough. So, might it have been this car Beach and Townes saw? The only thing that suggests it might not is that according to the landlord it was a big Essex saloon, so less open to confusion. It would be very hard to mistake an Essex for a smaller AC or Morris Cowley car, closed or not."

"Yes, Bradon," I tell him, "it's possible, but we may as well rule the Redesdale Arms party out too. Aside from the fact they were driving an Essex, if Ben Prior's timings are correct—and as a landlord he may have paid them more than average attention—they could not have been at Elishaw before five past seven. As for Mrs Charlotte Clark, we will come to her alleged involvement in due course. In the meantime, we should start heading back. The mist is closing in and we have work still to do."

I smile in apology for cutting him short. Maybe I should have paid better attention. I know times are a key element for us, but they are always prone to human error.

CHAPTER EIGHT

Otterburn: the present day, 22 January
Concerning 7.00-7.22 pm, 6 January 1931

"I think we should begin this stage with Margaret Foster," I suggest as we begin our journey back into Otterburn. "Set the groundwork, as it were. We might then consider what various people said about what they saw on the Otterburn main street that night and Evelyn's possible reunion with Bowler again at the bridge. After that, assuming we believe she did indeed make that link-up, we assess how her story of travelling to Belsay and back to Wolf's Nick stands up. Fair enough?"

"It sounds good to me," Frances says. "How long till it gets dark?"

"We have another hour or two, I think." I am hoping that once we climb out of the Rede Valley we might be clear of mist. As it is, entering Otterburn with The Kennels on our right and the garage on our left, from a landscape that resembles how it must have been in Roman times into a fleck of human settlement, the fine day has turned into gloom.

I hand out a couple of sheets of paper, to refresh their memories.

Mrs Margaret Foster's Tale (Part One) (ID1)

Mrs Foster testified at the inquest that her daughter had left The Kennels at 6.35 pm and returned from Birdhopecraig at 'about' 7.00. Evelyn had told her of picking a man up at Elishaw who wanted to go to Ponteland to catch a bus; there had been a car standing at Elishaw as she passed and he had hailed her. He said he had missed the bus in Jedburgh after having tea with the people in the car, that they had given him a lift and were proceeding to Hexham. He told her he had been about to phone from the AA box. Mrs Foster asked her daughter what the fellow was like: 'What kind of man is he?' Evelyn replied he was respectable and gentlemanly-looking, 'a bit of a knut.'

They exchanged a few words about the fare Evelyn proposed to charge. She had told the man £2, but that she would need to check when she got to the garage. Mrs Forster thought it may be too high and Evelyn said, 'get Daddy to work it out while I'm filling the car.' Mrs Foster then asked if the man was outside and Evelyn told her he had gone to the inn to see if he could get a free lift and would leave word there. She went to fill her tank and on her return her father advised that the fare should be £1 16s 0d (£1.80p) Her sister Dorothy suggested she should take George Phillipson along, a sentiment echoed by Mrs Foster. 'Alright mother,' Evelyn replied, and added she would take her mother's flashlight. She picked it up from the table as she left.

Margaret Foster next saw her daughter at 10.35 pm slumped in the bus, and 'knew there was something wrong.'

Gladys Tatham's Tale (ID1)

Gladys Tatham was the married daughter of the Percy Arms' manager and lived at the hotel. She testified at the inquest that Evelyn, whom she knew very well, had definitely not called at the hotel between 6.00 and 10.30 pm on 6 January. Gladys had been in charge of the lounge all day, and no one had come to ask her if there was the chance of a lift to Newcastle. She said Evelyn 'used to always come to the front door and ask if she had any message.'

John Scott's Tale (ID1)
Scott was a chauffeur and barman employed at the Percy Arms, and he lived in one of the cottages there. He testified at the inquest that he was on duty in the bar from 6.20 until 8.20 pm on 6 January. He knew Evelyn Foster very well and could definitely say she had not called in between these times to enquire about any man seeking 'a lift to Ponteland or Otterburn' (*sic*). There had been 'no stranger in the bar that night whilst I was on duty.'

Peter stirs on reading this again. "How strangely similar these two statements read," he says. "The word *definitely* rather stands out like a sore thumb, doesn't it? A touch of police coaching once more, don't you think? Putting words in one's mouth? And they both knew her *very* well. Am I right in thinking the same Otterburn Tower typewriter was used?"

"It looks that way," Frances says. "Of course, these two may have caused the police to doubt Evelyn's story. I wonder when their statements were made? They almost read as being corroborative. Otherwise, why bother? And why ignore people who may have had a different slant?"

"Quite," Peter says. "Plus, we have the probability that several people changed their stories immediately after the event, and certainly before they testified. George Maughan was one, a change of mind that caused Mrs Foster to jump to her feet in protest at the inquest, crying, '*Oh, no!*' She was quickly told to sit down by Dodds, who declined to listen to her reason for interrupting. Her reason being, of course, that on the morning of 7 January Maughan had told his boss, George Sinclair, and some customers in the Co-op, that he had seen *three* men the night before: Blackham, yes—except Blackham was betwixt school and village when Maughan saw him—Thompson, yes; but also a *stranger by the lych-gate* to the church. By the time Maughan spoke to the police, certainly by the time he testified, this third party had flown from his memory. Along with variations in Thompson's own statements in the weeks from January to February, it made villagers question the reliability, if not worse, of both. You will recall that Thompson had told fellow workers at Garretshields that he had seen Evelyn's Hudson passing the school just as he walked onto the road, *not* 100 yards east as his statement suggests. At the very least, this would concertina his time-frame into something closer to other people's. If it wasn't codswallop to begin with.

"Yet again," Peter adds, "these people were not questioned as they should have been, and yet again, the police emerge as manipulators."

George Sinclair's Tale

Sinclair, the Co-op manager who lived nearby, a man held in high regard by his customers and fellow-villagers, could very easily have ruined the police theory had he been allowed to testify. Instead, there is little doubt he helped do so in the confines of the jury room. He had given his statement to the police before receiving notice that he was to serve as a juror.

Sinclair's statement was very simple. Having worked beyond closing time to reconcile cash and check stocks, he left the Co-op at about 7.00 pm on 6 January. On exiting, he saw a stranger lurking near the Post Office (which also housed a sub-branch of Lloyd's Bank) next door. As Sinclair moved towards him, the man hurried off down the street towards the Percy Arms.

Annie Carruthers' Tale

Miss Carruthers was a school teacher at Elsdon, three miles east of Otterburn. She was later to marry the bus driver John Robson (see below). She was *not* called as a witness at the inquest.

Soon after 7.00 pm on 6 January she cycled into the village. She crossed the bridge over the Otter Burn with the Percy Arms to her left, and saw a man step off the kerb and try to wave her down. She did not know him. He asked if she could tell him the time of the next bus to Newcastle. Miss Carruthers told him she could not, at which point 'the man became very offensive and made suggestive remarks'. She wasted no time in leaving him there and later gave the police a description of him that matched very closely Evelyn Foster's. Like others, though, she did not see Evelyn pick him up.

Mary Ferry's Tale

Miss Ferry was also a schoolteacher, assistant to Mr Blackham at Otterburn School. Like Annie Carruthers, she was *not* called as a witness. At about 7.15 pm on 6 January she called at the Percy Arms to collect sausages which the Hexham bus had left at Reception for her. This was normal practice; she made sure her brother ate only the best sausages. On her way out, she saw a man standing to her right under a tree by the embankment of the Otter Burn. He was a stranger. She did not hang about to ask why he was there.

John Robson's Tale (ID1)

Robson was a bus driver employed by Joseph Foster & Son. He testified that he had been delayed leaving Haymarket Station in Newcastle due to the late arrival of the incoming bus but reached Belsay at 6.40 pm, stopping to allow passengers to disembark. Further north he stopped at Raylees so his conductor could 'put the papers on the wall.' A car which he recognised as 'Mr Foster's Hudson' approached from Otterburn. He checked his watch. The time was 7.22 pm (i.e. he had driven fifteen miles from Belsay to Raylees, possibly with additional stops, in forty-two minutes at an average speed of 21-22 mph).

He was temporarily blinded by the car's headlights so could not see its occupants (the *'s'* has subsequently been crossed out by an unknown hand), but said the Hudson was travelling slowly, no more than 10 mph, at the time.

(Coroner Dodds was later to point out that Robson was the only witness definitely to have seen the Hudson on the road, but its speed 'did not seem like a car hurrying with a passenger.')

"So," I ask them as we sit once more in the Zafira outside the Percy Arms. "What do we deduce from these statements?"

"We deduce," Bradon says, "that three witnesses—a store manager and two teachers, so presumably not idiots—saw a stranger within a hundred yards of each other between just after 7.00 and 7.15 pm. We deduce that he may not have been a particularly stand-up guy. We deduce that Evelyn had no need to enter the Percy Arms because she saw him by the creek, which renders Tatham and Scott irrelevant or stooges of the cops. And we deduce that between 7.15 and 7.22 pm, Evelyn set off from home, picked him up and drove him the next 2.5 miles to Raylees at an average speed, matching the bus driver's, of 23 mph."

"Bradon, my man," says Peter. "Would you care to be my editor? Or perhaps apply for the judiciary? That is as capable a job of summing-up as any courtroom could wish to hear. But I wonder who crossed the 's' out, and when? Dear me, how clumsy. I think if I'd been Chief Constable Fullarton James, I'd have had it retyped and re-signed post haste."

"Wait, Peter" I say. "First, would you all please note that it was 'Mr Foster's car' in Robson's eyes; indicative of the times we are dealing with. But more importantly, we still do not know that Evelyn picked this man up, do we? Assuming she picked him up at Elishaw in the first place."

I let that one hang in the air while they think about it.

"Reasonable doubt?" Sven says. "We have her word for it, of course, and she wasn't on trial here. Or shouldn't have been."

"We have a lot better than that," Frances says. "We have a positive negative. Three people, as reliable on paper as witnesses could be, saw an unknown man between 7.05 and 7.15 that evening. Four, if we include the somewhat flaky Maughan. If he did not get into Evelyn's car, where did the stranger go? Why was he never seen again? Why did someone not spot him at, say, 7.30? The bus had gone, yet he asked Miss Carruthers about a *Newcastle* bus, which fits Evelyn's story. Why? A chat-up line? There were few cars on the road. Had this man known anyone in the village, he'd have headed for their house, wouldn't he? He wouldn't have been loitering between the Post Office and the Percy Arms. Tatham and Scott may not be so irrelevant after all, although the police might gnash their teeth at it. On a cold winter's evening, the first place this stranger—Bowler—would head for, failing a lift, would be a nice snug bar. Yet both of them swear they saw no such person, at least until 8.20 pm when Scott clocked off. No one in the village did, after 7.15 pm, and we can be sure the police would have asked around in an effort to bolster their theory."

"It would help," I suggest, "if someone had seen a man get out of Evelyn's car, or on the street somewhere near it."

"That's true," Sven says. "But none of them were looking, were they? And we have Maughan again, his first unexpurgated tittle-tattle confirming a stranger at the lych-gate, and Sinclair seeing a stranger not fifty yards away, across the road at the Post Office. Robert Luke wasn't about to peer nosily into the Hudson, was he? He had no interest in it. Thompson heard Evelyn talking to someone, but didn't know to whom. Maughan was dazzled by the car's lights but concedes there may have been someone in the car. He was distracted, if not outright embarrassed, by Luke winding him up about his sweethearting. And surely Mrs Foster, knowing Evelyn better than anyone, would have known if her daughter was spinning a yarn, or would have picked up on something not quite aboveboard. Yet there is no trace of that whatsoever."

"Is there so far anything," Peter asks, "that any of us feels is dubious about Evelyn's story? Between Elishaw and Raylees, we have heard from eight witnesses at the inquest, out of a total of twenty-seven, and four who made statements but were not called. I am excluding Mrs Murray, but she was earlier. Unless Otterburn was invaded by strangers that night, three, arguably four, people saw our friend Bowler or something very like him. And these twelve statements are all to do with a short space of time, roughly half-an-hour between ten to seven and twenty past. Does anyone feel there are any gremlins in there?"

"Only George Phillipson," Bradon says. "Perhaps."

"In what way?" Frances asks.

"One," Bradon says, "why didn't Evelyn seek him out, take him with her as her sister Dorothy suggested, as she promised her mother she would? Two, Evelyn's younger sister Margaret said she had seen him in the village when she returned from conducting a Bellingham bus, but that could have been an hour after Evelyn left. It's unlikely, but could he have been the man some of these people saw on the street or at the bridge?"

"Good questions, Bradon," Peter says. "A pity they weren't asked at the time. As I recall, after Evelyn had been brought back to The Kennels from Wolf's Nick, she simply said she had not seen Phillipson in the village. She had 'not troubled' to call at his digs, the so-called bothy."

"I can understand that," Frances says. "It wouldn't have been a con-genial place for a young woman to go. It was full of men, wasn't it, Foster employees from outside the village? Her father had provided the place for them. It would have been nothing better than a doss-house. Who would do the house-keeping, if there was any? Had she called there, she would most likely have embarrassed both Phillipson, by all accounts a conscientious and upright man, and herself. She may also by that time even have seen Bowler down the street, waiting at the bridge. The bothy was south, or rather east, of the church, wasn't it? So when she reached it, she'd be around the slight curve and able to see him. And which girl of twenty-nine hasn't ignored her mother occasionally? She may have felt a touch rebellious, or simply couldn't be bothered."

"She may also have felt some attraction to Bowler at that point," Peter says. "Don't you think? She may even have put a little gloss on her description of him. A bit of a dandy? She may have been looking forward to a mild flirtation."

"Not in her character, I think," Frances fires back at him.

"Stranger things have happened," Peter says. "But as to the idea that Phillipson may have been the man everyone saw, I don't think so. He was known in the village, he'd worked at Foster's for a while, and was seen as Evelyn's future fiancé. He sounds to me like a fellow who was settling in quite well to his new community, integrating himself. If he'd been a wrong'un, Evelyn's Dad or her brother would have had something to say about it. He certainly wouldn't have been welcomed into the family. *One* of our witnesses may not have known him in the dark. But two? Three? Four? And I believe he was seeking her out at the garage at the time she left, so how could it have been him?"

Bradon has been flicking through his papers as this exchange is going on. "Your reference to a doss-house reminded me, Frances," he says. "Here we are; at the inquest, in answer to a question from Mr Smirk, Mrs Foster went further than Smirk would have wished. She confirmed asking her daughter to take Phillipson with her, and that Evelyn had agreed, but added, 'I've thought since that my daughter did not care to go to his lodgings', clearly meaning they were unsuitable for young ladies. It was a place known to host its fair share of brawls and cursing and raucous behaviour, and on reflection she didn't blame her daughter one bit for avoiding it."

"Plus the chance they would both have been fair game for derision and innuendo if George had been seen by his mates to be no better than a chaperon, or a kind of baby-minder," Sven adds.

"*And*," Bradon adds, "maybe most important of all, Evelyn was to tell her mother later that she hadn't called on him because 'it wouldn't take her long.' We can take from that, can't we, she was intending to return home that evening? It doesn't sound like a girl intending to incinerate her car and hoping she might hitch a lift later. Come to think of it, how did she think she was going to get home, if that *had* been in her mind? Unless she was desperate for a bit of cash, or quite mad, or there was something wrong with the car—and we can apparently rule out all three—why choose the darkest, coldest time of the year to do it?"

I start the engine. It is now after three and the light is fading fast. "Time to head back," I tell them. "We'll double-check times and distances en route. Provided everyone is still in working mode, of course?"

I take it from the injured silence that I've insulted them.

"So here we have it," Peter Maxwell says as I pull out. "Here we have a young woman, competent and friendly in all evident respects, a young woman with a secure homelife and possible forthcoming marriage, who enjoys her work and her cars, first preparing to take three people up the A696 towards Carter Bar, primping her hair and putting on her hat— talking with her brother, I believe, although we may yet come to that— behaving quite normally with them and chatting happily to her final passenger before dropping her off, stopping to pick up a well-dressed man at Elishaw in sore need of a lift, having a normal conversation with her mother and sister on returning home, checking a fare with her father's help, and duly picking up her passenger again near the Percy Arms."

I wait for the punch line. It isn't long in coming, and it's a beaut.

"Lady and gentlemen of the jury, I ask you, does that sound like a young lady who plans to torch her car and herself in the next hour or so?"

CHAPTER NINE

Otterburn-Belsay: the present day, 22 January
Concerning 7.22-9.50 pm, 6 January 1931

As we leave Otterburn I am not inclined to bother about times any longer. The mist is like cotton wool over the Rede Valley and if I were to dawdle at 10 mph we would be in serious danger of having an uninvited truck in our boot. I tell them so, and judge 30 mph to be a safer option. As we pass Raylees Farm again I am encouraged to meet vehicles without headlights, and sure enough, as we begin the climb to Ottercops Moss, the conifers on our right are strung with mist but not shrouded in it. Late afternoon sunlight, gold and red, shafts through the rear window.

I have handed out their final pages of notes for the day:

Mrs Margaret Foster's Tale (Part Two) (ID1)
Continuing with her statement, Mrs Foster said that during her interview Evelyn confirmed twice she had driven through Belsay. She had seen two cars she thought she knew; one was Mr William Kirsopp-Reed's but she wasn't sure of the other. She believed she'd passed Mr Kirsopp-Reed near Capheaton (4-5 miles north of Belsay). At Belsay, her passenger had said, 'Well, there's no bus here' and, when Evelyn replied it would be further on, said he would turn back. When she asked why, he retorted, 'That's got nothing to do with you.' After the car was turned she 'felt him creep along the seat towards her,' taking hold of the wheel and saying he would drive back. When she objected he 'hit her over the eye.' She said she tried to see someone in Belsay, but her eye felt sore 'as though she had sand thrown over.' Mrs Foster was unclear whether Evelyn had been struck again before Wolf's Nick. Her impression was that she had not changed seats but the man was sitting up close to her.

Evelyn said they stopped at the top of the hill at Wolf's Nick. The man offered her a cigarette, and when she declined he retorted, 'Well, you are an independent young woman.' He then began 'hitting her and knocking her about' and 'chucked her into the back of the car.' He kept nipping her arms. Mrs Foster asked what had happened after she was knocked into the back seat: had he 'interfered' with her? Evelyn said, 'Yes.' Her mother said, 'Oh, my God.' Evelyn replied, 'Oh, mother, but I couldn't help it. I fought for my life.' After that, she said he had taken something from his pocket and threw it over her. It was 'out of a bottle or a tin.' She said it 'just went up in a blaze.'

When Mrs Foster asked how had she 'taken alight,' Evelyn said she didn't know; she could recall nothing more until she felt a 'bump bumping' like travelling over rough ground. She said this 'sort of roused her up' and she somehow got out of the car, 'all alight,' and 'tossed her coat off.' Choking with fumes, she heard a whistling and screeching, and a motor stop. No one came. She tried to creep to the road, hoping to see the bus, but she was there for a very long time and tried to quench her thirst with frozen blades of grass.

Mrs Foster asked if she had no suspicions of the man before Belsay.

Evelyn answered none. What had he talked about on the journey? Nothing much, Evelyn replied; he had talked about cars, and said he had one of his own. He was 'not Scottish or broad Geordie.' He did not know much about Newcastle for 'he was from the Midlands.' He smoked a lot. As a driver, he was 'alright' but not as fast as she. He had hit her twice, once on each eye. Why, Mrs Foster asked, hadn't she stopped at Belsay and phoned? She replied 'with emphasis,' as if her mother didn't understand her predicament, that she *couldn't*. She had not 'kept hold of the car' as she was afraid of an accident.

Robert Harrison's Tale (ID1)
Harrison was a bus driver for Robert Tait and lived at Longwitton Station. On 6 January, he testified he left 'the house' at Knowesgate at 7.30 and drove his bus south to Belsay. He met a car heading north near Ferney Chesters, north of Belsay, but did not recall any other cars passing him. He did not recognise this car, nor saw its occupant(s). He did not know Miss Foster's new car.

Peter, predictably, is onto this offering like a farmyard moggie onto a rat. "What on earth?" he says. "What conceivable reason did the police and coroner have to introduce this red herring? Am I missing something? This bus was going south, well ahead of Evelyn. Were they trying to give the impression it had exclusive use of the road all evening?"

"They may well have been," I tell him. "This non-statement *might* be taken as an attempt either at obfuscation or to place the idea in the jury's minds that Evelyn's car was not at Belsay, or heading north from Belsay, five minutes or so either side of 8.00 pm. Which would have suited the police theory that she never got there, or attempted to get there."

"So what?" Peter says. "If she was at Raylees at 7.22 pm and had to climb this hill we're going up, she would have been *behind* the bus." He snorts. "We are dealing with rank *amateurs* here, trying to be clever."

William Kirsopp-Reed's Tale (ID1)
Kirsopp-Reed was a farmer living at Old Town, Otterburn. He testified at the inquest that at about 6.45 pm on 6 January he left Gosforth in Newcastle (he was a County Councillor, so had presumably been to a meeting) with his sister and small son. 200 yards north of Belsay he met a car going south; it would then have been 'between 7.15 and 7.20 pm.' He did not recognise it or see what occupants it held. Similarly, 'about 7.25 pm' he met a 'large saloon car' just north of Ferney Chesters, again not recognising the car or seeing anyone who was in it. He then met a large lorry with no headlights and 'one of Tait's buses at Harle Post Office' and got home at 'approximately 7.55 pm.'

Previously, a handwritten addendum to his statement read that he 'knew Miss Forster's car and had not seen it.' In answer to the coroner, he conceded it 'may have been' her car. Pressed by police solicitor Smirk, he said the times he had stated were accurate 'to within five minutes.' Asked by Smirk if he happened to know whether Miss Foster, or anyone associated with her, knew he was going to Newcastle that day, he replied, 'Gordon, probably.'

John Kennedy's Tale (ID2, 3 February, the second day of the inquest)
Kennedy was a roadman employed by the County Council and lived at
Knowesgate. He testified that on 6 January he had been with his wife to choir
practice at Kirkwhelpington Chapel. They left just before 8.00 pm. After three
quarters of a mile walking north towards Knowesgate they were overtaken by
a dark saloon, travelling 'exceptionally fast.' At this point, 'Easton's Corner,'
it was by Kennedy's reckoning 8.20-8.25 pm. A man was driving (Kennedy,
when asked, could not say if he was wearing a bowler hat) and there was no
one beside him. His statement said its rear number plate included the figure 13
and that he noticed such things. He and his wife were passed by two other cars
going south before the saloon appeared; he was surprised he had not seen its
headlights coming when he glanced round to watch the southbound cars.

50-60 yards later, reaching the brow of a bank, he could see three
quarters of a mile along the road towards Otterburn. The saloon could have
gone left or right at Knowesgate cross-roads, but in any case had disappeared;
he could see no headlights. The next morning Kennedy saw the burned-out car
on the moor. He said he knew Miss Foster's old car but not her new one.

(Police solicitor Smirk tried to give this witness a hard time. He looked
angry and sounded angry and set out to prove him hostile.) Smirk asked first if
Kennedy knew William Herdman and that he drove a car, number BR 6123.
Kennedy said 'Yes' to both and then shot Smirk down by adding that he could
definitely say it was not Herdman's car he had seen; Herdman would not drive
at such a furious rate and on the car he had seen at Easton's Corner the
numbers 1 and 3 were there; he thought adjacent but couldn't be sure. Smirk
then changed tack, asking if Kennedy had spoken to the police at Wolf's Nick
on 7 January about seeing a saloon the night before. After some equivocation,
Kennedy replied he was 'hazy' about it, and agreed he may only have told the
police ten days later when they approached him.

William Herdman's Tale (ID2)
Herdman was a farmer who lived at Hawick Farm, Harle, five miles west of
Kirkwhelpington. He owned a blue Morris Cowley saloon, registration BR
6123. Called as a witness at the inquest, he testified that he finished a house
call in Kirkwhelpington and left the village at about 8.10 pm. He travelled
north to Knowesgate and west to Ferneyrigg to his home, arriving at about
8.30 pm. He had no recollection of seeing any vehicle or pedestrian en route.

(Except for a short distance from Kirkwhelpington to Knowesgate on
the A696, Herdman's journey was on minor roads westwards).

Sidney Henderson's Tale (ID1: inserted here for chronological sequence)
Henderson was a shepherd at Harwoodhead, Cambo, and lived there. He
testified that at about 8.45 pm on 6 January he was walking about halfway
between Harwoodhead (close to Winter's Gibbet) and Harewood Gate (three
miles distant, on a minor road roughly parallel to the A696). He looked to his
right two miles across the moor in the direction of Wolf's Nick and saw a fire;
he thought it was on the main road, maybe campers. It 'was then very bright.'
By the time he reached Harwood Gate at 9.00 pm the fire was going down. He
returned on the same road about 10.45 pm but 'saw no person at that time.'

(He was not asked if he had looked across the moor before 8.45 pm.)

Beattie was a motor salesman employed by a firm of motor engineers in Hawick, Scotland, and lived in Hawick. At the inquest he gave a long and rambling account of his work and journeys, the salient points being:

- on 6 January he had collected a Morris Cowley car in Darlington
- from Ponteland to Hawick, over Carter Bar, he averaged 25-30 mph
- about 9.50 pm, at Wolf's Nick, he saw a 'practically burned out car'
- it was 30-40 yards off the main road and he stopped to take a look
- he was not aware of whistling or of his brakes squealing
- he saw no movement, but the two offside doors of the car were open
- thinking it was an 'ordinary' case of a car taking fire, he moved on
- he thought he might see the occupants later on the road, but didn't
- after seeing press reports, he reported to Hawick police on 8 January

"Well, team?" I ask. "Peter having discounted Harrison, and excluding Mrs Foster for the moment, we have three witnesses—Kirsopp-Reed, Kennedy and Herdman—to help us in trying to track Evelyn from Raylees to Belsay. Or not, as the case may be. The last two, Henderson and Beattie, have to do with after she got there. What are your thoughts?"

We are parked once more at Wolf's Nick in clear evening air, the ocean of dormant heather and waving grasses infused with fading tawny light. A kestrel hovers, hunting across a sky so big it feels liberating. I reflect the day has gone well; they have seen a great deal they needed to see. Sven Carlson apart, they have seen *more* than they needed to see.

"Frankly confused," Bradon says. "I hope Coroner Dodds knew the finer points of this countryside, place names like Easton's Corner and Hawick Farm. Before this, I'd kinda thought Hawick was purely Scottish. If he *didn't* know, what was he to make of all this?"

"If he cared," Peter says. "That is, if he was interested in listening, or in those finer points, and hadn't already made up his mind. But let's try to make sense of it, however much he and the police and their brief might have been trying to pull the wool over everyone's eyes. Let's look at it from their point of view for a moment. And let's forget the hundred and one questions that should have been asked to clarify matters but weren't. I believe the maligned Kennedy—maligned, that is, by Smirk—holds the key. He and his wife were walking, and they were observant of their place and time." He smiles. "I went to choir practice myself in days gone by, and unless the choir master was ill or in bad humour, they started and ended pretty well on cue."

"You need to sift through them all, Peter," I say, "not just the ones that appeal or make most sense to you."

"I appreciate that. Bear with me. Here was a man, not forgetting his wife, who more than likely saw Evelyn's Hudson between Raylees and

Belsay. He was the only one, excluding Kirsopp-Reed, to suggest as much, although he admitted he did not know her new car. This was dangerous to the police and their reaction, through Smirk and the evidence of Herdman, was to try to discredit him. It's the way the forces of the establishment behave, isn't it, and they are just as inclined to do it now as then. As the world has developed, so they have tried, not always successfully in contexts like the internet, to keep ahead of the game." He looks around. "Anyone else like to come in?"

Frances, OS map once more on her lap, says, "Kennedy's sighting at 8.25 pm or thereabouts, short of Knowesgate, would fit in okay with Evelyn's story. He and his wife had come out of the Chapel a minute or two before 8.00 pm. These are his exact words after that: '*After leaving the Chapel I stood for about 5 minutes and it would take me 15 to 20 minutes to walk to Easton's Corner.*' Easton's Corner is not marked on this map, but 'Heeston Bank'—I assume the first word has evolved down the years—is shown north of a bend. From the Chapel in Kirkwhelpington, which sits back off the A696, it is, as Kennedy stated, a walk of three quarters of a mile. Easton's Corner is still well over two miles short of Wolf's Nick, so from Raylees to Belsay and back Evelyn would have needed to drive, let's see, um…24 miles in about an hour. Even I can work out *that* average mph. Kennedy says the car was travelling very fast, which makes up for the bits when it couldn't; on her journey up from Raylees to Ottercops masts, and turning around at Belsay. After Kennedy saw it, the Hudson would have been at Wolf's Nick within minutes, giving Bowler time to manoeuvre it onto the moor, assault Evelyn, and set her and the car alight. By 8.45 pm, the fire would have had time to really get going."

"And the part recognition of the number plate, although it's by no means infallible, helps too," Sven says.

"Yes," Bradon says. "The cops did their best to confuse things. They tried to drag this guy Herdman, plate number BR 6123, into the frame. His evidence otherwise seems unnecessary, except as Peter says for purposes of discrediting Kennedy, whom he might have seen but didn't. They may have even tried it with the auto salesman Beattie, whose trade tags were 031 KS. But Kennedy wasn't having any. He didn't catch the Hudson's full number, TN 8135, but he caught enough to say there was a 1 and a 3, and finally confirmed they were adjacent. And he wouldn't have mistaken a Cowley for a saloon; a roadman would know his autos."

"On another point," Frances says, "Herdman, whether the police knew it or liked it or not, became irrelevant. It was understandable that he may not have seen the Kennedys leaving Kirkwhelpington. He said he left the village at about 8.10 pm, but could have taken a different route onto the A696, and the Kennedys may well not have reached the main road by then. But more than that, it would have been almost impossible for Herdman to have seen the Hudson. It was pointless for the police to imply he should have. Even at his slow pace, he would have turned off the A696 westwards to his home well before the Hudson came past at 8.20 or 8.25. He was, after all, on the A696 for much less than a mile."

Frances reaches to switch the Zafira's reading light on and shows us the exit routes from the village of Kirkwhelpington to the A696, the short distance to Knowesgate and the four miles of unclassified road that Herdman would then have driven along to his farm.

Sven eases back. "Thank you, Frances. I was struggling with the geography and that makes things clearer. It also confirms that beyond Heeston Bank there is the straight stretch of road Kennedy mentioned, on which, when he reached the brow, there was no sign of the Hudson."

"I am sitting here in some admiration of Kennedy," Peter says. "He was no fool, although Smirk did his best to make him out as one. Bates, of course, was as usual inept and when he did ask a question he blundered too far. But I see here he did one good thing, although whether he thought of it himself, or Gordon pushed him forward, is debatable. He recalled Kennedy to the stand and asked him if he had noticed how the driver was sitting in the saloon that passed him. Kennedy replied that he seemed to be sitting sideways rather than straight on. Bates should have left it there; it would have gelled with Evelyn's version of this apparently awkward journey. Instead, he confused things by asking if anything—another person or luggage—had impaired Kennedy's view. When Kennedy said 'No' it was all Smirk needed to confuse things further. He proceeded to ask Kennedy the same thing several different ways; we have all seen it done, and done cleverly it can be effective."

"But then," Bradon says as Peter stops for breath, "Smirk ventured into cheating, which is not so clever. He started asking questions framed around untruths. First, knowing that the Hudson was dark in colour, he asked Kennedy if he'd known it was light-coloured. He got the answer 'No.' He then asked if Kennedy knew it had been 'put in evidence' that the man Evelyn Foster said had taken over the driving, drove slowly. This was putting a seriously wrong slant on what Evelyn had told her mom, but having received another 'No' Smirk could at least sit back believing he may have confused the jury. If not Kennedy himself."

"And what of Kirsopp-Reed?" I ask. "What are your impressions of his evidence?"

"Nothing much," Bradon says. "His timings are suspect; driving fourteen miles out of the northern part of the city to reach Belsay in thirty minutes was fast going even if he knew the road, especially with a kid in the car. But *if* his timings were right, the large saloon he met couldn't have been Evelyn's Hudson. At 7.25 just north of Belsay he'd have been way too early."

"Precisely why the police threw him in there." Peter waves a hand. "He *should* have seen the Hudson, but was at first convinced he didn't, although he seems to have been far less sure when asked about it. And, of course, he may not have known Evelyn had recently bought another car, and there again Bates was as silent as the proverbial grave."

"But Evelyn says she saw *him*, or *his* car," Frances says. "If she wasn't on the road, how could she have said so? It has been suggested, I think by Goodman, that the police may have wanted everyone to believe that, having heard he'd be in Newcastle, she was lying in wait for him to appear so she could say without fear of contradiction she had driven to Belsay and at what time. She could then set fire to her car and attempt to dupe people with her Bowler story, which the police by then had decided was a figment. How far-fetched is that? Machiavelli would have been proud of such a scenario. Even accepting that Kirsopp-Reed had told her brother he was going to Newcastle that day, how could she have known the time he'd set off back from his business in the city? Clairvoyance? She thought she saw him in the Capheaton area, which would fit exactly with Kirsopp-Reed seeing a 'large saloon' north of Belsay. In fact, Ferney Chesters is just across the A696. But the timing is crazy; Kirsopp-Reed would have had to be fifteen or twenty minutes out. If Evelyn was at Raylees at 7.22 pm, as I think we believe, she could not have reached the Capheaton turn-off, even at 25 mph, until around 7.45 pm. And if Kirsopp-Reed was right in saying he got home at 7.55 pm, that part fits with *his* timings, assuming he was correct. Half an hour from Capheaton to Otterburn, fourteen miles, is maintaining his Newcastle-Belsay speed of between 25 and 30 mph, and he *would* have known the road. But how reliable *are* his times? Nowhere in his statement does he say he consulted a watch. It is all 'the time would have been *about* this, that or the other.' Empirical evidence. The sort of times he'd done before."

"Just hold on, people," I say. "And look again at the statements of Harrison and Kirsopp-Reed. I freely confess they are summaries, but these statements from what we might call the lay contingent, and with the exceptions of Mrs Foster, Kennedy and Beattie, were usually concise." I wait a beat.

"Oh, my," Frances is onto it. "They *saw* each other…and maybe—"

"They did, but we have a conundrum wrapped inside a mystery. Peter was keen to dismiss bus driver Harrison earlier, but Harrison says he met a car close to Ferney Chesters. Kirsopp-Reed says he met a bus two miles north of there, at Harle Post Office. Taking Reed's own estimates, he would have met this bus at 7.30 pm. But Harrison says he left his *house* at Knowesgate at 7.30 pm, and had to get to his bus and start it. There is a conundrum here, because if Harrison lived at Longwitton Station, he was five miles east of Knowesgate to begin with. But let's be kind and say he meant a house in Knowesgate. If it *was* his bus Reed saw, and it couldn't have been any other, Harrison could not have been at Harle Post Office much before 7.40 pm, and not at Ferney Chesters much before 7.45. It sounds to me as if Reed got either his times or his places wrong; most probably his times, as a bus would aim to run to its timetable. By any criterion, he may not have been a totally reliable witness, a possibility that like many things seems to have escaped our Mr Bates. In short, if Reed met his 'large saloon car' fifteen minutes later than he thought, that would begin to fit with Evelyn's story. She could well have seen him where she said she did."

"Hats off to you, maestro," Peter says. "I'll be less hasty in future." Then he spoils this gracious compliment by adding, "It's impossible to do more than surmise, you know; to try to claw our way logically through these inadequate and often conflicting statements which went totally unchallenged at the time. And, by the bye, what happened to the other 150 statements the police took but were never used in evidence? Was the coroner even privy to them?"

"I'd imagine they were filed away, out of sight and out of mind" I tell him. "Especially after the police decided the jury verdict was unsound and a line should be drawn. The same thing is by no means unknown today. But remember we are dealing with a balance of probabilities, which for the moment we might translate as a reasonable doubt, so do your best to act as Devil's advocate if you think we are in danger of bias. And by this, I mean all of you."

I think it has become time to wrap this session up; it is now quite dark and we need to get back to the city. I start the car.

"On our journey north," I add, "Sven remarked that times and distances in this case were crucial. I think you will all agree. It seems that both the police and the coroner paid insufficient attention to them, or the fact that many people—Kirsopp-Reed, Beattie and bus drivers among them—seemed to have no trouble in driving at 25 mph that night, or quicker. Beattie achieved it over a much longer distance and, after Otterburn, over no less a climb than Carter Bar, with serious hairpins as he entered Scotland—and presumably, being 1,000 feet higher, with a more severe covering of frost and ice. Why then couldn't Evelyn, with arguably the most powerful motor of all? I would like you now to reflect on what you have learned from today. Our next session, which I have pencilled in for Tuesday in Newcastle, will turn to the events that took place at ten o'clock on the Twelfth Night of 1931, and the police activities that followed on."

"I think I speak for all of us when I say we'll look forward to it," Peter grins. "Onwards and upwards. Am I hearing the sounds of Roman legionnaire's marching feet? This has been a revealing day."

I'm sure he means it. But I am looking forward equally to my weekend, and to a trip to Durham.

CHAPTER TEN

Durham City
The present day, 24-25 January

"If you apply the balance of probabilities test," Molly says to me, smiling over the table. "I think you may already have passed it. The likelihood that Evelyn could indeed have made the journey in the time, plus the sightings of the Hudson between Knowesgate and Belsay—one possible, the other more clear-cut—suggest serious flaws in the police theory. You've picked a winner, I think. It sounds to be a worthwhile project for your students, if they handle it correctly." She pauses. "Under any yardstick it has to be worthwhile for Evelyn's family, or her descendants. There'll be what?…grandnieces and nephews now, maybe still alive, and you should be able to add one or two 'greats' in front."

"I'm not totally sure if there are, or if they still live in the village."

"You should find out. You never know what kind of family folklore has been passed on to them. There could be nuggets in there you'd never get from the police or archives. Your father gave you this nugget in the first place, remember, and just think of all the tales your grandma or grandad could tell of his and *their* early lives."

Professor Molly Malone (yes, I know, when I heard her name for the first time I laughed too, then tried unsuccessfully to cover it with a cough: she said her father had no doubt had a good laugh long before me) is my—what shall I say?—my lover, I guess (I despise the word 'partner' in this context; it really belongs on a golf course or tennis court). So, yes, Molly is my lover, and she's very good at it, as I hope I am to her. I have no reason not to believe so, since we have been this way for pretty much the entire three years I've been in Newcastle. You notice I said 'this way', and if you were to ask me I couldn't tell you exactly which way that is. It is not married, or engaged, and at the other end of the spectrum is no casual thing either. We have said we love each other (many times) and I'm sure of it. But neither of us wants to change things, and we have said that often too. Why this should be so is complicated (not insuperable, but tricky) since Molly lives and works in Durham, and I live and work a mere twenty miles away. But we both rather like where we live and work. And please don't mention commuting, my friends; we are each within fifteen minutes' walk from our work, and we both like that as well.

Molly, no surprise, is a member of staff of DU's Criminology Department. She also, no surprise, is an alumnus of Trinity College Dublin's Law School, the oldest and many would agree most prestigious in Ireland. I tell her that in Durham she took a step up, since Durham University is ranked in the world's top 100, in the UK's top 10, and has been a centre of learning for over 1,000 years, tracing a continuous line of scholarship from the times of the Saints Bede and Cuthbert. A former Chancellor, one Bill Bryson, said 'it had a capacity to astound out of all proportion to its size.' I think in many ways he was spot on, but then I am a fan of his.

There, however, I tell Molly, the compliments must stop. Because, in the realm of law, Durham is ranked somewhat higher than its offshoot in Newcastle and I'm jealous. (In fact, Durham currently lies fourth in the UK behind Oxford, Cambridge and LSE). But recent trends are up in both cases, and more so in Newcastle's—which I'm modest enough to confess will have little do with me: less than two percent on a simple calculation of members of staff. And there is always the fact that these rankings change year-on-year and in most cases you could not insert a sheet of tissue paper between them in the first place.

But this aside, Molly is two years younger than me, more ambitious than me, brighter than me, and about ninety percent more beautiful than me. In fact, her male students drool over her and her female students idolise her: I've watched them. On the surface she is 5'7", slim and fair (she usually has her hair in a pony-tail but not tonight) with a well-sculpted and no-nonsense face, delicious curves and legs and a stunning smile. Below the surface she is—well, that is for me to know, and you will not be finding out.

It is now evening and we are having supper in a bar restaurant 200 yards above the Wear, at the neck of The Bailey—the horseshoe that post-glacial rebound and the river have fashioned down the centuries—a shade further from the Castle and the same again from the Cathedral. Oldfields Eating House is a weekend habit of ours, and we both like their flat iron steaks, medium rare with a side salad and French fries. That said, I am trying (not very hard) to wean us off this habit, as I am not really a creature of habit and the place does not seem to be quite as well-run as previously. But that is maybe a case of familiarity breeding ennui.

I have, of course, told Molly of my Otterburn adventure, and how it came about, but we have not discussed it in any detail since last week. She certainly knows enough to form some judgements.

But having had a week of law, and being someone with great empathy for people anyway, she is less interested in that side of things than in Evelyn Foster and her family. I can happily go along with this, as my head is spinning with times and distances and calculations of speed. Or at least it was until this afternoon, after we had greeted each other properly (i.e. improperly) and then taken a long walk along Durham's

Heritage Coast from south of Shippersea Bay to Liddle Stack and back. It is a dramatic stretch of sea and shore, with headlands, cliffs and pinnacles, shingle beaches and sandy bays along the way, but we all have our favourites—at least those lucky enough to have them do—and my favourite stretch of coast is some way north, almost the furthest extremity of Northumberland, the stretch from Beadnell north to Lindisfarne, including the Farne Islands thrusting from the sea two to five miles offshore. The sweeping beam of Longstone light will be branded in my mind for as long as we both exist, indelibly associated with falling gently asleep on childhood holidays spent in Seahouses Clifftop caravans.

Still, the Durham Heritage Coast did a good job of blowing away any cobwebs that remained after our reunion in Molly's flat. Hmm…I say 'flat', but it is a suite of upper-level rooms in a building of such character that really nothing less than 'apartment' does it justice. It is situated in an area of the city centre called Elvet, just across the River Wear from where we are eating. Which is another reason we like to visit Oldfields: except in the worst of weather, it is a pleasant walk across either Baths Bridge or the Elvet Bridge, the latter a river crossing that dates back to the 12th century and is a Grade 1 listed building.

"Yes, I know," I tell her. "I'll set one of them on it. I think Sven might enjoy it, or Bradon. Peter would be bored inside a minute."

"You should do that part yourself, I think. You know the area, you speak the tongue."

"I've tried the paper route, but it's not my forte. I was able to track Gordon, Evelyn's elder brother, who married a local girl called Mary Luke in 1924. And I got as far as four children in quick succession: Joseph in 1926, Kenneth in 1927, Sheila in 1929 and Joy in 1930, after which they seem to have felt their family was complete. I can find two records of a Margaret Foster, Evelyn's youngest sister, being married, one in 1933 and the other in 1934, both in that part of the world but not in Otterburn, to either a Drinkwater or a Brewis. Neither ring any real bells, although date-wise either bride *could* have been our Margaret Foster; we know from the headstone in St John's Church that she died aged sixty-eight in 1979, and in the early thirties she'd reached the age of majority and had been working as a bus conductress for several years. I got stuck at that point, mainly because, as you know, we only have access to Census records after a century. So the last Census available is that of 1911, and parish records haven't always been updated on websites. And I seriously object to paying for historical data which should be available to all; I don't know what the National Archives think they're playing at."

Our steaks arrive and look as appetising as ever. I know restaurants need to ring the changes to keep their regulars interested, but I'll be sad if these delights were to disappear.

"If Margaret is interred with Evelyn, it might suggest she never married," Molly says, dabbing mustard on. "Had she been, it would have been more usual for her to be interred with her husband, wouldn't it?"

"Either that, or there was some split or divorce. Or it may have been her wish. But yes, you're right. I'm afraid I gave up trying to find her."

"And the middle sister, Dorothy?"

"Dorothy's name is on Evelyn and Margaret's gravestone in Otterburn as the surviving sister, and quite possibly she is the person who had their headstone and the matching one of her parents put in place. I believe, but I could be wrong, that she died much later than her sisters, in 1994, by which time she'd have been eighty-five or so."

"Did Dorothy marry?" Molly asks. "I'm thinking, quite apart from everything else, how traumatic it must have been for the family to believe that a daughter and sister died in such horrible fashion and not a great deal was done about it."

"You're wondering if it may have caused the girls to develop a wariness of men?" I replenish our glasses with some palatable Malbec.

"How are we to know? These things live on, don't they? They have repercussions, some expected, some not."

"Well, I believe Dorothy did get married, a few years later. In fact, I'm certain of it, and it explains why she is missing from the Foster family plot. There is a record of a marriage between a Dorothy Edith Foster and a John Wright in late 1940, and three earlier birth registrations which could be her husband's. Strangely, they all refer to a John Nesbit Wright, two in Bellingham in 1900 and 1906, the third in Corsenside, West Woodburn in 1911. I'm not sure what to make of that, except that as Dorothy was born in 1909 any one of them, if they're not the same person, *could* have been her husband age-wise."

"Maybe the 1900 and 1906 were two original and rather faded or badly written records, later transcribed by two different people? The 0 and 6 simply being a little illegible?"

I nod. "That's possible."

"Any children? Dorothy, I mean."

"None I could be sure of, or anywhere near sure of. A score of Wright children were born between 1940 and 1950, but only one in the registration district of Northumberland West, which included Otterburn and Bellingham. And none where the father's name was given as Wright and the mother's as Foster. Three with the alternative spelling, Forster with an 'r', but they were all registered in Newcastle."

"They could have moved, of course."

"They could." I surreptitiously take out a page of notes.

Molly, typically, won't let this go. I have time for only a couple of mouthfuls of my steak before she comes at me again.

"So your best route is with the four children of Gordon and Mary, Evelyn's nieces and nephews, any of whom might still be alive today. If they are, from what you said earlier, they would be well into their eighties now. But it's not impossible, is it? And surely one or two would have married and had issue." She smiles. "A job for you next week. What are you fidgeting with under the table?"

I swallow a piece of steak and lift the wine bottle. "More wine?"

She laughs. "Come on, Matthew. What is that piece of paper?"

"I did try to go a little further before giving up," I tell her.

"You aren't playing hard to get, are you? It's a bit too late for that, isn't it? Not to mention out of character."

I glance down at my notes. "Of Gordon and Mary's four children, their first-born Joseph died when he was little more than a year old; his grave is next to his aunts' in St John's churchyard. So there was another tragedy in this family some years before Evelyn's." I shake my head. "Of course, children in those days were much more prone to illnesses and diseases we barely think of now as common killers. Polio, whooping cough, TB, measles and the like. Kenneth married a girl called Doreen Robinson, who seems to have been from nearer Newcastle, in 1959. He took over the business from his grandfather and father, who remarried after Mary predeceased him in 1952 and died himself in 1968. Kenneth died in 1994. He and Doreen may have had two children at least. His son Christopher may have married in Essex in 1983, Alison a man called Richard Forster, with an 'r', in north Tyneside in 1989. I'm not sure.

"Evelyn's niece Sheila may have married a local man, Thomas Scott, in 1956 and died in 1995, also in north Tyneside. They may have had three children; Catherine, born in 1958, Susan in 1959, and/or Jacqueline in 1962. Sheila seems to have drifted south towards Newcastle with her family. I apologise for all the 'maybes', but it's the best I could do and none except Kenneth—Joseph, of course—are guaranteed to be accurate. I wasn't able to find any further reference to Joy after her birth. As you say, she may have moved. I just hope it wasn't yet another family tragedy."

"This is the work of a dark horse, working behind the scenes."

"Only a case of some preparation," I say modestly. "And I haven't even touched on a possible wider family; this all has to do with Evelyn's siblings and *their* possible offspring. They could, some of them, still be known in the Otterburn area but there has clearly been some movement away and this is all a long time ago. So, when you suggest I might do a bit of digging around, I would shy away from dragging them back uninvited into a sensitive area of their family history."

"Well, there is one thing you can do for them, and for yourself. You have the means to provide some solace. And if it is an indirect means, you shouldn't cause them heartache: with luck, the reverse."

"And that is?"

"You are already more than a little dissatisfied with the way this matter was handled initially, as I gather your students may be, too. You are also dissatisfied with the various attempts that have been made to investigate it by true crime authors, given that most were written a long time ago. You, my love, and your merry band, need to write your own version, and dedicate it to any remaining members of Evelyn's family you have semi-tracked or not been able to track. There must be some out there, connected with the names you've mentioned."

I take a sip of wine and think about it. "It's an idea, provided we feel when it's all over that we have something useful to contribute."

A little later over coffee, as though she has heard my earlier thoughts, Molly says, "We're lucky people, you know, you and I."

"Yes, but what makes you say so?"

"We are both only children, although that has its disadvantages when it comes to family support structures. But we had, or have, parents who devoted themselves exclusively to us, and provided us with secure childhoods. We both retain strong connections with those childhoods; you with Hexhamshire and the north Northumberland hills and coast, me with the stud countryside of Kildare and the coast and mountains of Kerry and Killarney. Our parents saw that we were both well-educated and encouraged us to make good use of it. Birthdays and Christmases and holidays were happy, memory-filled times. Our parents are—in one case were—secure in that knowledge. They know they've done a good job. We ourselves have enjoyed, so far, except for a marital error apiece, an untroubled and fulfilling existence. And now we've won each other in the love lottery. I could go on, but I'm sure you get the message."

"You are saying the Foster family had these things removed."

"I'm saying Evelyn ran out of our kind of luck. I'm saying she may have been victimised twice over. I can only begin to imagine the anguish it caused her family. She died in a brutal and inhuman way, in an excruciatingly painful way, and then seems to have been dismissed as someone of little value, not worthy of sustained or genuine effort, by the authorities of the time. They lit upon a theory or excuse that suited them, and rammed it home to the point where only her family and friends in the community held on to a nastier truth. People forget, they put such things behind them, but her sisters never forgot. Her sister Margaret is on record as saying so, isn't she? We've talked before about the many forms hypocrisy can take. We're still puritanical, aren't we, when it comes to such events? We still live in a world in which, when women are victims, they remain liable to be judged as having brought it on themselves, whether or not it's the case. Except for dedicated care workers and priests, that is often and sadly the first response. And more so then, when there was not the veneer of political correctness we have now; when the authorities' word, except in radical circles, was taken as their inalienable right. Am I saying anything you find questionable or invalid?"

"I'm glad you said 'dedicated', and assume it included the priests."

Molly gives me a quick smile. She says, "And let's think about this: in the days of their lives afterwards, her family members, especially her parents but also her siblings, would have occupied themselves with their vehicles and their chores, doing housework, buying food and clothing and making ends meet. All the everyday things we do on automatic pilot and are far easier now than they were then. But their nights would have been another matter, wouldn't they? In their beds, in the wee small hours, they would have been treated to a long-running horror movie, with no means short of drugs to stop it playing."

She tells me the Evelyn Foster case study has inspired her to do something similar with a class in Durham. She has researched other local unsolved crimes, including the murders of May Thompson, 18 years old (stabbed 36 times but not raped or robbed) in Low Spennymoor in 1952; John Bianchi, also 18 (shot once in the stomach from behind a hedge) in the Biggs Main area in 1919; and William Abbey (a Ferryhill bank clerk hit with a paperweight and stabbed with a cobbler's knife by Norman Elliott in 1928). But nothing, she says, seems to have the same resonance as the case of Evelyn Foster. Although equally tragic for their families, none of these deaths, or others she has found so far, offers a depth of material suitable for a case study. She adds that the Bianchi case is more my territory anyway and she wouldn't like to encroach. (Biggs Main was where Wallsend Golf Course is today and has been called 'The Village that Died'—although there are quite a few others of that ilk in the former mining areas of Northumberland and Durham.) As for Norman Elliott, she says *The Northern Echo* has recently been on the case.

Whilst doing this, Molly tells me she checked out every murder committed in the UK from 1920-40. Two—and only two—stand out as having elements in common with Evelyn Foster's death. We spend time over dessert discussing the crimes of Alfred Rouse and Ernest Brown.

Our meal finished, we meander back arm-in-arm through Palace Green and across Kingsgate Bridge, a longer route but one that enables us to enjoy the Castle and Cathedral sitting atop their leafy hill. It may be a World Heritage Site, and deservedly so as the resting-place of two great Northern saints, but it also makes for a delightful lover's walk.

I have my own version of the horror movie that night. I see flames leaping from molten metal and wood and upholstery, licking my face and chest, burning my flesh, blistering. There are sounds of creaking, crackling, sizzling, spitting. There is a stink of charring pork and pus and acrid smoke and petrol, a display of fireworks arcing against a darkened sky, a shadowy figure stumbling away, a wailing that might be coming from my own throat. I collapse on the ground, a hard arctic earth that fizzes and melts as I fall on it and try to crawl, twisting, turning, tearing at my clothes, fingers clawing at icy clumps of turf…I wake up with a cry, throwing bedclothes off myself, and an instant later find myself slumped pitiably on the floor.

Molly is kneeling on the carpet beside me in the blink of an eye. I had forgotten she was there, that anyone else was in the room.

"What on earth…?" She puts her arms around me and strokes the back of my head. I am still shuddering, trembling, sweating profusely, and try to catch my breath.

Finally, I manage to say, "A bad dream…just a bad dream."

I start to apologise and she shushes me.

"Don't be silly," she says, "you were having a five-star nightmare."

A dreadful thought occurs. "I didn't hit you, flailing about, did I?"

"No, no," she says, "of course not. The first thing I knew was when you gave a shout, and then crashed onto the floor. You aren't hurt, are you, Matthew? No bones broken? You didn't bang your head?"

"No. I'll be fine. Just give me a minute."

She holds me close, her skin as cool and soothing as silk, and tells me to relax, that we will go downstairs and have hot chocolate and a brandy, maybe a shower as I am perspiring so much. Eventually she stands and takes me by the hand.

This is why I feel safe with her, as I hope she does with me. Other than mundanities, neither of us talks about the other to our colleagues; we are private to the point of impoliteness. Molly is confident and secure and practical enough to take things as they come and deal with them: no games, no artifice, no dramas. She also likes us to shower together, and it never fails to put things in perspective.

"I hope that doesn't happen again when I'm not there," she says as we move away from the bed. "You need to step back a little, sweetheart. This is reaching somewhere deep inside you, as if it hadn't done enough to people already."

But stepping back from people is not in Molly's make-up. In the kitchen she says, "We should call her Evie, don't you think? I'm sure her friends would have called her that."

CHAPTER ELEVEN

Newcastle Law School: the present day, 27 January
Concerning 10.00 pm, 6 January 1931, and later

Needless to say the case study goes on, and I have had two good night's sleep, the first with Molly in Durham and the second back here in Newcastle. Maybe my dream was a one-off: I hope so. We have discussed it again several times, Molly and I, and know beyond doubt that Evelyn's torture was one of millions of such cases, many of them much worse. With luck, you will not see this weakness recur. I have told my students what happened, so they will be forewarned and will not feel embarrassed should they experience anything similar.

It is a bitter January morning, a cutting wind blowing in from the northeast, an inch of snow on the ground. Foot traffic is already dirtying it, turning it to slush, but the tracery of branches and twigs above still looks attractive. As I walked to work past Brandling Park, diverting for a coffee-to-go at Hugo's window, ominous grey clouds were building over the rooftops and it was clear more snow was in the offing.

We are once more gathered in a Law School seminar room, the table spread with maps and notes (largely Bradon's): in fact, it is not unlike an incident room. Before we begin on the later part of Twelfth Night 1931, I ask them to look again at bus driver Cecil Johnstone's statement. This is for no other purpose than to emphasise something. He had left Hexham for Otterburn at 5.00 pm that night with fifteen passengers, stopping on his way to drop people off and pick them up: he mentioned Wall, Swinburne, Colwell and Woodburn. He arrived in Otterburn at 6.20 pm with three passengers remaining; those Evelyn had taken on to Rochester.

"Twenty-five miles in eighty minutes," I point out. "About the same distance and time that the police later concluded Evelyn could not have achieved in her Hudson. Johnstone was driving a bus, for much of the way on a Roman military road notorious for making no concessions to topography, with blind summits, minor diversions and stops en route."

"Was that a drum-roll I heard?" Peter puts a hand to his ear.

Cecil Johnstone's Tale (ID1)

Johnstone, 28 years old, was employed by Joseph Foster & Son and was called as a witness at the inquest—an important if unlucky one. A dark good-looking man with a firm chin and deep-set eyes, rarely seen without a pipe, his next journey of the evening began at 6.30 pm in Otterburn. He arrived at Newcastle's Haymarket station at 8.00 pm (30 miles in 90 minutes, with a few stops, the climb from Raylees and the northern part of the city to negotiate).

His return journey to Otterburn, with Tommy Rutherford conducting, began at 9.00 pm, with no suggestion of a bad moon rising. At 9.20 he was in Ponteland, a time-check (8 miles/24 mph). When he reached Knowesgate, (with stops at Belsay, Ferney Chesters and Kirkwhelpington) it was 9.55 (16 more miles in 35 minutes/27 mph). Here, his bus emptied of passengers.

After two miles he told Rutherford, who was practising his driving, to stop at Wolf's Nick 'in consequence of seeing a fire on the moor to my right.' He got out to investigate, at first not recognising the car that was on fire, or even, in the dark, that it *was* a car amongst the heather. He then heard a keening moan and saw 'a dark object' lying on the moor nine yards away 'on the opposite side of the car from the road.' Walking over and kneeling down, he recognised the object as his employer's daughter. As she had 'no clothes on the lower part of her body' he took off his overcoat and wrapped it around her. He saw the skin of one of her palms was almost burned off and her eyes were puffed-up. When he asked if anyone else was with her, the first thing she said was, 'Oh, that awful man,' and 'he has gone in a motor-car.' Then, as he lifted her to carry her to the bus, she said, 'If you get me onto my feet I will try and walk.' He ignored this and carried her, and she repeated, 'Oh, that awful man.'

Johnstone put Evelyn on the bus, tried to make her comfortable, and secured his scarf around her so she didn't slip off the seat. He noticed that the skin around her eyes was discoloured, 'as if black and blue with blows.' She kept staring at her hands and asking for a drink. He stopped at Blaxter, a cottage some three miles towards Otterburn, where Rutherford got her a drink of water. Johnstone then drove directly to The Kennels, seeing no strangers or cars on the journey.

In response to questions from Bates and Smirk, Johnstone said when he arrived the car was burning and 'red inside'; he could not judge how long it had been alight. Its two offside doors were open, the nearside doors closed. They were in the same position when he returned at 1.00 am with Thomas Vasey, P.C. Fergusson, P.C. Proud and Sgt. Shanks (see later). When they left, one of the nearside doors had been opened but not, he stressed, by him.

Thomas Rutherford's Tale (ID1)

Rutherford was a bus conductor employed by Joseph Foster & Son and lived in Otterburn. In his late teens, a brown-haired stocky youth with a wide mouth, he was Cecil Johnstone's conductor on their trip from Newcastle on the evening of 6 January. He told the inquest the burning car was 'about 30 yards from the road.' On approaching it (in some trepidation), he noticed part of the rear was on fire but the inside of the car was burned out. He, too, had seen a 'black object' lying on the grass 'between the car and road'; he, too, had heard a moan and Evelyn say, 'Oh, that awful man'; and he, too, had noticed the bad black-and-blue marks around her eyes. Rutherford assisted in getting her into the bus and home. He escaped without being questioned.

Thomas Vasey's Tale (Part One) (ID1)

Vasey was a motor mechanic employed by Joseph Foster & Son and also lived in Otterburn. He was on night shift that evening. A tall, strongly-built man with dark straight hair, he had gone to the bus as it pulled up outside The Kennels at about 10.30 pm and saw Evelyn 'propped up in a seat.' He saw she was 'terribly burned' and as soon as she saw him she said, 'Oh, Vasey, lift me up.' He tried to calm her and, with her brother Gordon's help, carried her upstairs to bed in the family home. On the way upstairs, he asked, 'Who did this, Evelyn?' She replied, 'He threw something over me and set me on fire in the car.' In response to police solicitor Smirk, Vasey also confirmed that Robert Luke had been in the garage earlier at 7.00 pm.

"Comments so far, people?" I ask.

"Obviously all *these* people had no problem in breezing around the countryside at 25-30 mph that night," Peter says sardonically. "The fact that the fire was almost out an hour later fits in with the shepherd Henderson's story, but I wish we knew exactly when it was lit. Two minutes before he spotted it? Five? Ten?"

"She was a brave girl," Frances says. "Asking Johnstone to get her on her feet, and in the circumstances being able to talk at all. She must have been in agony, half burned, half frozen. Certainly in shock."

"No clothes on her lower body?" Bradon asks. "And no questions asked? Had they been taken off, ripped off, burned off, or what? And how come the bus guys saw her on different sides of the car?"

"Everyone seems to have rallied round," Sven says. "No matter how sickened they must have been by the sight and smell. I mean, these weren't medics or fire-workers or soldiers, were they? Just normal guys, looking forward to finishing work and getting home."

"What was this fellow Smirk about?" Peter asks. "Trying to cast doubt every which way till Sunday, trailing detritus across everyone's path? Okay, these are prosecutor's tricks, but had he no sense of justice for this family or their friends at all? These days, he'd have needed an armed escort to get him out of there in one piece. And the police were short of vehicles? No doubt they could have bought half a dozen for the money they paid him for this unsavoury piece of work."

"But they were different days, Peter," I tell him. "And I'm sure we'll see many more examples of just how different. As for Bradon's points, we will certainly need to revisit the question of clothing. I can only assume Johnstone walked around the car to look into the open offside doors, or was confused. Evelyn seems to have been trying to crawl towards the road for help, so I'm sure Rutherford's version makes sense."

Mrs Margaret Foster's Tale (Part Three) (during ID1)

As her statement moved towards a conclusion, the emotional pressures on Mrs Foster cranked up. Evelyn was brought to The Kennels at 10.35 pm. On hearing she was burned, her mother asked Dorothy to phone for the doctor and call a neighbour, Mrs Christian Jennings, to come to the house, and to waken her sister Margaret. Mrs Foster then hurried upstairs to prepare Evelyn's bed. Gordon Foster ran to the bus, having been told by Johnstone that Evelyn was in a bad way. Dorothy evaded Johnstone's attempts to stop her, asked him to fetch the nurse, and followed Gordon. Evelyn told them: 'It's been that man. He hit me and burned me.' Gordon asked her to describe him: 'About your build, a little taller (Gordon was 5'6"), not quite so stout. He was dark, wore a suit, and had a bowler hat and dark overcoat.'

Lying at last on her bed upstairs, still wrapped in Johnstone's coat, Evelyn told her mother she was cold and something was hurting her back. Mrs Jennings arrived and Dorothy came back inside. In the confusion, no one had forewarned the three women of the extent of Evelyn's burns. When they removed the coat, they met a sight that would stay with them till their dying day. 'It was hard to believe the flesh was human,' Dorothy would later say.

The district nurse arrived soon after 11.00 pm, having been brought from Elsdon by Johnstone. Nurse Lawson confined her attentions at first to Evelyn's facial burns; the rest were beyond any treatment she could offer. It was only when Evelyn asked her to see to the burns on her legs that the nurse tried her best. She was still trying when Dr Duncan McEachran, a young assistant in the Bellingham practice, arrived. He helped the nurse finish the task and treated Evelyn for shock. He was followed at 11.45 pm by Dr Miller, the family's GP, who had been on a call and had travelled from Bellingham when told by his wife that Dorothy had phoned. (Miller was almost brought to tears when Evelyn apologised for bringing him out on such a cold night). The doctors conferred, and then took Mrs Foster and Dorothy downstairs. McEachran told the family there was no hope of Evelyn recovering. Miller said, 'It's amazing she can talk. I wish for her sake she wasn't so strong. We can only hope and pray she doesn't rally.' It would be as well, he added, if the police came quickly while she was still able to answer questions.

Joseph Foster's Tale (Part One) (ID1)

Evelyn's father was 57 when the tragedy occurred. He had not seen her leave for Rochester but saw her when she returned. Through her mother, he had provided the estimate for her trip to Ponteland but had no direct conversation with her at that time. He overheard her say she going to fill the Hudson up, saw her leave for Ponteland and said the time then would be about 7.20 pm.

When Evelyn was 'brought home by Johnstone' Joseph Foster followed his son Gordon to the bus. Until that point neither had felt concern that she was late returning home; they assumed she may have picked up another fare or had met George Phillipson in the village. Evelyn asked him to bring her a drink and he took her some coffee. In the kitchen, he asked if anyone had called the police and when Dorothy told him she thought not, said he would phone the village constable. When he returned to Evelyn and asked her what had happened, who had done this to her, she 'simply held up her hands.'

Mr Foster testified that the Hudson was Evelyn's own car. It was sea-green in colour and the interior was 'sort of a green plush.' It was a right-hand drive, had three gears forward, one reverse, its brakes were 'alright' and it was 'a very fast car.' There was a luggage chest at the rear, never locked, which had two retaining clips. A 2-gallon Pratt's petrol can wrapped in a sack was always carried as a spare. He had last seen the can ten days before, when it had 'a piece of wire on it'. He said Evelyn was an experienced driver, had owned several cars, the Hudson was in perfect order and her driving licence was in force. She had paid over £200 for it in a lump sum fourteen months previously. It was insured, but on 6 January the road licence was not up-to-date; he had renewed it on 14 January. He was asked by Dodds to provide details of Evelyn's finances and the insurance policies, which he agreed to do.

He knew of no worries Evelyn may have had, financial or otherwise.

"We have a small example here of people's time-keeping," I tell the four students. "Mr Foster says it was about 7.20 when Evelyn left, but that would not have given her time to reach Raylees by 7.22, Robson's estimate. Minutes either way are critical, but we have no means now of asking for verification, and even if we did it is unlikely the two times could be reconciled exactly. In Mr Foster's case his estimate was qualified, as usual, by the word *about* 7.20 pm, and if he were standing here before us he would be unlikely to be able to improve on it. We need to think our way through Evelyn's journey, and the statements we've read."

I see Bradon is getting to work. I hope it's as useful as his last effort.

"I know the Fosters would have been reading prepared statements," Frances says, "but they seem genuine throughout. No 'spin', nothing covered up, no attempt made to do so. It could even be said that Joseph did himself no favours with some of his evidence. He could, for example, have made a bigger issue of Evelyn's 'holding up her hands.' He could have said she gave him chapter and verse on her assailant. Who was to know otherwise? He could have said he'd watched her leave and there was no sign of George Phillipson on the street."

There is no dissent. I'm pleased Frances picked up on the nuances.

"I've done some basic stuff on times and distances," Bradon says, nodding at the papers strewn on the table. "Or as near as I could calculate. Except for the two miles from Raylees up to the Ottercops, where I've halved the speed to 12 mph, I've used an average of 23-26 mph throughout, and think I've been generous with time at Wolf's Nick."

I look at his notes. Bradon is proving to be a very valuable member of this small group, not least because he directs his efforts to areas in which he is more than competent and thinks will help everyone:

Place	Distance	Time	Notes
The Kennels	(departure point)	7.15 pm (say)	Stop at Percy Arms
Raylees	2.7 miles	7.22 pm	Av. 23 mph: bus met
Ottercops masts	+ 2 miles	7.32 pm	Av. 12 mph
Belsay (south)	+ 13 miles	8.02 pm (arr.)	Av. 26 mph: K-Reed
Turn at Belsay	-	8.05 pm (dep.)	J Kennedy/Mrs J K
Wolf's Nick	11 miles	8.31 pm	Av. 25 mph
Car off road	-	8.33 pm	-
Assault on EF	-	8.37 pm	-
Set car alight	-	8.41 pm	Car ablaze 8.45: SH

Peter says, "Bradon, yo da man, if you know the expression. I struggled to get a pass mark at maths—sorry, *math*—and here you are again with data a dolt could grasp. And there, in ten simple lines, is the destruction of a good chunk of the police's theory; namely, that Evelyn could not possibly have driven to Belsay and back. For heaven's sake, she could have slowed down and still driven it. And what evidence is there to suggest she wasn't going even faster? We have Evelyn herself, from Otterburn to Birdhopecraig, doing an average of 28 mph; we have buses from Hexham and to Newcastle, stopping and starting and matching Bradon's times; we have John Kennedy saying the car that passed him was going exceptionally fast; we have Joseph Foster saying it was a very fast car; we have Walter Beattie going as quickly as Evelyn *couldn't* go over a much longer distance between Ponteland and Hawick; we have County Councillor Kirsopp-Reed, child in tow, rattling along between Gosforth and Belsay, and then between Ferney Chesters and Otterburn Old Town Farm, at 25-30 mph. Assuming he knew his times, that is."

He pauses. This is an impressive off-the-cuff catalogue and he has the others appreciative, if not spellbound. All of them are smiling.

"I'll tell you what happened here, and please feel free to give me a roasting if I prove to be wrong. What happened here is that the police quickly realised they had got off on the wrong foot and made serious errors of both commission and omission. They hadn't found this man, they were fed up with the local flak they were getting, they felt hounded by the criticism daily being levelled at them in the press, so they decided: why bother with all this grief? What have we done to deserve it? Let these yokels rot. They don't deserve our best efforts, or any efforts at all."

"Well now, there's a forthright statement," I say. "And it may be, Peter, you are partly right. That table of Bradon's—give or take a minute, as before—does seem to speak for itself, and fits broadly with Kirsopp-Reed, Kennedy and Henderson's evidence. If anything, she may well have been faster going south. *But* you are jumping ahead of the game again. We undertook to be careful, meticulous in our approach. We have not yet looked at the police side of this story, nor considered how their efforts may have been decided or viewed. They may have thought it would have been difficult for her to drive the distance in the time she had available, but at no point did they openly say as much. Symons says only that 'it was suggested by the police that Evelyn Foster had driven no further than Wolf's Nick', but he doesn't say who said so or when. Dixon builds part of his thesis around the suggestion, but also without citing a source. He says 'the police attempted to form a theory that Evelyn drove her car no further than the point known as Wolf's Nick', and worse, that 'they were in a passion for it' although they 'failed to show any proof'.

Later, he repeats, 'the police maintained their theory that Evelyn Foster did not drive as far as Belsay, in fact went no further than Wolf's Nick'. He claims it was odd that Sidney Henderson was not questioned about his evidence since his statement, 'if the times were noted, proved beyond all doubt that Evelyn Foster never travelled as far as Belsay; she simply did not have the time'. Yet Dixon himself calculates that Evelyn drove to Birdhopecraig and back earlier at 23 mph, and otherwise uses 16-20 mph as pretty much his marker for speed that night—until, somewhat out of the blue and towards his conclusion, he says, 'given her average speed of 14 mph, and there is no reason for believing she drove any faster, she could only have driven as far as Ferney Chesters road end...and back again'. Goodman suggests that the only reason the 'irrelevant witness' Harrison was called was to mislead the jury into thinking Evelyn had not driven past Knowesgate; that Kirsopp-Reed's evidence was presented with much the same motive in mind; and that Herdman was there simply to show that the car Kennedy had seen south of Knowesgate was his, not Evelyn's. Goodman also says that Kirsopp-Reed also stated, 'about 200 yards north of Belsay, about 7.20, I met a car at Ferney Chesters'. Which is odd to say the least, given that Ferney Chesters is four miles from Belsay, and throws additional doubt on Kirsopp-Reed's evidence.

"In any event," I add, "we need to consider what the police actually did say, so I suggest we do that now, and in our next session."

"That should be fun'" Frances says. "For us, if not the ghosts of that poor family. We should apologise in advance for raking over old ashes."

"I hope 'old ashes' was just a Freudian slip, Fran," Peter says.

What to do with him? He is incorrigible to the point of infuriating at times. And yet...

"That is not amusing, Peter," I tell him. "Not even close."

"Sorry," he says, looking me straight in the eye.

I wish.

CHAPTER TWELVE

Newcastle Law School: the present day, 27 January
Concerning 10.45 pm-1.00 am, 6-7 January 1931

I direct their attention to the police activities in the hours immediately
following Evelyn's return home. But first, a word on the hierarchy:

Although in the days afterwards, members of the Northumberland
Constabulary were active in following up reported 'sightings' in parts of
the county and (belatedly) patrolling roads and cross-roads, there were
principally ten officers with starring or supporting roles in the case; a case
which at the outset they believed was a murder investigation. From the
top down they were: Chief Constable Captain Sir Fullarton James; Supt.
James McGilvray Tough; Supt. Thomas Shell; Supt. Thomas Spratt;
Inspector Edward Russell; Sgt. Robert Shanks; P.C. Andrew Fergusson
(the Otterburn bobby); P.C Henry Proud (Bellingham); P.C. William
Turnbull (Ridsdale); and P.C. Francis Sinton (Kirkwhelpington). First on
the scene, or at least at Foster's Garage, was P.C. Fergusson.

These policemen are now all dead, along with every other actor on
the stage you have met so far, so it may be unfair to be critical (as much as
it would be unfair not to be). But there are grounds for believing that this
line-up could have been inverted, flipped, with no adverse effect on the
conduct of the Evelyn Foster inquiry. There is no evidence I know of that
trauma and distress, self-inflicted or inflicted by others, severe or not so
severe (I am thinking of everything from childhood anxieties to abuse to
imprisonment to the theatres of war), can prolong active life, but there *is*
evidence to suggest that in many cases—not all, but many—they can
shorten it. I have little doubt that some of the actors you have met so far,
excluding incidental witnesses, will have had days of their lives stolen
from them, and likewise some of those you are still to meet.

I remind my troops that, in 1931 as now, murder cases in rural
Northumberland were rare—which partly explains the high profile in this
case of the Constabulary's highest-ranking officer. But Capt. Sir Fullarton
James and his deputy Tough were no newcomers to murder. They had
presided over the notorious Sun Inn triple murder case in Bedlington
eighteen years before, and Fullarton James in the case of the John Nisbet
murder on a Morpeth train three years before that. Less easy to explain is
the Constabulary's shortage of motor vehicles. Cars had been used in the
Sun Inn case (one to convey Fullarton James to the scene), and eight years
earlier four motorbikes were commandeered to escort the Prince of Wales
on a visit to Alnwick Castle. But it was not until 1930 that any serious

cash was laid on the table—to purchase a car and four motor-cycle combinations. Most neutral observers believed that Fullarton James was a man out of his time and place; his time was fifty years earlier and his place was a gentleman's club. It was only partly his fault he got where he did. Born in Dublin, he was the archetypal retired army officer, having resigned in 1897 from the Royal Scots Fusiliers to become Chief Constable of the Welsh county of Radnor. Three years later he was appointed to his Northumberland post. He was then 37, a youthful age, but the words 'innovation' and 'initiative' seemed to have been censored from his dictionary. He confined himself to matters such as ensuring his officers ceased to use their night-shift waist belts as razor strops, and that they complied with a system of coded postcard messages (specifying uniform or plain clothes, with bicycle or without) in their attendance at parades. Perhaps he missed more suitable vocations as a cryptanalyst or spook.

Sherlock Holmes may have worked his fictional cases only a few years earlier, but the Chief Constable seemed oblivious to any benefits his force might gain from either forensic science or the appointment and training of detectives. The Northumberland County Constabulary, an entity of 300-400 men (no women then) had none. It was not until 1935, after Capt. Fullarton James had retired (he died twenty years later), that a CID was created by his successor. Meantime there were a handful of designated plain-clothes officers—one, John Eckford ('No. 7'), took Mary Murray's statement—all stationed in urban areas around Newcastle, which had its own separate force. None had received training in detective work. Before 1931, there was only one recorded instance of forensic science being used to help solve a case, and it was due to the initiative of a constable in Ashington. He noticed fingerprints on white panelling at the scene of a shop-breaking, removed the wood and sent it with a list of known felons to Scotland Yard, who found a match.

This was therefore a police force, I tell my four students, which embarked on the Foster case labouring under severe disadvantages. Some of its own officers, let alone the fellowship of local crime reporters, recognised its inadequacies. The expectation that Scotland Yard personnel would be brought in to lead the investigation was immediate. It did not happen; it was apparently not even considered by the Chief Constable, or if so it was soon dismissed. This left the local policemen literally and metaphorically stumbling around in the dark. Some may not have been the sharpest knives in the rack, but the rack was no work or art either.

P.C. Andrew Fergusson's Tale (Part One) (ID2)
Fergusson, a heavyset and deliberate man, 35 years old, was in the Police Office at Otterburn at about 10.45 pm on 6 January 1931 when he received a

phone message from Joseph Foster to say that his daughter Evelyn had been brought home in one of his buses at 10.30. She was severely burned.

Fergusson immediately phoned Sergeant Shanks, his superior officer, in Bellingham. He then went to the garage, where he met Vasey (Joseph at this point was waiting for him in the house). He did not call in to see Miss Foster.

While Fergusson was at the garage Shanks arrived, a passenger in Dr McEachran's car. The two policemen had a brief conversation, after which Shanks asked Joseph and Gordon Foster to repeat what they had already told the constable. Shanks then wandered over to the bus, in which Johnstone and Rutherford had taken up residence—presumably waiting to be asked to do something useful. Shanks didn't speak to them, instead falling into deep thought and viewing the bus as if it were the crime scene. He went back into the garage and told Fergusson to phone Supt. Shell in Hexham. There was some discussion with Mr Foster about the easier option of phoning from The Kennels but Fergusson, with Shanks's approval, declined (this may have been in order to keep his police records straight). He and Shanks set off back to the police house at 11.45 pm. Neither at that point had visited The Kennels.

After this phone call, Fergusson and Shanks returned to the garage at just after midnight and were shown across the road and upstairs into Evelyn's bedroom. In it with Evelyn were Dr McEachran, Dr Miller, Nurse Lawson and Mrs Foster. Fergusson could not recall if Evelyn's sisters were present.

He started to take a statement from Evelyn, making notes himself while her mother asked the questions. Fergusson and Shanks left the house at 12.30 am and shortly afterwards headed for Wolf's Nick in one of Joseph Foster's cars. They were driven there by Vasey, accompanied by Johnstone and P.C. Proud from Bellingham, and arrived at 1.00 am. Fergusson then set about examining the burned car and its surroundings.

"Apart from noting that Fergusson did little or nothing between 10.45 and 11.45 pm, except chatting to Vasey and the male Fosters, are we sure we have covered all the main points of this so-called interview already?" Peter asks. "I know we've relied on the various parts of Margaret Foster's statement for most of it, but what about the tone, the set-up? For instance, it seems very strange that neither policeman asked questions directly. Fergusson more or less acted as an amanuensis, and Shanks took on the role of Lot's wife. He seems already to have been floundering."

"The interview lasted no more than twenty minutes or so," I remind them, "and Dr McEachran had made it clear they would be well advised to get on with it. It has been suggested that Fergusson said he was having difficulty in hearing what Evelyn was saying, but this seems to have been a tale which grew without real foundation. In any event, Mrs Foster took over the questioning and Fergusson jotted down both the questions and Evelyn's answers. It wasn't comprehensive, it wasn't sequential, it was messy, but it was done after a fashion. And it may be that Shanks decided it would be best if Fergusson took the lead role as he was well-known to everyone present."

"Yet we don't know which questions were asked on Mrs Foster's initiative or the police's," Frances says. "Who precisely made the running during it? At the inquest, Dr McEachran said it was Fergusson, who in turn—perhaps in deference to seniority—said it was Shanks, who wasn't even called as a witness. Which is weird in itself. I mean, had he said or done something to offend his superiors? Or *not* done something?"

"I think all we can say," I tell them, "is that Evelyn was consistent throughout. None of the statements or answers she gave in that room, as available to us now, were materially different to those she had earlier given her rescuers and family members. From Elishaw, to the car she'd seen this man emerge from and who was in it, to her description of the man, to Otterburn, Belsay, Wolf's Nick and the assault she'd suffered, nothing except the odd word here or there changed. It may have been incomplete, sometimes vague, but it held together. Simple questions she should have been asked—for example, how she had come to meet Bowler again at the Percy Arms; whether he had been awaiting her; whether she had needed to go into the hotel; whether she had noted the time on any part of her journey; whether Bowler had used a lighter or matches on his cigarettes; whether he had actually taken the wheel and trapped her completely against the door—were ignored. Having been told by the doctors and *knowing* she was close to death, the police left The Kennels at half past twelve apparently without reviewing any gaps they may have left behind or wondering if their questioning had achieved all it should. It almost seems as if they couldn't get out of there quickly enough, although to be fair the doctors may have objected to their continuing any longer. And they were not to know at that stage anything about the theory they would eventually pursue, so some questions would not have occurred to them. What *should* have occurred to them was to make absolutely sure, in their own minds, that she was telling the truth.

"From the perspective of Evelyn's story, I believe the ambiguities or inconsistencies, such as they are, mainly revolve around four issues: precisely what nature the assault on her had taken; their modus operandi in driving back from Belsay, assuming they did; how and when Evelyn was forced into the back seat and/or assaulted; and how and when she and the car were set alight." I let them ponder that for a moment or two.

I then say, "We should consider the mother-daughter relationship first, I think, and the moral code of that era."

"She would have been reticent at describing anything of a sexual nature to her Mum," Frances says. "They both used euphemisms, words like 'interference', and both no doubt knew what *they* meant by them. But did they know what the *other* person meant? Or was hearing?"

I say, "Precisely, Frances."

"I imagine there was very little coarse language used between mothers and daughters—at least those who were respectable, and respectful—in the 1930s. There was nothing like the prevalent and casual use of profanities we know today. At puberty, there'd have been lessons in personal matters like menstruation, but little talk of sex acts or sexual urges. Add a policeman or two into the mix, and *nothing* of a risqué or embarrassing nature would have come out of Evelyn's mouth or her Mum's. You talked of coded messages earlier but I doubt whether even they would apply in this scenario. It would have been uncomfortable for them and they had much more important things to worry about."

"Which is one of the differences we mentioned," I say to Peter before he has the chance to launch into another compelling theory.

"Some mothers and daughters would find it hard now," he replies.

"But," Frances goes on, "I'm thinking about something else we mentioned. I'm wondering *why* at this stage, if anyone—her family, the police, Johnstone, Rutherford, the doctors, the nurse, the neighbour—had even had a whiff of something not quite right in what she was saying or in how she was behaving, they didn't say so. Apart from the fact that it seems an extraordinary story to concoct, inconsistencies and all, and knowing or suspecting that she was fading fast, why would she persist in it if it wasn't true? What had she to gain at that stage? Her dying words to her mother were, *Mother…I have been murdered.* I know I'm jumping the gun, Matthew, but for heaven's sake, if she had been lying, wouldn't she have been more inclined to say, 'I'm sorry I've been such a fool' or 'this is all my fault' or 'I've made an awful mistake?' If she had been lying, she'd have been more likely to have sought forgiveness, wouldn't she? Cards on the table, and I know we have a lot of details still to consider, but this to me is the central issue in this case. *Why on earth would Evelyn not only lie, but also continue to lie?* Sorry, Bradon, you boys can play around with cars and times all you like, but she was saying someone had killed her, and amongst all the pain and drugs and shock and weariness she was groping for a grain of comfort. And where better to turn than the person she had relied on all her life for comfort? I'm sorry, but I need to tell you all that as far as I'm concerned she was relating what happened as best she could. She was leaving whatever legacy she could and hoping it would not be thrown away. She may even, at some instinctual level, have been appealing to her mother not to *allow* it to be thrown away. Isn't that what a lot of victims try to do if they get the chance?"

"I'm being careful," Bradon says. "And not just about cars and times."

"Sorry if I offended you," Frances says. "I didn't mean to."

"No, no. I mean we have to be careful with the inconsistencies, or things maybe not quite adding up or being neatly packaged. Ralph Waldo Emerson once said that 'a foolish consistency is the hobgoblin of little minds', and I think we shouldn't try to force consistency on situations where there is none, or where there's uncertainty or trauma."

I think Bradon has made an excellent point, one which I hope everyone will digest and act on, but keep it to myself. I wonder if he is a fan of Emerson's, who I believe once met Brigham Young, among others, during a journey across America. But that may be for another day…

P.C. Henry Proud's Tale (Part One) (ID2)

Proud, a constable stationed in Bellingham, testified that at about 11.25 pm on January 6 he passed the home of Dr Miller (rtd) at Roseneath, Bellingham. He noticed the doctor's car, lights on, in its garage and the doctor coming out of his house. Dr Miller told him that Miss Foster of Otterburn had been seriously burned in her car, the family needed a second doctor and as he was the only one available and the family's former GP, he was going there to give whatever help he could. As the doctor had a game foot and was glad of some assistance, they set out with Proud at the wheel.

They arrived at Foster's Garage at midnight: Proud looked at his watch. He enquired where the other officers were, was told they were at the Station, and made his way there as soon as the doctor's car was under cover. At the Station, Shanks confirmed to him that Miss Foster was badly burned and had said a man had thrown something over her. Proud told his colleagues Dr Miller was at The Kennels. They made their way back, Shanks and Fergusson going into the house and Proud into the garage. He found Joseph Foster engaged in heating oil to put in a car 'to take us to the scene of the occurrence.' Proud said they would need a car as they 'had none of our own here.' Joseph Foster told Vasey to make himself available to drive it.

The constable waited on the road until Shanks and Fergusson came out of the house, 'keeping a watch for anyone passing.' No one did. Proud did not check the time but said that all three policemen, with Vasey and Johnstone, got into the car together. In the car, Shanks and Fergusson again told him that Miss Foster had stated that a man had thrown something over her and set fire to her. He did not take note of the time they arrived at the burned car.

"Before Peter goes off the deep end," Sven says, giving his crooked smile, "am I reading this right? Proud arrives at the garage at midnight. He hangs about while the doctor's car is safely housed. He walks the length of the village to where Fergusson's police house and the lock-up—'the Station' as Proud proudly calls it—were located. I believe they were both in the same building at Carter Cottages in those days. Where the B road turns off to Bellingham and the Mill; am I right? He has a brief chat with Shanks and Fergusson and they all walk back up the main street. The interview begins minutes later, when Shanks and Fergusson have made their way upstairs. According to Fergusson they were out of The Kennels at 12.30 am. And we thought earlier it lasted over twenty minutes? More like fifteen, unless those policemen were athletes, and they don't sound much like it."

"Did anyone up there know about Greenwich Mean Time?" Bradon asks. "I mean, even in New York City they kinda have a grasp of it."

"It does all seem rather slapdash," I offer. "But if the coroner didn't feel the need to probe further, there is little we can do about it now except think our way through the most likely sequence of events. Whatever views Frances has expressed, that is what we all must continue to do, and Frances will need to search as hard as anyone for something that could cast the shadow of doubt over her beliefs." I give her a pointed look. "Or even harder, in an ideal world. Anyway, before we immerse ourselves in the various police activities during the night and the following morning, has anyone anything to add?"

"What else did those cops talk about, going from Otterburn to Wolf's Nick?" Bradon asks.

"Where would be the best place to get breakfast?" Peter suggests.

CHAPTER THIRTEEN

Newcastle Law School: the present day, 27 January
Concerning 1.00 am, 7 January 1931, and later that day

While they are reading the next set of notes I wonder if I have presented this project in the right way, in doing things roughly chronologically. But what other way was there, to make sense of it? Now, Frances has thrown down the gauntlet (if Peter hadn't already) and there is a risk everyone will be swayed into indifference or inattention. I can't find it in myself to blame her, either. In these days, when we are all treated 24/7 to news reporters, inured to their task, covering unspeakable crimes as if only the minutiae of places, times and circumstances (and/or political ambitions) were of consequence, and words like 'tragedy' and 'terror' are used as indefinite pronouns, it is refreshing to hear someone think aloud about raw human emotions and interactions. I console myself with the thought that, whatever my students believe now, there are still things for them to learn. To start with, there is the whole police ethos.

To begin, I suggest to my team that perceptions of the Constabulary were not helped by Fergusson. He and his colleagues were not bad men, but several seem to have been employed or promoted beyond their capabilities and others were of the kind that nostalgia would have us believe we need more of today. We do not; we need better cops who are street-wise in the world around them and are of a mentality to engage in it, and a lot more of them. I have no doubt some of those in this story joined the profession to make that world a better place. Like the doctor and schoolteacher of their time, they were the pillars of the community.

Why review this now? Because Andrew Fergusson was a village bobby who, on receiving Joseph Foster's phone call, must frankly have taken fright. What, after all, had he been used to dealing with in Otterburn? Drunks, poachers, rowdy youths, fights, petty theft. This was something beyond his ken. His first reaction was to call Shanks. His second was to kill time in the garage with Vasey while Evelyn's family awaited him in the house. His third, when Joseph Foster and his son came in and began pressing him to start a search for Evelyn's assailant—to *do* something—was to say he was sure Shanks would have it all in hand. His fourth must have been relief when his superior finally appeared. But his and the Fosters' hopes were dashed like trust and loyalty in the Garden of Gethsemane. Shanks had done nothing—yet. His was an adroit strategy, conveying effort-free pensiveness, and one he would stick with all night.

When the two policemen began their interview with Evelyn, it was

Fergusson who first opted, for whatever reason, to leave the questioning in Mrs Forster's hands. And it was Shanks who allowed an unorthodox interview, with minimal police input, to proceed. To be charitable, he may have felt Evelyn would be more relaxed and open with her mother asking the questions. Or it may have been that he could not bring himself to imagine her pain, could not look at her without shuddering, or could not think of any useful questions to ask.

P.C. Andrew Fergusson's Tale (Part Two) (ID2)

On arrival at Wolf's Nick, Fergusson noticed that both offside doors of the car were open and those on the nearside were closed. He checked the front plate (the rear one was melted) but in any case knew the car well. He heard Vasey say it was in gear and told him nothing was to be touched until daybreak.

Fergusson tracked the route the car had taken over the moor; it seemed to have taken a shallow semicircular course and was facing north, angled towards the road facing north. Behind it was a 3-gill bottle, which smelled as though it had contained lime juice (confirmed later by the pathologist). On the carrier platform at the rear he found a Shell can in 'an upright position', its cap and neck missing. He assumed it was empty but didn't touch it.

He returned to the road with Shanks and Vasey at 1.30 am. Proud gave him a charred purse picked up near the car. At Kirkwhelpington, where they went to inform P.C. Sinton of the event, it was found to contain two 10s notes, 9s 6d in coins and two driving licences of Evelyn's; one current, one expired.

Fergusson, Shanks and Vasey stopped at Raechester Farm, the nearest south of the crime scene, on their return to Wolf's Nick. They searched the outhouses and woke the farmer. He had seen or heard no one. They picked up Proud and Johnstone at Wolf's Nick and headed to Ottercops Farm, the nearest north of the crime scene. They repeated their search of outhouses and again questioned the farmer. He had returned from Scots Gap near Cambo at 8.00 pm and likewise had not seen the fire or any strangers.

On the way back to Otterburn they stopped to search 'an unoccupied lunch hut' and called at Raylees Farm to search the property and speak to that farmer—again with no result. By then, it was 4.00 am. Fergusson returned to the Station in Otterburn and resumed his search in the village for 'any person answering the description of the man given by Evelyn Foster to her parents.'

"So at this point, I mean from about 2.30 am on," Sven says, "no one was guarding the car or the scene. They had carried out a search in the dark, presumably by flashlight, and found a petrol can, a bottle and a purse. They had picked things up and put things down without thought of fingerprints or marking the precise locations of items of evidence. But maybe that wasn't done in those days. They had called in at roadside farms on their travels—although Blaxter, Ravenscleugh, the hamlet of Knowesgate and various sheepfolds aren't mentioned—and no one they spoke to had seen or heard anything, not even a blazing fire. And what is this about 'the description given by Evelyn Foster to her parents?' Hadn't this constable been present at the interview, taking notes?"

"Let's refresh our memories a little more," I suggest. I confess at this point to being nervous that Peter and/or Frances might wade in again and start merrily shafting the police. There was also the question of why all three available policemen—Shanks, Fergusson and Proud—had gone to the scene, when one should have remained at The Kennels near Evelyn. They knew by then from the doctors that she was increasingly slipping into unconsciousness, yet they all headed for the hills.

Thomas Vasey's Tale (Part Two) (ID1: inserted here for chronology)
Vasey confirmed he had driven Shanks, Fergusson, 'another police officer' and Johnstone to the scene. He said that on their arrival 'both front doors were open and one of the back doors was ajar.' (Johnstone also noticed these positions had changed, but only later). Vasey tried the car's gear lever but couldn't move it; he believed it might be in low gear. He lifted the bonnet and saw the engine 'was not burned at all severely.' He went to the rear and saw an empty petrol can lying on its narrow side on the luggage carrier. Its handle was melted off and the can's neck was out, but he didn't see the neck. He touched nothing. He saw a police officer (P.C. Proud) pick up a scarf and what Vasey took to be a suspender near the back of the near front wheel.

P.C. Henry Proud's Tale (Part Two) (ID2)
The last part of Proud's statement mirrored much of Fergusson's. He added that Johnstone had shown them the route he and Rutherford had taken in rescuing Miss Foster. He was quite sure the two offside doors were open and the two nearside doors closed. In walking around the car, he stepped accidentally into a drain in front of the nearside front wheel. He picked up a length of 'dun-coloured cloth' near this drain and wheel, looked at it with his lamp, formed no impression as to what it was (it was Evelyn's scarf) and laid it back down. He told 'someone' standing nearby not to touch anything.

Just before Fergusson, Shanks and Vasey left for Kirkwhelpington he found 'a purse with a ten shilling note sticking out' a yard away from the nearside rear wheel. He picked it up, went over to Fergusson and handed it to him. He and Johnstone then resumed a search around the car, trying to find 'any article—a bottle or tin—which might have been used by the man described by Miss Foster.' They found nothing. Sometime during this search he saw a petrol can lying on its side in the burned out carrier, its cap and screw neck missing. He did not lift the can to see if it was empty.

Proud 'remained on guard at the car' until Shanks and Fergusson came back, returning with them to Otterburn and 'searching all farms etc. on the roadside on the way.' They saw no cars and no one on foot. He rejoined Dr Miller in Otterburn and drove back to Bellingham, arriving home at 5.00 am.

He added that whilst at Wolf's Nick he 'did not pick up anything which resembled in any way a lady's suspender.' (He sounded offended at the idea.)

"Inconsistencies," Bradon says, getting in first. "The doors. Did someone get to them before Vasey and/or switched them back before Proud saw them? The can. Upright for Fergusson, on its side for Vasey and Proud. But in all cases, minus cap or neck and surely used as the main accelerant. The cops seem to have been keen to have no one touch anything, but that keenness didn't extend to themselves. The purse. Why would Evelyn's purse have a bill sticking out? Why was it lying where it was, a yard from the *nearside* rear wheel? Had someone looked in it earlier? Or, at that point in the night, can we assume no one else had been there at all?" He stops, I think surprised—he doesn't need to be—by his temerity.

"I think we have to assume that," Sven says. "And apparently no other bottle or tin was found, then or later, that might have been the one referred to by Evelyn. Only what seems to have been a relatively harmless soda bottle and the petrol can itself."

"True," Bradon says, reviving. "But I'm thinking, if this guy was a heavy smoker, he'd have had a lighter or box of matches. Maybe he had one of those small tins of lighter fuel in his coat pockets; they'd be big enough to take it. That could have been what he threw or squirted over Evelyn to start the blaze, and it would have been pretty well indistinguishable in the lab from the petrol that was used as the main agent. He would have to put a small can like that back in his pocket, wouldn't he? He'd have been an idiot not to, with his dabs all over it."

"The way these cops were stumbling about," Peter says, "picking things up and dropping them, opening and closing doors like a scene from an Ealing comedy, he could have left it with his name engraved on it. It seems incredible, but they were behaving as though the crime scene didn't matter. A twenty-minute inspection? If Mr Foster hadn't prepared a car and driver to take them, it's debatable whether they'd have bothered at all. Their efforts, such as they were, became focussed on searching for a man in a bowler hat. But it's a good thought, Bradon. It makes sense."

On that happy note of accord, I turn their attention to the morning of January 7 1931:

P.C. William Turnbull's Tale (ID2)
Turnbull was stationed at Ridsdale, 7 miles south of Otterburn on the A68. He had a visitor at 5.50 am on 7 January: Inspector Russell, who instructed him to head for Wolf's Nick and take charge of a burned car that had been driven by Evelyn Foster. Turnbull got on his motorbike and arrived at the scene at 6.30. No one was there. He did not approach the car, being 'unaware what the investigations of the early morning had disclosed, i.e. footprints etc.'

His vigil ended at 1.00 pm when he was joined by Fergusson from Otterburn. Together they took measurements of the distance the car had travelled from the road and its direct distance from it. He said several people had been during the morning, most of them reporters, but he allowed none anywhere near the car.

He was relieved from duty at 2.00 by P.C. Sinton (Kirkwhelpington). (Note: another Turnbull, P.C. George Turnbull from Morpeth, made a brief appearance to take photographs of the scene on 7 January. His shots have appeared regularly in books and articles about the case.)

"Is anyone else struck by the similarity in content of these police statements?" Frances asks. "And for that matter Vasey's? Almost every one of them refers to the Hudson's doors and the petrol can. Almost every one of them says they hadn't touched anything or had told other people not to touch things. Being an average group of humans, surely someone would have seen or thought or said *something* different? There's very little variation, is there? Or was this all an attempt to direct people's thinking only into areas the police wanted them to go?"

"They had a lot of time to decide how they wanted to play it," Peter says. "But our good Inspector Russell at least saw other things."

Inspector Edward Russell's Tale (ID2)
Russell was stationed at Prudhoe-on-Tyne, 30 miles south of Otterburn. He set off for Otterburn at 4.00 am on 7 January and arrived at Foster's Garage some time after six, having called in on Turnbull. He went straight to The Kennels but was told Evelyn Foster was unconscious and unable to answer more questions. (He seems to have understood more questions were needed).

He then made 'certain enquiries' at Horsley, returning to Otterburn at 9.15 am, when he was told by Mr Foster that Evelyn 'had died at 8.55' (*sic*). He made further enquiries in the area and at 3.30 pm made his way to Wolf's Nick. He saw tyre marks cutting west to east across the road at an angle of 45°. Tracks across the moor indicated the car had travelled in a semicircular course 198 feet after leaving the highway, down an embankment 4'6" below road level and through a soft marshy ditch. It had come to rest 78 feet from the A696, facing north and at an angle of 75° to the road.

Russell then examined the car, the body of which was totally burned out with every window shattered or melted. He noted that both offside doors were wide open and an empty 2-gallon Shell petrol can was standing upright on the luggage box platform, the steel framework of which was all that remained. The neck of the can was 6" from it, its screw cap 10" from it, and there were the remnants of a brass funnel and two clips/catches from the luggage box. The grass and heather beneath the car were burned for a foot around it, but there were no traces of burning along its track from the road. Russell concluded the car had been burned where it stood and the fire had taken place at the rear of the car.

He thought he saw traces of blood on the near side door handle and mudguard, and removed both parts for analysis. He also picked up a piece of brown tweed cloth and another of burned linen close to the nearside footboard; a piece of dress material with narrow elastic in the hem; buckles from suspenders beside the nearside front wheel; and a piece of white wadding about three feet from the footboard under the nearside front door. He found a brown tweed scarf hanging on the nearside lamp of the car.

On the grass 5-6' from the front of the car, and again 12' from the front wheel he saw what seemed to be blood. He removed both these portions of grass. (Although subsequent forensic tests found no traces of blood, Russell remained convinced that was what the stains were).

At about 5.00 pm, after speaking to Supt. Shell, he had the car removed by lorry and taken to Foster's Garage, where it was kept under lock and key.

Two days later, on 9 January, he examined the burned debris inside the car. He found the remains of a notebook (Evelyn's) and pocket flashlight, and a cone-shaped portion of burned material. He took possession of these articles.

Two days later again, he visited Wolf's Nick 'after the frost had given' and removed some heather near the ditch where 'the offside wheel marks appeared slightly scorched.' He handed over all the items he had collected to Prof McDonald at Newcastle College of Medicine on 15 January (see later).

"Well," Peter says, "do we finally get to meet a meticulous, methodical policeman, albeit late in the day? I believe I'm inclined to give him the benefit of the doubt. It is not his fault, after all, that people have been trampling the ground ahead of him, picking things up and putting them down elsewhere, taking some items away but not others. Or, as the senior policeman to appear so far, the man who might arguably have taken control earlier, *is* it his fault? Maybe that would be too severe on him, as he would not expect his constables to be a wrecking crew. But it gives us a problem in any case, doesn't it? If, *if*, we could be sure all the items he found on the nearside, the *passenger* side, had not been moved in the previous fifteen hours—this crime scene has been dying a slow death—it might help us to conclude that someone had been sitting on that side, and/or had got out that side, and/or some kind of action had taken place there. I'm thinking of the doubts expressed about Evelyn and Bowler being able to drive from Belsay in some kind of Siamese-twin position, or with Bowler still on the passenger side scrunched up towards her. I'm thinking of him assaulting her, first in the front seat, by hitting her and forcing her into the back, second by emerging from the nearside himself, getting into the back and assaulting her again more forcibly. With intent, as it were. It's what may have happened, isn't it? But *can* we believe all these bits and pieces lying on the car's nearside? We might just be able to, for two reasons. One, in lurching about in the dark, Fergusson and Proud and the largely absent Shanks, assisted by Johnstone and Vasey, missed seeing any of them. If they had, they would have been strewn dear knows where, and the same thing would apply to any insomniac who may have visited the site between 2.30 and 6.30 am. Two, while *some* items could have been moved and brought to the nearside, it's unlikely *all* of them would. But were they torn and thrown by Bowler or shed by Evelyn as she crawled across the moor? Or both? Or *collected* by someone?"

He looks at us in some perplexity. "Something is niggling with me. I have a feeling I've missed an ingredient and don't know what."

"Two *Evening Chronicle* reporters were on the site before 6.30 am, at least according to their paper," I remind him. "They moved things."

He snaps his fingers. "Of course. No wonder it was niggling."

I am almost more impressed by this admission than anything else he has said.

Gordon Foster's Tale (ID2)

The role of Evelyn's brother at the inquest was limited. He was asked to repeat the description that Evelyn had given him of her assailant ('about your build, a little taller, not quite so stout, wearing a suit, a bowler hat and dark coat') but his main evidence was to do with the retrieval of the Hudson from Wolf's Nick. He was asked by Russell on the afternoon of 7 January to take a wagon and bring it to the garage. He got to Wolf's Nick at about 3.30 pm.

Gordon Foster examined the Hudson in Russell's presence and found it was standing in low gear. He had to put it into neutral to have it winched and removed by motor lorry. Back in the garage at 5.00 pm, he returned the car to low gear. (It wasn't long before he was thinking it was salvageable, although he didn't say so at the inquest.)

Joseph Foster's Tale (Part Two) (ID2)

Evelyn's father was recalled towards the end of Day Two to explain his daughter's finances and produce the Hudson's insurance policies, which he had been unable to do off-the-cuff the day before. (In essence, this was the first evidence, concrete or otherwise, of the police's main line of attack.)

Evelyn's day-to-day account book had been destroyed in the fire, but as this was confined to transactions such as fares and fuel purchases it was not crucial to the inquiry. (The coroner expressed surprise that such a document should have been carried in a car, but perhaps didn't understand the difference between running expenses and an Annual Report and Accounts).

However, at the second time of asking, Joseph was able to produce a statement of Evelyn's bank account at Lloyd's Bank in Bellingham and her credit at the Post Office. The two accounts totalled £489 10s 0d, the equivalent of £28,000 today. (In fact, this was an underestimate of Evelyn's wealth, since her will was later probated at £1,442, the equivalent of £82,000 today, although it is not known how the other £952 10s 0d was calculated.) Joseph explained that the Hudson was insured under two policies, both taken out by the firm although the insurance company understood the Hudson was Evelyn's. The first was not applicable. It insured, up to a maximum of £450, any vehicle stationed in Foster's Garage against fire. The second covered third party risks, fire, accident and theft of the Hudson—or any other of Foster's vehicles below 30 horsepower—*up to* a value of £700.

(It was to become clear that some policemen believed Evelyn needed money and had set fire to the Hudson in order to claim against the second policy, accidentally causing her own death. The theory had three serious flaws: no one knew why Evelyn should suddenly have developed a need for money and the police failed to offer any explanation; she was a comparatively wealthy young woman; and the General Accident Assurance Company's assessment of the sum she would have received in compensation was £45.)

"What is the British phrase for frugality?" Sven asks. "Waste not, want not? The amazing thing to me, or one of them, is that Gordon Foster and the mechanics at the garage seem to have had every intention of resurrecting this wreck of a car. They did it, too. I suppose mechanically it was okay, but it was still remarkable. These days, it would have been written-off for sure, whatever the insurance people had to say about it."

Frances smiles. "It was a company, Sven, that from its inception had 'make do and mend' as a watchword; another turn of phrase for you. Look at Joseph's blacking boxes and how he adapted those. Nothing was thrown away until there was no option. It had to be total rubbish."

"Tell that to the average Yank," Bradon says. "We didn't just invent the throwaway society, we made sure everyone else fell into line."

"It's appalling," Peter says when the laughter has died down, "that this grieving father should have been badgered into explaining his dead daughter's finances at all. What had the police been doing? Surely if they were serious about this theory of theirs they might have had the decency to investigate leads that could just possibly have given it credence. Or had they already done so and found there was *nothing* to give it credence? A word with George Phillipson to see if this rumoured marriage was on the cards? A phone call to the bank? To General Accident? But oh, no. That piece of dirty work was left to the coroner, trying to dig what he could out of Joseph Foster. And hats off to Mr Foster for playing it straight, however he must have felt. The man was amenable beyond a fault."

"But hey," Bradon says, "please tell me I'm wrong. Did this guy Russell have to *cycle* all over? From Prudhoe? Two hours to Ridsdale?"

We look at each other uncertainly. Peter is the first to start chuckling again. Bradon could be right, and I'm grateful. He has relieved me of the fear that Peter will wind up into top gear and throw more strictures at the coroner or police. That time is inevitably coming.

"That *would* be different." Peter grins. "Dedication with bells on."

"We will meet again on Friday, if that's acceptable," I tell them hurriedly, before he regroups from his little joke and starts up again.

As we've been talking the snow has been falling continuously, wet flakes slowly trickling down the panes. At times they've been distracting. It would be as well to warn Molly she should make the train her Plan B.

I have invited her to join our Friday session, friends. Well, I could hardly have avoided it, the way the hints were flying.

CHAPTER FOURTEEN

Newcastle Law School: the present day, 30 January
The immediate aftermath (1)

"We have a guest today," I tell my troops, who are gathered around the table as before. "This is Professor Molly Malone from the Criminology Department of Durham University. She is here as an interested observer but has my permission to tell us when and how we're all going wrong."

She will do more than that, but at that point I was not to know.

I then introduce the students to her. "May we call you Molly?" Peter asks, a gleam in his eye. "I believe you are a friend of Matthew's?"

"More than a friend," Molly tells him. "And yes, you may."

With the ice broken — and I'm pleased to see Peter blushing slightly, although that may just be the effect Molly has on men — I begin.

"There are few notes today. And before we look at the inquest and forensic evidence in detail, I would like us to spend some time on the immediate aftermath, and then consider what we've learned so far. In particular, I would like us to consider possible explanations of the various aspects of Evelyn's story I suggested on Tuesday and others I've added since. But first, what happened in the days following Evelyn's death?"

I make sure they all have soda (Bradon) or coffee (Molly and I had deluxe ones earlier, a pit-stop at Willi's Café) and remind them of the many cases they have come across where media interest, for good or ill, has had an impact.

In the USA, the OJ Simpson case in 1994-95 in Los Angeles and the prosecution of Timothy McVeigh in 1996-97 in Denver were, in their times, unrivalled in the intensity and endurance of media coverage. Closer to home, and more recently, the Angelika Kluk murder in 2006 in Glasgow and the Joanna Yeates murder in 2010 in Bristol had thrown up once again issues ranging from contempt of court and media commentary on witnesses' characters, to the filming of court proceedings and the reproduction of trial-related material.

So what did we have in 1931 in the Evelyn Foster case? We had reporters combing their dictionaries for other ways to describe a bleak moor and remote village; to find synonyms for mystery strangers (and wolves); to pile adverb upon adjective in illuminating the most *dramatic* man-hunt the county of Northumberland had ever seen (until Raoul Moat, that is). We had local and national newspapers churning stories out (the *Daily Express* became prominent, but not for the most salubrious of reasons) and international interest (e.g. the *Sydney Morning Herald*). We had reporters and photographers huddled in their cars along the A696, waiting for a break in the weather (or the crowd) so they could get an uninterrupted look or shot. But we did not have television, and we had only one official police statement. It was issued on 7 January and it read:

> About 10 pm last night Miss Foster, of The Garage, Otterburn, was found by a bus conductor (*sic*) about three miles south (*sic*) of Kirkwhelpington, on the Newcastle-Jedburgh road, lying beside one of their own cars, badly burned, and the car was still burning. She was taken home to Otterburn. Will any person who may have been on that road between the hours of 7.30 and 10 pm please communicate with the police at Hexham or the Chief Constable, Morpeth?
> Will the party who were travelling south from Scotland in a motor-car, and from which a man whom they gave a lift alighted at Elishaw Road Ends, north of Otterburn, about 6.30 pm (*sic*), kindly communicate with the police?

Although a pen-portrait of the man the police were seeking was not included in the statement, Evelyn's description did appear in most papers. It was vague, though; it could have applied to a quarter of the male population, and it was unlikely that had friends dropped him off at Elishaw—or had *anyone* dropped him off who would rather not be part of a police investigation—they would willingly have come forward. Like the confiscation of guns or knives, those with most reason to hide them are the last to give them up.

In any event, the *Newcastle Daily Journal* (now *The Journal*) broke ranks. Someone, perhaps a member of the Northumberland police force, had given two competitors a scoop during the night. Two morning papers, the *North Mail* and the *Sporting Man* (!), both part of the *Newcastle Chronicle* group (a rival then, but now a sister publication of *The Journal* under Trinity Mirror ownership), had carried reports of the assault on Evelyn Foster. This injustice clearly infuriated *The Journal*'s editor:

> The police have a difficult task. It might have been less difficult had the newspapers been notified immediately of the crime, so that a description of the passenger in Miss Foster's car could have been circulated throughout Northumberland and further afield. What a curious thing it is that if the police desire a dead body to be identified they will notify the Press immediately, but if it is a live body, urgently wanted for some horrible crime, they are not so quick to seek the aid of the most efficient publicity medium.

A description of 'the passenger' had at least been circulated, on the morning of 7 January and under the direction of Superintendent Shell, to all the policemen under his command in Hexham Division (which included Otterburn). They were ordered to patrol the roads and keep their eyes open for a man, *Height 5ft 6ins, slim build and wearing a bowler hat, dark (blue?) overcoat and suit.* This was relayed to the superintendents of other divisions in the county so they could follow suit, and to the HQs of surrounding forces. The question was, of course: was it all too late? In Otterburn and its immediate area, local policemen may have geared themselves up within twelve hours after the fire, or about the time in the morning when Evelyn had died, but the results could have been no better than patchy and time-delayed elsewhere.

"The first hint of them and us?" Peter points a finger to the editorial.

"I imagine that might have come some hours earlier," Molly says. "At least as far as the local community was concerned."

He looks at her quizzically.

"When P.C. Fergusson declined the use of Joseph Foster's phone," Molly says. She has read all my notes, of course. "Bad move."

Frances smiles at her. "And raising all those farmers from their beds on a wild goose chase."

She receives a smile back. This is very worrying, if the two ladies, you might say the Yin team, are planning to gang up on the rest of us.

"But I imagine," Molly says, "that 'them and us' may have been an incremental process, an accumulation of things, rather than a sudden rupture. Don't you think? I'm speaking of this case only, setting aside the certainty that relations between the police and media would have had a history, good or bad. Editors may have liked and trusted Fullarton James and his senior people, but on the other hand they may not. And personal issues and characteristics would have come into it in another way. Evie's father, for example, would have been patient and stoical and ready to forgive, wouldn't he? Whereas her brother had a lower flashpoint. I think Fergusson and Shanks may have got off on the wrong foot with Gordon, and of course the whole community would have had an opinion on Fergusson's capabilities in the first place."

"In any case," I say after a beat, thinking she had demonstrated both her perception and credentials rather well, "I don't intend we should sift through all the media coverage the case received. You have already received a good flavour of it in the reference books and articles. Apart from the police statement, which is important as much in getting things wrong as right, I think it's as well to emphasise that it was a triangular relationship. We have the impact of media coverage on the community. Ditto on the police. And then we have leaks by the police, reported by the media, making a further impact on the community."

"The local people were nervous," says Sven, "in the days just after

Evelyn's death. And who can blame them? They thought this stranger, Bowler, could still be in the area. He may, for all they knew, be surviving in an old bastle or barn until the hue and cry died down. He may even have had a shepherd pal somewhere in the hills, someone sheltering him: we've read it was a strong rumour at the time. In British terms this was, and is, a vast area of moorland and forest, the biggest in England certainly, with lonely farms and cottages. So doors were locked at night. Windows were blacked out. People kept handy tools like chopping axes and kitchen knives by their beds. The bus driver, Cecil Johnstone, is on record as saying he carried some sort of cudgel, a 'clout', when he had a late shift on the buses and had to walk home. *School*children would be walking back and forth along that road, both ways in the dark. And as the days went by with no arrest, the feeling of unease would have ratcheted up before it reached a peak and then began to fade. And it would partly have translated into criticism of the police. It's human nature, isn't it?"

"And daily there were searches and reported sightings that came to nothing," Bradon says. "Dozens, we've read. All those guys working on the moors, shepherds and farmhands, flurries of activity from the Tower as cops set off to follow up another lead, people reporting every stranger or bowler hat they saw, every instance of anyone on foot or in the hills. No wonder sales of bowler hats went down the tubes. And some of those cops were drinking in the Percy Arms each night. They'd have been got at once or twice, and people would have eavesdropped on what they were talking about. And if any of them were to say anything pessimistic, or critical of Evelyn's story…" Bradon draws a finger across his throat.

"The fact is," Peter says, "none of these things, not one in all this churning activity, did any good. Bowler was never found. Not a sniff."

"I will read out parts of just one article from *The Journal*," I tell them. "It paints as good a picture as any of the flavour of the day."

> …(most) police activity is centred on scouring the district, and shepherds and farm workers have been asked to keep a sharp look-out for anything that will assist in tracing the assailant.
> …Among the country folk…is a strong belief that the assailant is still at large in the district, although they do not believe he is a local man. They say there is no reason why, even in this cold weather, a man may not hide for days in the many shelters and 'hemmels' which abound in the moorlands.
> As one (shepherd) pointed out…an aeroplane was lost (in the hills) for many days before search parties found it…There is a most uneasy feeling throughout the area, and cottage doors are being more securely bolted than ever. Last night a motor-cyclist, seeking assistance, had the utmost difficulty in getting a cottager to open his door.

"So where do we think Bowler, assuming there was a Bowler, went?" I ask. "*Why* was he never seen or found?"

"He'd long gone," Peter says. "He'd walked thirty yards to the road, brushed himself down, toddled off as far as Knowesgate cross-roads maybe—a mile or two, half an hour?—and hitched a lift in any direction but Otterburn. He could even have been wearing Evelyn's felt hat by then; it was never found either, was it? And the bowler, let's face it, was his most distinguishing feature. Every newspaper article that came close to giving a description featured it up front. He could have thrown it in the fire before he left, shredded it, dumped it in a burn or woodland. Or maybe the whistle Evelyn heard was Bowler hailing a passing car; she wasn't to know exactly when she'd heard it. It could have been ten, twenty minutes after he set the car alight, although he wouldn't have hung around for very long. And then he spins some yarn to whomever picks him up about crashing his car onto the moor, a patch of black ice maybe, and could he cadge a lift to Ponteland or wherever?" Peter gives his wolfish smile. "Preferably Newcastle, of course."

"Has anyone else any ideas?" I ask.

"What Peter says makes sense," Sven says. "It isn't as outlandish as having him hiding in the hills for days or having an accomplice of some sort pick him up. The man was respectably dressed and in those days there was no taboo about giving people lifts. And if he was a shade untidy or scuffed-up, so what? He'd just emerged from crashing his car and walking across a boggy moor."

"Look at the police statement," Frances says, "and ask yourself who vetted it before it was released. It asks for information from anyone on the Newcastle-Jedburgh road, three miles *south* of Kirkwhelpington, almost Capheaton in other words, seven miles south of Wolf's Nick, to check in with the police. *And* between 7.30 and 10.00 pm; quite a time-span. Even if someone read the reports, and had picked up an apparently respectable and unlucky driver around Knowesgate, would it have clicked? They may even have felt sorry for him; why cause more trouble for the poor chump? And Bowler may have told them he'd have to report the crash anyway to his insurance company and/or the police. Would they have bothered? Especially, as Peter says, if Bowler was no longer *in* a bowler. It took Kennedy, a local man clearly reluctant to talk to the police, ten days to tell them anything, and then only when he was asked."

"By noon," Peter says, "he could have been in York, within twenty-four hours after the fire in Birmingham or London. Or he could just have stayed in Newcastle a day or two, lost in the maw of the big city. He's two hundred miles from Dodge before the Sheriff and his posse are out of their beds." He throws a grin at Bradon. "Right?"

"Anything to add?" I ask Molly before we get into the Wild West.

"Only four things," she says. "The first three are apropos of nothing much, but worth remembering. Bowler hats were common headwear in those days, worn by everyone from coroners, if you'll forgive the word, to grooms and valets. Goodman, in his book, builds a theory about this man possibly being a groom and Evelyn's description, if nothing else, would have fitted such a man. If he were a groom, he may very well have visited Jedburgh and other horse or cattle sales in southern Scotland from time to time. *But* he need not have been a groom.

"The second is that two characters in this story, at least the parts I've read," (as far as I know she has read *all* the parts) "came to the view that Bowler must have had—I quote—considerable local knowledge. One was Mr Foster, I think on the assumption that Bowler knew where to pick his spot on the moor to assault Evie and burn her car. However, it has to be said that Mr Foster developed some eccentric ideas, I imagine partly due to the stress of seeing no progress day after day. The other was John Kennedy, on grounds that the saloon he saw was not only travelling fast but also had its lights switched off and on as it approached a bend in the road after Knowesgate. Frankly, I'm not sure how much weight to give either, but put them forward so the possibility isn't totally ignored.

"The third goes back to something both Sven and Peter mentioned: woodland as a hideaway. I would only caution you to be careful about assuming what you see today existed then. Certainly, there are patches of mature trees which would have been part of the landscape, albeit smaller patches and smaller trees. But Kielder and Redesdale Forests, those vast areas of sitka spruce and Norway spruce and pines, along with smaller plantations close to Wolf's Nick, are of more recent duration. The first experimental planting in Kielder Forest was in 1926 near Falstone, less than five years before Evelyn's death. Just how huge the forest and its timber turnover are can be gauged by the fact there have been years when two million trees have been felled. You could hide herds of elephants in it now, but not then. Blackface sheep were the main inhabitants."

Molly is now in full flow and the four students are mesmerised. It's as though she is providing information that only they deserve to hear. She is stating simple facts but they sound like state secrets.

"The fourth and most important is this: the efforts of the police by all accounts were concentrated on roads and road traffic as well as on the moors. But what of trains, of rail traffic? There was a single-track rail line, was there not, that ran across country through Knowesgate, to Morpeth and places *east*, north and south, eventually including Newcastle; and to Reedsmouth and places *west*, north and south, including Hexham? What was to stop this man spending a few hours until morning in or near a station, then catching the first train out in *any* direction? Many small rural stations had sheds and empty or disused carriages standing in them, some converted to stores. Tramps could and did find temporary homes there, if they weren't chased away. It would have been rather less of a hardship than spending days and nights in a hemmel, wouldn't it?"

"Holy smoke," Peter says. "Was Knowesgate Station functioning?"

Molly smiles and looks at a page of handwriting in her file. "Although called Knowesgate Station, it actually served the village of Kirkwhelpington. It was operated by the Wansbeck Railway Company, subsequently LNER. The station opened in 1865. It closed to passenger traffic in 1952, to freight in 1966. At Reedsmouth Station, two miles east of Bellingham, it connected to the Border Counties Railway which ran between Hexham and Riccarton Junction in Scotland. We tend to forget railways these days, don't we, since the Beeching axe—which we may judge today as a woefully short-sighted surrender to the motor vehicle— wreaked its havoc on rural communities? It seems the Northumberland County Constabulary in 1931 may have done so too. Rail does not feature in any document I have read about their investigation."

Peter laughs. "Molly, please tell us that at eight in the morning there was a train from Knowesgate, would you?"

"Are you a late riser, Peter?"

"Umm…well, not particularly. Depends who I'm with."

That loopy grin of his is getting on my nerves.

Molly comprehensively ignores it. "If Bowler, as you call him, had made it to Reedsmouth Station—it should have been r-e-d-e-s like the village, but BCR and North British Railway refused to change its name— by quarter to eight in the morning, he would have had a choice of trains, either to Hexham, where he would have arrived at half past eight and could have caught a connection to Newcastle, getting him there just after nine, or Riccarton Junction in Scotland—clearly a less appealing choice— where he would have arrived just before nine. Redesmouth, as I'm sure you all know, is an eight mile trek—two or three hours?—across country from Knowesgate and past Sweethope Loughs on country lanes. The same route, or part of the route, that our farmer Herdman drove along an hour or two earlier. Even on an evening with a waning moon it would not have been impossible to walk it—and with little chance of being seen. I don't believe it will have changed radically, other than in terms of surface improvements. And you have all read of witnesses in this case using Shanks's pony. It is what people did. Sidney Henderson walked six miles that evening in the Harwood area. Beach and Oliver thought nothing of walking from Elishaw into Otterburn and back, just for a beer or two. Thompson walked in from Garretshields, Mrs Murray three miles to

Cottonshopeburnfoot, the Kennedys to and from their choir practice. If this man was a groom or similar you can be very sure he was used to walking. It would be second nature to him. And if he did use this means of escape, it *would* rather confirm Mr Foster and Mr Kennedy's opinion that he had knowledge of the area. After Herdman, there may well have been no vehicles at all along that track on that evening.

"But more to the point, the Border Counties Railway operated about five trains each weekday, and the 'Wanney Line', as it was called, maybe three or four through Knowesgate. I should add, at Knowesgate or West Woodburn stations, Mr Bowler would have needed to avoid soldiers going to or from the Camp if there were any about. Whatever he did or did not do, I think he may have been wary of soldiers."

Did I mention Molly's Irish accent caresses people? They are looking at her open-mouthed.

"The Wanney Line," she looks at her notes again, "was perhaps in years gone by the best-loved railway line in Northumberland. On October 2 1966, an 11-coach special was laid on from Morpeth to Woodburn and back, celebrating the last run of the *Wansbeck Piper*. It sold out. There are old black-and-white photographs on the internet which feature some of the stations on these lines, and the beautiful engines that used them. They've clearly been taken by people with talent, because you can almost walk into them, smell the steam and smoke, join people from all walks of life who are waiting on the platforms; solicitors, farmers, railwaymen, businessmen, people going shopping or for a day out, children, grooms, some with bowler hats, some with flat caps, some bare-headed."

She closes her file, firmly. "Now, I am not proposing to bore you with any more details of the Wansbeck Railway or its connectors. The point I am making is this: if you were *not* a Mr Bates, but a good and competent barrister fiercely defending the reputation of Evelyn Foster in a court of law, would you not offer up this hypothesis in her defence? Would you not ask if it had been looked into? Or, if you were a diligent policeman conducting an investigation into her death, would you not have taken pains to assess it as a possible escape route for her assailant?"

Silence. Then:

"Molly," Peter says, "before Matthew asks, will you do me the great honour of becoming my wife?"

CHAPTER FIFTEEN

Newcastle Law School: the present day, 30 January
The immediate aftermath (2)

"So," I resume, and I have difficulty making myself heard, "we seem to have provided some answers to my question about why Bowler was never seen again. I believe we may have come up with some credible scenarios, some breaking new ground. But please remember we need to focus on Evelyn's story and whether there are aspects of it which cause us concern. So far, it appears not. That may change: we will see."

Of course, I am wasting my time; they are all still laughing.

Frances busies herself going around the table with a jug, making sure everyone has liquid. Sven and Peter, the great coffee drinkers among us, accept; Molly and Bradon opt for water. Nitrous oxide is not on offer.

I carry on regardless of the fading titters. "I'm sure these ten bullet points are not by any means mutually exclusive. I offer them as areas to consider. I've added a few since Tuesday. Please add any you think I've forgotten." I jot on a whiteboard:

- Elishaw: the pick-up/where the second car went;
- Bowler's change of mind/behaviour;
- the nature of the assaults on Evelyn;
- how two people could 'share' driving a car;
- how/when Evelyn came to be forced into the back seat;
- how/when she and the car were set alight;
- the initial reaction of the police;
- the effectiveness of their response;
- Evelyn's funeral/related issues;
- the souring of police/community/media relations

Frances, who is still on her feet, sets the ball rolling:

"The main thing about Elishaw is that if you believe Evelyn there, you may be set on a course of believing her throughout, or vice versa. I think that would be why, of the witness statements we've seen, nine of the twenty-four—I'm including Mrs Murray and I know there are three experts to come—have focussed on Elishaw, and later along the main street. And they seem to have been selected to give minimum support to Evelyn. There are, as we know, omissions from the list. There is Townes, Sinclair the juror, the teachers Misses Carruthers and Ferry, our two West Woodburn cyclists, and a man you, Matthew, talked of on our visit to Otterburn; the headmaster Blackham. We can't be sure who else was missing from a pick-and-mix selection offered by the police but there must be many, certainly more than were called. But among those who *were* called none, at the end of the day, cast any real doubt on Evelyn's veracity. They could have been clearer, more certain of what they saw and when they saw it; but they saw cars, and in some cases what could have been Evelyn doing what she had told her mother she was doing. And to disbelieve her must mean, in those respects, also disbelieving her mother, her father, her brother, and Foster employees. The only other explanation is that Evelyn duped everyone from Elishaw down the line and I think, to put it mildly, that is unlikely. I assume no one, not even the police, disputes that she took two men and Mrs Murray to Rochester and beyond. The crux, first of all, is what happened at Elishaw Road Ends."

"I'm struggling to better Jonathan Goodman's theory," Peter says. (Peter, struggling? I almost make it the eleventh bullet point). "It hits all the right notes." He seems to have regained some equilibrium.

"I've been doing some research on Goodman," Bradon says. "He's not unknown in the States, you know? Among other things, he wrote *The Passing of Starr Faithfull*, a daughter of Manhattan socialites, whose body was washed up on Long Beach, Long Island, also in 1931. He received the CWA Gold Dagger for non-fiction in 1990. He's known to have been a meticulous researcher, and the American critic Jacques Barzun described him as the master of true-crime literature. Goodman died in 2008 but years before had interviewed as many people as he could find who had known Evelyn Foster. Including her two sisters."

Peter nods. "I found little wrong with his theory about the car that left Elishaw, even though he was discreet about the identity of Mrs X, as he called our mystery driver. But that was perhaps because she was still alive at the time his book first hit the shelves." He shrugs. "I'm not sure, because two Charlotte Clarks seem to have died in the Newcastle area in the mid-1960s and others elsewhere, and I'm not into this stuff."

I see Molly give me a subtle wink, recalling our talk in Oldfields.

"You could be right," she tells Peter soothingly (and vaguely).

'Mrs X' was identified by Robert Dixon in his book as Charlotte Clark, wife of John Clark, whose family owned the thread company J&J Clark of Paisley (later to merge with J&P Coats to become Coats Paton, Coats Viyella, and then Coats plc). The Clarks lived at Troughend Hall; they had done so since about 1920, and it could well have been their first home. The Hall was a three-storey Georgian mansion built in 1758 by Elrington Reed, possibly a Kirsopp-Reed ancestor. The grounds in which it stood, 2.2 miles down the A68 from Elishaw, had long been the home territory of his ancestors, the Reed family of Border Reivers. The site was reputed to have been haunted, and maybe still is, by a dog mourning its master, Percival Reed. There have been a number of chilling encounters with Parcy Reed's unquiet soul in the hills and moors of Batinghope and Redesdale, his sticky end being a choice example of Reiver methodology.

Several versions exist of *The Death of Parcy Reed*, a ballad relating a kind of Middle Marches variation on Glencoe, but most agree he was awakened and hacked into pieces by the Crosiers of Riccarton in cahoots with the Halls of Otterburn Tower and Girsonfield:

The slightest wound might caused his deid/And they hae gi'en him thirty-three/They hacket off his hands and feet/And left him lying on the lee is one take on Parcy's last moments. 'Mad Jack' Hall will take a bow shortly: something for you to look forward to, friend. By all accounts he seems to have been more likeable than some of his ancestors.

Troughend Hall was badly burned in 1952 and demolished in about 1956. Long before then, John and Charlotte Clark had moved a couple of fields down the hill to Dunns Houses. In 1931 they had two cars. Mr Clark used his for trips to Scotland on his Coats business and outside interests such as his membership of Berwickshire Naturalists' Club. He was a gentleman farmer who owned Troughend Tofts Farm (John Thomson was recorded at one time as being his farm bailiff, although there may be no link with the John Thompson who was a farmhand at Garretshields in 1931) and he became an air raid warden for Troughend in World War II. Mrs Clark used hers for social purposes, involving frequent journeys outside the area. She was rarely seen in Otterburn.

Charlotte Clark, one of the wealthiest women in the district, had the reputation of being a lady who used her husband's absences to seek alternative male company—both at home (drinking parties, for which she often dressing up in her wedding outfit) and away (trips to Jedburgh, Newcastle, Hexham and elsewhere). Nor, allegedly, was she choosy in the male company she kept. Goodman, employing the French phrase *nostalgie de la boue* for this aberrance, cites two brothers, small-time crooks from Jedburgh, as regular (or irregular) visitors to Troughend Hall. Their trips to her home were reciprocated by Charlotte in visiting a cottage they occupied—I hesitate to say owned—near Jedburgh. Goodman was able to talk with people who knew Charlotte and her reputation, and were still alive in the 1970s. As far as I can see he did his usual thorough job. Peter is latching onto it like an otter after a fish:

"One," he is saying, "Mrs Clark had only months before bought a Morris Cowley, which could quite easily have been the car seen 'tearing' down Dere Street from Elishaw by the steam-roller driver Beach and his pal Oliver. Two, the car quickly disappeared from view. Where better than into the grounds of Troughend Hall, semi-enclosed as it was by trees? She could even have driven into those familiar surroundings without lights. Three, Evelyn said she thought a woman was driving and someone else was in the car. She did not identify the woman, but may not have wished to add further fuel to the gossip about Mrs Clark. Or she may not have seen her clearly in the dark and failed to recognise the car because it was a new acquisition. Four, if Mrs Clark had a male guest in the car with her—perhaps one of these Jedburgh johnnies—she may not have been too keen on a threesome that night, especially one involving a relative stranger, so was quite happy to dump Bowler. Five, she would not have wished Bowler in those circumstances to know where she lived or that she had no intention of going to Hexham. Six, she couldn't safely take him into Otterburn because she might be recognised by someone on the street. She *may* not have known it was Evelyn picking him up but if she had may have felt secure in Evelyn's discretion. Evelyn, after all, would have been party to all sorts of conversations in her taxi and would quickly have lost custom if she was known to be a blabber-mouth. Seven, on the day after the fire, the day of Evelyn's death, Mrs Clark developed a debilitating bout of influenza, so debilitating that when the police called to interview her she was unable to speak to them. Whether they returned at all or left with a large flea in their ear after meeting Mr Clark, who *may* have got home by then, is unknown. She was certainly never called as a witness and there is no record of any statement made by her. And eight, we have Mr Blackham, the headmaster. You described his input, Matthew, if I recall correctly, as having 'some interesting if rather gossipy things to say about the car from which Bowler may have emerged.'

"I did," I say, mainly to allow Peter to catch his breath if he needs to. In this mood he is not susceptible to prolonged interruption.

"Blackham, like many others," Peter resumes, "was not called as a witness although we have it on Maughan's authority that he was on the main road, albeit not where Maughan claimed, around seven o'clock that night. In fact, Blackham was much nearer the school, possibly even near enough to have seen the lights of Mrs Clark's car turn into Troughend across the Rede Valley. That aside, we have, via Goodman's research, the word of Blackham's daughter, Mrs Dorothy Groves. Mrs Groves said her father refused to speak about the Foster case in the presence of his children. That, too, may have been to do with an unappetising sexual content. But we have him pointing out to an old friend of his, a visitor to the school, 'that house on the top of the rise': Troughend Hall, across the valley of the River Rede. *That is the home of the woman who drove the car,* he is alleged to have said. *There is no doubt about it in my mind.* His daughter was found eavesdropping by her mother and packed off to do her homework. Goodman goes on to make three points: that Elishaw was, for Mrs Clark, the most convenient point to drop Bowler off; that she knew

Evelyn's habit of meeting the bus and transporting people onwards—she had once or twice availed herself of that same service; and that Charlotte had good reason to hide any connection to the Foster case. As Goodman says, she would have needed to explain other things. She would have dragged her clandestine lover, or lovers, into it; she would have needed to reveal how she had spent the day before and the night. In short, her double life would have unravelled. It would have come down to a question of priorities; Evelyn's reputation, or hers."

I look at Molly and raise my eyebrows. She stands up and moves over to the drinks table to refill her glass, looking over her shoulder.

"You like things to be tidy, Peter, don't you?" she asks. "The train option appealed to you, because it was an elegant construction."

Peter nods, not quite sure what is coming.

"And here, you have constructed something very elegant, and very persuasive, yourself."

"I hope so," he says. "With Goodman's help," he adds modestly.

"But the world is not tidy or elegant, is it? It's a mess, imperfect and annoying, and refuses to fit neatly into our best constructions."

"We have to do our best," he says. "Take the world as it comes."

"I agree, but let's look at some of the untidiness in this elegant theory you—not forgetting Mr Goodman—have constructed. And, what is more important, let's then ask ourselves whether it was necessary to try to make it such an elegant structure in the first place."

"Okay," he says. "I think it answers all the questions, though."

Molly nods. "I'm sure it does. But with flaws." She begins to tick them off on her fingers, like an echo. "One, with due respect to Bradon, we are not in *Perry Mason* country and you would not be allowed to float theories about Mrs Clark. She had done nothing criminal. Two, there is doubt about the Morris Cowley. Beach thought it may equally have been an AC car. No one positively identified it, certainly not as Mrs Clark's. Three, there is doubt about how it vanished and where to. Troughend Hall, as I understand it, sits close to the brow of a hill. This car, any car, could have gone over the top of the hill and southwards down the road. It could have swung off at the crossroads two miles later to Bellingham, or even towards Newcastle via the Mill. In either case it would have avoided our two cyclists on their way from West Woodburn."

Sensing an interruption, Molly holds up a hand. "Let me finish, please. Four, there is further doubt about who saw what, and where and when. Townes seems a more credible witness than Thompson, but was not called to explain his sighting of the car that stopped near Elishaw and started up again. It is difficult to speculate why, without besmirching the police, but in Townes *we* have part of a jigsaw that was *not* presented to the jury. Beach doesn't mention that he or Oliver saw this; only that a car of some description headed into Otterburn. Five, *none* of these people say a woman was driving *any* of these cars. The only person we can rely on for that suggestion, although she seems to have said it more than once, is Evelyn. The police thought they may be onto something when the Redesdale Arms landlord, Ben Prior, said three people had been in his bar on the evening of 6 January, but the car Prior saw was an Essex, all were men, and they were able to clear themselves. You made a convincing case for Mrs Clark wishing to drop a man off at Elishaw, but what if there had been a trio of strangers to the area in that car? They could well have seen a convenient AA box, stopped to use it, and quite fortuitously found Evie bearing down on them. Six, the police made great efforts to track this car and these people down. At that stage, they were committed to investigating a murder case and I have no doubt were doing the best they could. I agree that Mrs Clark's bout of influenza was convenient, and in a perfect world, even an untidy world, she should have been revisited whatever her husband's standing in the community. But was any of your argument, or Goodman's, clever as it was, necessary at all?"

"In what way?" Frances asks. "*Some*thing was needed to highlight the gaps and the police's failings."

"That was Mr Bates' job as things turned out, and the coroner's, and both failed miserably. Mr Bates was out of his depth, and I hesitate to speculate what the coroner was thinking. But there was *reasonable cause*, given what the jury heard, to believe Evelyn was telling the truth without the Mrs Clark construction. There was nothing at that stage, in the police's minds, to suggest she was lying, or had any reason to. That came later, didn't it, when they failed to find anything? No man, no stranger, no car, no driver of either gender, no other passenger at all; an abortive investigation on all fronts. In the absence of all these things, including their failure to interview Mrs Clark, the police had to find another explanation and make a liar of Evelyn. But we are not prosecuting the police, are we? To do Evelyn justice, I think we would be better served by looking at how and why that came about, don't you?"

"Quite happy to do so," Peter says. "I'm sure the Charlotte Clark connection is significant, though; you won't change my mind on that."

"I wouldn't try to, unless it begins to cloud other things," Molly tells him. "But please remember that the police were doing a lot of interviews and searches on 7 and 8 January. They were being diligent. On 8 January Superintendent Tough and three officers from Morpeth were back at Wolf's Nick inspecting footprints and the like; a lost cause perhaps, but they tried it. Perhaps even more of a lost cause occurred on 16 January when an attempt was made by Spratt and Russell to remove a 10 by 8 feet area of turf on which the car had stood. By then the ground seems to have thawed, been rained on, possibly snowed on, frozen solid and thawed again. What they hoped to achieve, publicity aside, is questionable.

"Back again to the previous week, three officers were in Jedburgh with Roxburghshire colleagues, interviewing people in hotels, guest houses and cafés. There weren't many to call on but they covered all they could find. Even Ernest Primrose, Foster's former bus driver and Evie's ex-boyfriend, on whom suspicion had originally fallen, was interviewed up in Scotland and managed to clear himself. So, *at that stage*, with or without Mrs Clark, the police appeared genuinely to believe they were seeking a murderer. Through carelessness or haphazardness they had allowed a potential crime scene to be destroyed, they had ducked the thorny question of fingerprints—I mean that literally since the Chief Constable was asked about it after the inquest and ignored the question altogether—but were pinning their hopes on a nationwide manhunt. In other words, they believed Evelyn's version. It was only later they gave up on it and her, although doubts may have started to creep in when they interviewed Tatham and Scott in the hotel and learned that neither had seen Evelyn or a stranger, and more so when they received McDonald's post mortem findings. And it was only *much* later when they put together their witness list and gave us *six* witnesses who said they had not seen the man, and/or were so vague as to be useless, and *none* who may have. The question, in this untidy world, is why."

"Let's skip a few bullet points for now," I suggest. "It seems a good time to look at the police's reaction and the efficacy of their response."

"One of the first things to upset the local cops," Bradon says, "and it would have been humiliating, was being asked insistently by the media and local people to bring in Scotland Yard. No one likes being told they're not fit for purpose. It would have gotten their backs up, and it seems to have gone on far beyond the inquest."

Frances nods. "Lack of judgement. It was a bad tactical decision by Fullarton James, I think, as well as a bad operational one. Had he brought them in, he could have washed his hands of anything that turned sour on him subsequently. Whether he consulted his colleagues about his decision, who's to know?"

Peter, however, is not prepared to give up his 'construction' quite so quickly. He has been leafing through his notes again.

"Hold on," he says, "before we forget Mrs Clark, let me just add two things. First, having interviewed her daily woman, Goodman writes that in the midst of this debilitating bout of flu on 7 January Mrs Clark twice visited a copse of conifers at Troughend Hall, a place she had never been known to take an interest in before, a place where a man could hide until the hue and cry died down. Whatever Molly said earlier about the origins of Kielder Forest, this copse was present then; Goodman would not have invented it. It would presumably be there for him to see. So how do we explain Mrs Clark's departure from the norm except to say it was too much of a coincidence to have zero connection with the night before? Second, here is an excerpt from the *Newcastle Daily Journal* a fortnight later. It seems to be dated 21 January, after Mr Joseph Foster had tried to float the idea, unsuccessfully and no doubt desperately, of a reward being offered for information about our mystery woman:

> There may be private reasons for hiding an indiscretion; there may be the possibility of someone having a car out without authority of an employer; there may be many reasons which make a driver hesitate to come forward and say where he or she was on a certain evening, and none of them may be criminal. (There are) grounds for saying that any such reason should not be a deterrent to coming forward. The police are more anxious to investigate Evelyn Foster's death than to be inquisitors of the private affairs of a kindly-disposed motorist who may have unwittingly carried the man who holds the secret of the Wolf's Nick tragedy.

"…in other words, please step up to the plate, Mrs Clark, and tell us what you know. Had this journalist been fed a line, or what? And Goodman tells us something similar appeared in other newspapers. It got no response. It was too late, and the lady had already decided to clam up. In the circumstances, who can blame her?"

"But how would Bowler, if it were he lurking in this copse, have got to Troughend?" Frances asks. "Thumbed a lift? Walked across the fells? Avoided cars and policemen along the roads, including the Bellingham road? He could hardly have phoned for a lift on his mobile, could he?"

"No," Sven says, "but Peter could be right. He *could* have thumbed a lift. That may have been the whistling Evelyn heard. He *could* have gone to earth in this copse for a day; the lady may have phoned for someone, maybe the second of these Jedburgh brothers, to pick him up. No one has claimed their tea party in Jedburgh was the first time Bowler had met these people. It just wasn't followed up, was it? *And* it seems the Scottish papers may have paid less attention to the case than the English ones."

Molly smiles at me and lifts an eyebrow. "It's possible," she says. "But that seems to have brought us neatly to the actions of the police and their interactions with the media. So perhaps we should shelve Mrs Clark for the moment and concentrate on that?"

CHAPTER SIXTEEN

Newcastle Law School: the present day, 30 January
The immediate aftermath (3)

We call a halt for more coffee and biscuits, but it's a pointless exercise for no one seems interested in topics of conversation other than the case in front of us. And somehow, in some mysterious way known only to the fair sex, Frances has conveyed the message to the three guys that she is here to work, not flirt or fool around over coffee tables, and they have somehow got that message. If they needed to, I add to myself, thankful that their concentration on the case now seems more or less absolute.

So Molly and I, after a quick review of city centre eating houses for later in the day—nothing, given the ice-bound conditions, too far from my flat—turn our attention back to the white board. She thinks the ten bullet points are fine as they stand. She should do. She helped identify them, and no one else has suggested improvements.

I put a red tick next to Elishaw and say, "This is not to suggest we won't come back to it, but for the moment it's done. Bradon, you were about to make some points concerning Scotland Yard?"

"I'm intrigued as to why they *weren't* brought in, as much as by the anticlimax local people must have felt when they realised it wasn't going to happen," he says. "In my country I can see how the FBI wouldn't get involved—it wouldn't be seen as a federal case—but here the situation was different, wasn't it? The guys at Scotland Yard were used to being called in to help in cases outside London, they had the expertise, and this was a big enough manhunt to warrant it. Am I right?"

"You are," I tell him. "Their absence took the local press, everyone, by surprise. But it seems the Northumberland police, led from the top as Frances said, decided it would not be necessary. And up to a point, I can see why. Initially they were confident of getting their man, as the saying goes. Maybe over-confident. It didn't look too difficult, after all. Here was a rural area, an inhospitable countryside covered in frost and a flurry or two of snow, a clear lead from Wolf's Nick north and south—most likely south—along the A696, a semi-workable description, a local community anxious to help, and a decidedly burned car which could offer up pieces of evidence. All systems go, except that point was quickly reached, as soon as the police realised their target wasn't about to fall like a ripe plum into their hands. *Then,* I can only think the shunning of Scotland Yard became a matter of pride, of not admitting that the local force couldn't cope. And we can imagine whose pride was first and foremost at stake."

"So Sir Fullarton James, or maybe Dudley Do-Wrong would be a better handle, had every confidence in his men to crack the case," Bradon says. "That wouldn't be a bad idea, if his men deserved it. Plus, he got mad at the press, or most of them, who seemed to have got it into their dumb heads that his men actually *didn't* deserve it and, worse, kept banging on about it. Result: no Scotland Yard."

"Couldn't have put it better myself, Bradon," says Peter. "If I may say so, you are developing a nice touch of British irony. And after a few days, seeing the mess the locals were creating, the Yard wouldn't have gone near it. But this surfeit of pride on Fullarton James' part would also have offended the good people of Otterburn. What were they to think? That the death of one of their own, a girl who'd left their local school with no great accomplishments to her name but who was making a good fist of creating her own business and providing a valuable local service, was worthy of no better than the spastic attentions of a bunch of local Plods."

"Nevertheless, Peter," I try to bring them back to a more positive focus, "they were making every effort to track this man down."

"And how!" Peter says. "Molly has put up a good defence of their actions in Jedburgh, but what of Otterburn? First, they go to the garage and worry their fingernails. Then they conduct a cockamamie interview through the victim's mother. Then they go up to the crime scene and tramp about with two civilians, allowing them direct access to the Hudson. They take no fingerprints or footprints. They fall into ditches. They pick up and drop bits of evidence like sweetie-papers. They head off halfway through to tell a colleague and wake a farmer up. They come back and tramp around some more. They pack it in and head home, leaving crime scene containment to the sheep and random nosey-parkers for four hours. You use the word effectiveness, Matthew? They make Inspector Clouseau look like the answer to a maiden's prayer."

I take his point, of course: who could fail to do otherwise? But the quiet strategy that Molly and I had devised last evening, in the hope of bringing balance to the debate, seems to have backfired. Wouldn't you say? Peter, far from seeking balance, is now lashing out in every direction that threatens his conviction that a dire injustice has been perpetrated. It has to be said, he is doing it well. The cumulative force of those few words, had they been directed where and when they should, might have given a whole new meaning to the phrase 'best practice' as applied to the Northumberland police force.

"Meanwhile, Peter," I tell him mildly, "Shell and his senior officers in Hexham were treating the situation very seriously indeed. They had barely learned of Evelyn's death before the description of Bowler was being conveyed to their foot soldiers and other divisions. Shell drove to

Morpeth that morning to consult with the Chief Constable and Tough, and a call was made to Scotland Yard to issue an appeal for information on national radio. This was in addition to the statement we've read, which was issued to the press that morning. The appeal was aired, along with Evelyn's description of her assailant, after the evening's six o'clock news. Unfortunately, it could be said to have gone too far. Apart from a minor blip in giving the time that Evelyn had been found as 10.30 pm, it directed attention to the trio who had been in the Redesdale Arms. The driver checked in with Doncaster police and the rest is history." I take a sip of coffee. "The media did their best; they were efficient, but they were not Sky News or the internet or social media. Not back then."

"And this is leading us where?" Peter asks.

"I am making the point that we cannot dismiss the entire police and media effort on grounds of local police mistakes at dead of night at Wolf's Nick. Some of the right steps were taken, some good work was done, but it came to nothing. A lot of damage had already been done."

"Total snafu," I hear Peter mutter to Bradon, but Sven steps in.

"At what point exactly," he asks, "can we say the police changed their focus from a murder inquiry to a theory about insurance fraud or even hallucinations on the part of Evelyn herself? And where did *that* idea come from?"

"When they knew they'd lost the plot," says Peter. "When it struck them, to paraphrase Bradon a few days ago, that they couldn't find their backsides with two hands."

"As Molly suggested earlier," I say, ignoring him, "it would have been an accumulation of things, over the next two weeks. By the end of January their theory was in place to the point of finalising the witness list and briefing their solicitor. At that point it was firm. I have little doubt its origins were early in the process. Molly may only have been half serious when she said it began in the garage and house the night before Evelyn died, but first impressions take flight, don't they? It was not helped by the failings at the crime scene, which Peter has catalogued. Johnstone and Vasey would not have been silent about what they had seen and heard. The refusal to request help from Scotland Yard was, as far as the villagers were concerned, another departure from common sense. The Yard went so far as to issue a statement a day or two after the event in response to an enquiry by the *Newcastle Evening Chronicle*: '(We are) taking no part in the investigations,' they said. 'If that were the case we would have been called in long before now.' The police had been housed in Otterburn Tower, where it was said search parties had to be launched for *them* when they got lost in its rambling interior. They drank in the Percy Arms when they should have had their noses to the grindstone; leaving, in another cliché, no stone unturned. Some local people felt that their interviews had been amateurishly conducted; some contacted the police afterwards to tell them points they wished to make had been missed. Others felt that their reported sightings of strange or bowler-hatted men had not been properly followed-up. And they would have been critical of being kept away from the crime scene when VIP sightseers in the company of Fullarton James, including magistrates and members of his supervisory body, the Northumberland Joint Standing Committee, were poking around."

"There was a leak to the *Newcastle Evening Chronicle* after about a week, wasn't there?" Bradon asks, and I'm glad most us are continuing to sift through everything carefully. "Here it is," he goes on. "It sets Evelyn's statement that Bowler had struck her with his fist against an early report by the pathologist, Professor McDonald, that he had found, quote, no sign of violence whatever, unquote. It couldn't have been more at odds."

"No," I reply. "And this came after a week during which all the efforts of the police to trace this man, the car, or anyone connected with them, had come to nothing. Having already lost face with the media and most of the community, they *would* be losing heart. I think the story you've highlighted, Bradon, may have been a catalyst. To the police, already disheartened and beginning to wonder if there would ever be a positive end to their efforts, a serious doubt, as Molly said, crept in. Had they been wasting their time? Had Evelyn been lying from the start?"

"You said most of the community," Frances says. "Why not *all* the community? There wouldn't be anyone left by mid-January who was taking the side of the police, would there?"

"There may have been at least one significant person," I reply. "The victim's father, Joseph Foster, had reason to be supportive of the police, although it seems even he was getting discouraged and impatient."

"And you can understand it," Molly says. "Here was a bereft man who had lost his eldest daughter in terrible circumstances and was only interested in one simple thing: who was responsible? His best route, his *only* route, was through the police. Add to that Joseph's character. He was not a confrontational man; he was an honest man, almost to the point of naivety, but a man who had made his own way in life without much help from others and had married a devoted woman. Add to it also the nature of the times; an era when authority was not questioned, when people in important positions were believed — not just assumed, *believed* — to behave responsibly and with the best interests of others at heart. An era when there was a quid pro quo of general goodwill and probity in society among all but the criminal classes."

"This is important," I add, "because Joseph held to that belief, the belief that somehow the truth about his daughter's death would be found, long after the dark days of January and even after the coroner and police had failed his daughter and family at the inquest. His growing frustration with the lack of progress, however, had manifested itself first when he spoke to the police about offering a reward for information—even if, as he said, it ruined his business. He was rebuffed.

"A few days after the inquest this stoical man was driven, perhaps at his son's urging backed up by family members, to write in protest to the Home Secretary pointing to the injustice of the inquest's proceedings. We shall get there in due course. Suffice it to say the disquiet rumbled on, and during those dark days of January the press produced every story they could, some having only marginal relevance to the investigative activities or prowess. Breaches of security, so-called human interest, the hopes and fears of local people, landscape descriptions, the manhunt and the never-ending parade of alleged sightings, were favourites."

"And there were some doozies," Bradon says. "We have a guy being reported for buying a pack of smokes because Evelyn had said her fare was a heavy smoker. We have an American being sought by Liverpool cops, not because he had any connection with Evelyn's death but because he fitted the definition of 'stranger' and had been to Newcastle. It turned out the Consulate were seeking him because he'd asked for help in finding a passage back home. We have another Newcastle joker claiming there was a body in his trunk. We have a guy picked up because he was carrying a bowler hat, leading the cops to think he was trying to hide it. It seems he was afraid of telling his wife he'd lost his job and had been sleeping rough. We have another guy who *was* sleeping rough with a farm dog. He turned out to be a deserter from the Royal Scots and the dog had taken a shine to him. We have a guy in a tweed cap and yellow shoes, nothing like Evelyn's description, wandering on Bogswood Moor—*there's* a name—who seems to have done as good a vanishing act as Bowler. We have numerous stories about the possibility Bowler was still on the loose, hiding out in the hills, rampant speculation about where he might be, who might be shielding him and, in a few cases, how he might have met his death in the crags or…um, loughs, or from exposure."

"And one of the effects all this had, apart from causing people anxiety, was to waste police time," Sven says. "Along with the sightings they had two confessions to look into, both proving as groundless or attention-seeking as usual. But each sighting had to be considered and many had to be followed up in the hills. Cold, debilitating work." He pauses, and where he comes from he should know all about cold and ice. "It wouldn't have taken long to get disillusioned. As far as we can judge, the police began to look at Evelyn's story with real suspicion and develop their own ideas in mid-January. It *might* have been before, as Molly said, when they heard from Percy Arms staff that Evelyn had not called in to enquire about her hire, but if so it would only be something they felt didn't add up; something not too significant at that stage."

"Okay," I say, "I think we've explored the police-people-press angle sufficiently for the moment, except for one area of speculation that leads us into the next two bullet points: Bowler's change of behaviour and the nature of his assaults on Evelyn. Now these, of course, assume her story was genuine, and the area I'm referring to was her statement that he had thrown something over her from a bottle or tin. In the press, this was translated into a vitriol attack. It was led by a story in the *Newcastle Evening Chronicle*, who floated what they called a startling new theory."

"They had some grounds for it," Frances says. "Both Johnstone, when he found her, and Joseph Foster later in The Kennels, said they'd seen what seemed to be evidence of burning by corrosive acid. Johnstone said he saw it on the coat he'd wrapped round her, Foster on the bedclothes she'd lain on. The idea was dismissed by the police, who said they had no information about corrosive acid, but you wonder, don't you? Apart from the police's incompetence in other areas, which may have found its way into this one, both men would have been familiar with acid, what it could do and what its effects looked like. They were used to dealing day-by-day with vehicle battery acid, weren't they? And if I remember my elementary physics, a lead-acid battery is based, by any other name, on diluted sulphuric acid."

"I've scoured the web," Peter says, "and I could find no explanation, then or now, as to why someone would be carrying ammonia or bleach in his pocket. Neither, by itself, is instantly or highly combustible. Nor is blue vitriol, although some of its uses are interesting, especially if this man worked with animals: fertilisers; providing a source of copper in animal feedstuffs; controlling algae, moulds, fungi and so on. I could find no mention of pocket-sized flares being sold in the 1930s. And I could find no earthly reason, but a lot of unearthly ones, why anyone would be carrying sulphuric acid about their person. It's simply not credible. It is also used in the manufacture of fertilisers, in petroleum refining, in metal-processing, in making rayon and in batteries, but who except in labs and factories would be carrying it around? Unless of course they *planned* to disfigure someone with the stuff." He smiles somewhat evilly at Molly. "I do, though, have another *construction*, if you'd like to hear it."

"Love to," Molly smiles back. I know that smile. It's a 'come into my garden' type of smile.

"But first," I tell them, "some lunch. I'm sure Peter will use the time profitably to prepare his next tour de force."

CHAPTER SEVENTEEN

Newcastle Law School: the present day, 30 January
Revisiting Evelyn's journey, circa 7.00-8.45 pm, 6 January 1931

We settle for sandwiches; Molly and I have our evening meal to consider. Peter, Sven and Bradon head for the Students' Union to stock up. While Frances tinkers with her smartphone, we tuck into a corner to review the morning. Molly tells me I did a fair job in righting the keeling ship, but reserves the right to pick more holes in Peter's beliefs if necessary.

She quietly gives me her assessment of the students which baldly runs like this, and I'm pleased we are more or less unanimous:

Peter Maxwell, 4.8* bright, full of himself (and sometimes b.s.)

Frances Wentworth, 4.7* bright, headstrong, intense;

Sven Carlson, 4.6* bright, thoughtful, rational;

Bradon Young, 4.6/7* bright, helpful, the eager puppy; a gem;

The team as a team, 4.9*, great combination (she never gives 5*s).

"I'm quite looking forward to hearing what Peter comes up with this time," she says. "It may have faults, but we can be sure it'll be good."

Here is Peter's *re*construction of the events of Twelfth Night 1931:

Money, sex and power, he says: the three great champions of crime. The police know them well, and they knew them then, and this above all is a tale of sex. There is an element of power, granted—because, when it comes to motivation, misogyny and sadism often appear in the mix. But not money; there was cash, he reminds us, in Evelyn's purse. The police, in their bafflement, their *pride* and *prejudice*, opted for money. That is the cross they have to bear, the guilt they have to live with. He hopes they are living with it still, as there has not been as much as a concession that they may have been wrong. The story won't die; it has run again in NARPO magazine without direct police input. But Peter assures us, except at the outset, he will drag no more third-party names into this, no more polemics directed at Mrs Clark; her involvement is plausible but incidental from this point on. He will deal only with Evelyn and Bowler.

Bowler may have been a cruel man, of the kind who populate the world's nether-regions, or he may simply have been a frustrated, angry man. But let us give him the benefit of the doubt, Peter says. Let us assume only that he was feeling annoyed and jilted when asked to get out of a car at Elishaw and grab a bus. His feelings would be understandable. He'd been receiving encouraging signals over tea in Jedburgh; the woman had seemed up for it. In the car, even on this frostbound night, there had been a sense of warmth and belonging, of anticipating pleasures to come. But now, at a road junction in the frozen wilds of Northumberland, he was being cast off like a soiled shirt. She had made a choice.

When he reaches Otterburn he has no intention of entering the Percy Arms. He seems to have been offered an ounce of good luck; his cabbie turns out to be a young woman; not mouth-wateringly sexy but decent enough on the eye. He would prefer not to be seen at all in the village, and makes a decent job of it. He eases out of the Hudson, sidles down the street, and makes good use of dark corners and shadows. One or two people are about but there are no street-lights and he is clad in dark clothing. He turns away when anyone comes near, exchanges no words. In the shelter of the trees by the bridge he tries his luck with a girl he sees on a bicycle, but gives it up with a few well-chosen epithets when she rebuffs him. His anger and lust rise up another notch.

Evelyn doesn't keep him waiting long and sees him at the bridge. She has topped up her tank with petrol—sorry, Bradon, *gas*—and has told her mother she is heading for Ponteland. She doesn't waste much time wondering about George Phillipson. She doesn't like the bothy or most of the men who use it, who can best be described as coarse, and she doesn't see him on the street. With luck, even though there is frost on the ground and more in the air, she can be in Ponteland and back at nine or half-past and can maybe meet up with him then, perhaps in the Percy Arms.

At 7.22 pm she drives carefully past John Robson's bus at Raylees Farm—his conductor is slip-sliding across the road to deliver papers—negotiates the bend and begins the haul up to the Ottercops. Her passenger seems to be smoking a lot, preoccupied. They don't have much conversation; bits and pieces about where he comes from, about cars. He tells her he can drive, so good for him. He can't be a pauper.

Bowler is looking with interest at the passing countryside and it seems to him deserted. There are one or two lanes leading off the road, small clumps of trees, a barn here and there. He lights another cigarette to soothe his nerves. Once or twice, fishing for his lighter and fags—sorry, Bradon, *smokes*—he touches the girl with his right elbow. He has a sideways glance at her now and then. She is small and a bit on the plump side, quite sturdy but nothing he can't handle. She doesn't seem at all interested in him. His anger and lust rise up another notch.

The night is quite clear, not sparklingly so; some cloud, a low moon, and by the time they reach the Capheaton turn-off Evelyn can see the faint glow of city lights on the forward horizon. She thinks, but can't be sure, that she passes Mr Kirsopp-Reed's car. He'll have been to one of his meetings in County Hall (it relocated to Morpeth in 1981), heading home.

Bowler can also see the glow. If he is going to make a move he needs to do it now. He peers out of the window as they go through Belsay. His watch tells him it is 8.02 pm. As they come to the centre of the village he says, 'Well, there's no bus here.' Evelyn replies, 'There will be further on.' He thinks of telling her a bus is the last thing on his mind, but simply says, 'We'll turn and go back.' He senses the girl look at him in surprise. They are approaching the turn-off to the Hall and Castle. He tells her this is a good enough place to turn the car. Perplexed, she asks him why he is thinking of going back when he has come so far. He retorts, 'That's got nothing to do with you.' *Who does she think she is,* to question him?

Evelyn begins to feel nervous and slightly afraid. She has no idea why her passenger has suddenly changed his mind and seems to want, of all things, to return to Otterburn. She asks herself if it could be something to do with the car he left at Elishaw, or the people in it. Maybe he hopes to meet up with them again. But how? He said they were going to Hexham, and they'll be long gone—or maybe, if those rumours about Mrs Clark are true...but, no, she won't allow herself to delve into *that*. Still, this man is her fare, and the customer is always right. She feels him getting impatient, so manoeuvres the car around, looking back the way they've come, hoping to see someone. She doesn't; there is no one about. People will be putting their children to bed, listening to the wireless.

Then, after she turns the car, she feels him shuffle along the seat, squeezing up against her. At no point has he seemed drunk to her but she does smell alcohol, stale on his breath. He says he will take over the driving and pushes her against the door. When she objects he punches her over her eye. She sags sideways against the glass, sure now that something is very badly wrong, and again tries to see someone she can call for help. But her eyes are watering with the sting of the blows and she can't see clearly. Evelyn's mild concern at the change in her passenger's behaviour is now developing into full-blown panic. She tries to keep hold of the wheel, to stop him.

Bowler pinions her hard against the door and handbrake. He tells her to cut it out or she'll feel his fist again, another harder blow. He is now more or less behind the wheel, Evelyn crunched up to his right and unable to move in any direction. Their little altercation has aroused him. He has smelt her body odour; not at all unpleasant. He needs to get away from these fields and farms and back into the moors. It won't be far: ten miles? He has travelled this road several times before but doesn't know the area well, so misses a couple of possible turn-offs. But there are still lights in houses set back from the road so he isn't too concerned. Better to get right away from habitation. This is awkward, driving this way, but the girl at least seems to have given up squirming. By the time they stop she may be halfway receptive. If he can feel her warmth, she can feel his.

Evelyn's mind is in turmoil. She can't move; she can only look out and hope she sees someone so she can signal her distress, but can barely move her arms and is so low on the seat she can only just see out. The man seems to be a competent driver, not quite as fast as she was doing on the southward journey, but fast enough. She begins to wonder what he might be planning when they reach Otterburn; he'd better make himself scarce or he'll have her father, her brother, maybe George to contend with. She wishes she had stopped to pick George up but shudders again at the thought of going into *that place*. She is conscious of passing a couple walking along the road at Easton's Corner, but they are gone before she can move. She briefly sees the man turn around, looking startled as they surge past. Two miles further, over the rise past Raechester Farm, Bowler tells her they'll stop here. He brakes and pulls in to the verge.

Bowler reaches into his pockets for his cigarettes; it's been a while since he had a smoke. The moor stretches ahead and to their right, empty, ghostly, only a glimmer of light showing in the distance; a farmhouse. This is as good a place as any to get off the main road. He makes an effort to calm the girl and offers her a cigarette. She declines. So much for the milk of human kindness, he thinks. He says, 'Well, you're an independent young woman' and offers her a smile which even to him feels false.

Evelyn tries to push him away. He puts his cigarette to his mouth and pins her arms, then begins hitting her. This girl has to be brought to heel, Bowler thinks; the only thing she seems to understand is violence. He delivers one or two punches and then moves away along the seat to give himself room to manoeuvre. With a bit of a struggle he manages to force her over into the back seat, but the fight has gone out of her. She lands in a heap, stunned, showing a flash of thigh.

Bowler (no bowler now, his hat has come off) puts the car in low gear and drives it slowly across the road at an angle and down a short slope onto the moor. It feels precarious, he wasn't expecting such a dip, but it rights itself on the level and he begins to inch across the rough terrain. He feels it hit a ditch and thinks to himself, enough is enough. Nothing, human or animal, is stirring. They could be alone in the world.

The car grinds to a halt, stalls, still in low gear. He gets out, leaving the door open and opens the rear door. The girl is looking up at him, groggily. Time for action, he thinks. He climbs in beside her, runs his hands down her thighs and under her skirt. He tears at it, and then her knickers. She tries to fight him off. It feels about as effective as being flapped at by a moth. Suspenders; he has always been a sucker for suspenders, that little gap of warm soft skin they leave between knickers and stockings. His hand moves higher...

What the...?

A sanitary towel. She's having a period. For God's sake, the bitch is having a period. (Five years were to pass before Tampax came to the market.) He reels back in distaste, thwarted, rage rising as she tries to sit up. Bowler hits her again, harder, reaches in his pocket for his lighter fuel and pours some over her, *there*, in her lap, where that offensive, bloody, piece of cloth was hidden, waiting for him to *touch* it. He flicks his lighter to it, jerks back as flames flare upwards, backs out of the car.

It takes him a moment or two to regain his senses. When he does, he is incandescent with rage. Not only that, but the realisation quickly comes: this stupid, *filthy* girl has to be silenced. He takes a look into the luggage carrier for a hammer, a spanner, a weapon of some sort, and finds…a 2-gallon can of petrol.

Well now, there is a solution; no accusations of rape to worry about. There's not going to be much trace of this fracas left when this is over.

He quickly unscrews the cap and pours the can's contents over her, directing as much as he can onto that unclean, offensive part of her. When the flames become too much for him, he reels away, dumps the rest in the well of the car and throws the can down. It won't be long before the whole lot goes up. Maybe he has the presence of mind to pick up his hat, or hers, or both, from the front seat. He doesn't hang about. The girl has come to and is flapping her arms at her thighs and belly, struggling to beat the flames out, but they are steadily engulfing her. She cries out in fear and pain. Bowler runs for the road. Half a minute later Evelyn crawls out of the car and onto the moor, tugging at her clothes, hugging the ground in a desperate attempt to put the flames out.

The time is 8.42 pm.

Peter looks around. "And so it came to pass. Don't you think?"

The others are looking at him in some wonderment, and not a little admiration. Frances smiles and gives a thoughtful clap.

"It hangs together, Peter," I tell him. "The witnesses, such as they were, and your timings all make sense. There may be elements here and there which aren't perfect, but if ever there was a case of making evidence fit a theory, I think you just hit on it…Molly?"

"Good job in general, Peter," Molly says. "Most 'i's dotted and 't's crossed. Most of Matthew's bullet points dispensed with, too."

"Most?" he asks, offended. "What did I miss?"

"Not so much what you missed, but what you skated over."

"Such as?"

"Four points which, if roles were reversed, would cast sufficient doubt on your scenario to risk a conviction for your client. One, the contorted driving position: is it feasible? Two, the fact that the pathologist found no evidence of bruising: how could that be if Bowler had hit her as hard as she implied? Three, the arson attack: how could Bowler throw petrol at close quarters over a fire without risking himself? Four, Evelyn said the bumping roused her; she was unconscious before she was set alight. You'd need to have answers ready, Mr Maxwell, because in a court of law these questions could undermine your case."

"Very well," he says. "To take the last two first. He may well have scorched his own clothes, but if he then thumbed a lift—you'll recall one of my earlier *constructions*—it would only add credence to his having crashed his car. But beyond that, Evelyn was confused. By then, she had been manhandled and beaten, and *was* unconscious or very nearly so. Bowler could have poured the contents of the can in her lap and then set it alight. She came to, and crawled out. We have still to analyse the forensic evidence, such as it is, but that's where it's pointing. She may only have been vaguely aware of him, quote, throwing something over her from a bottle or tin, unquote. Perhaps it was his lighter fuel. I'm tempted to believe he may have done this while they were parked on the road—Evelyn's statement can be read as implying as much—and then drove as quickly as he could, 'bumping' across the fell before completing the job with the petrol can. Or he may have doused her lap directly from the can once they'd stopped on the moor, and then set it alight. Inspector Russell didn't find any trace of scorching along the cars tracks, but at that point either Evelyn was lying stunned in the back or a more limited fire may have been started from lighter fuel and confined to Evelyn herself. In any case, we are dealing with someone who has literally been burned to death; or, when she gave her statement, was four-fifths of the way there. She was groggy; how could she be expected to get every detail right? If the roles are *not* reversed, and she was innocent until proven guilty, there is more than enough to give a jury reasonable doubt."

"Let's say we accept that," Molly says. "And I don't believe eight decades on we are likely to do better. What about the lack of bruising?"

"I think that's the easiest of your concerns to answer," Peter says. "This was a pathologist who was unused to criminal forensics. He was not a hands-on guy. The suggestion has been made that he was brought in as a 'name' rather than as a skilled practitioner. He was first and foremost an academic, and he was assisted by his son and a young doctor whose experience of such cadavers would be limited or non-existent. There were signs of burning, discolouration, on Evelyn's face. Who in those days would have distinguished them from skin-deep bruising? Might she have rubbed her eyes, left traces of smoke and ash? How much of a blow would it take for her to faint? Johnstone and Rutherford, amongst others, noticed her eyes seemed to be puffed-up. Who are we to believe? The on-the-spot evidence of men used to seeing faces damaged by brawls, or the opinions of an occasional criminologist two days later? The pathologist's own admission at the inquest, and he was no Bernard Spilsbury, was—I quote—'anything superficial could not possibly be detected. I found no evidence of any deep bruising.' I ask again: what would it have taken, in her state of fright, to render Evelyn unconscious? Would it really have needed a heavyweight boxer's uppercut?"

I hold up my hand. "So far so good, Peter. We have yet to come to the inquest so leave it at that for the moment."

"Glad to," he says. "I confess the driving situation has me foxed. You'll probably say again, leave it till later, until we've looked at the evidence of motor engineer Jennings. I see, incidentally, he had a silent partner from this part of the world called Hodgson who may well have been better qualified to testify, but for the moment let me make three points. One; the Hudson Super-Six was a big, roomy saloon with plenty of head clearance. Two; the seating configuration was of a low-backed, bench-style type rather than the individual or bucket seats most cars have today. I agree it would have been uncomfortable to drive in the way implied by Evelyn's statement and it would have taken effort to force her into the back seat, but neither would have been insurmountable. Perhaps back in Belsay he had come to the conclusion it was more trouble than it was worth. But three, while at no point did she say they'd changed seats, we only have Mrs Foster's *impression* that this was how they'd done it. Everyone at the inquest and later seems to have taken it as gospel."

"Okay. That's good enough for today, Peter," I tell him. "In our next session I suggest we deal with the motor engineer, the doctor, and the pathologist's report. We can also consider the question of 'interference' or rape, and variations in the spectrum. In the meantime, you may not have given us a cut-and-dried solution, but to my mind you've come close. Given the bits and pieces of evidence and the circumstances, the sex angle especially rings true. Unless anyone has any other ideas?"

"Only that she may have given him some encouragement," Sven says. "Or something that could have been misread for it. But as Fran said, it wouldn't have been in character." He shrugs. "She could have upset him in some other way, but it would have played out much the same. It's difficult, when books and articles at the time tell conflicting stories. We have one press article suggesting he began to hit her at Kirkwhelpington; another that he pushed the car over the verge and onto the moor; another that he set the car alight and then pushed it onto the moor. But how anyone could figure why a man would get inside a burning car to drive it sixty metres is hard to understand. It's hard enough to understand why he wanted it on the moor at all, except to put distance between it and any passing spectators. Maybe he thought the fell was firm ground, hardened by frost, and he'd be able to drive it out of sight. It's why I suspect he didn't at first intend to set the car alight and didn't do so on the road. That only came about on the moor when he found the sanitary towel."

Molly nods. "It's possible, and best of all is that you're getting inside this man's head and trying to make sense of these bare bones of script."

"Unless there is something truly questionable," I tell them, "we are bound to use as our main source the statement Evelyn gave, as recounted by her mother at the inquest—however lacking or untidy it may seem, or however untidily it was recorded. Remember Bradon's Emerson quote."

Then Bradon says, "There's something else we may have ignored. Peter spoke of it a week ago, and if it doesn't add anything it tends to confirm some things. I'm talking of her purse, by which I understand the British mean a small money bag with a clip or zipper rather than a handbag?" He raises his eyebrows and I nod for him to continue.

"Well, looking at officer Proud's statement again, he says he picked it up after one in the morning a yard from the rear nearside wheel. It kinda suggests no one was at the scene between ten at night and one in the morning, so all the contamination was the cops' own doing with help from the garage guys. It suggests if anyone else had been roaming about, a tramp or shepherd, the money would have gone. And it suggests, to get where it was, someone must have thrown it or kicked it. It was burned, but not so badly that the notes and driving licences were burned, which figures if Proud found it a yard away. It couldn't have been on Evelyn while *she* was burning, could it? And if she'd crawled out of the auto from the *rear offside* door towards the road past the *front* wheel, as all we've read suggests, how did her purse get behind the *rear nearside* wheel? There had to have been some other agent, am I right?"

"You are," Peter says. "I'd forgotten that little item. Unless she'd been crawling around in circles, but if she'd found herself at the nearside rear wheel she'd have made for the road." He snaps his fingers. "If Bowler didn't move it or kick it, maybe those early-bird reporters did."

There is silence while they digest it.

"It must have been Bowler," Frances says. "The reporters weren't there till six. And if they'd got to it first they'd have pocketed the money."

Laughter again breaks the spell.

"So there is nothing so far that would have any of you disbelieving Evelyn's story?" I ask, and by this time I would be amazed if there were.

More silence. Obviously not.

"Think hard," I tell them. "We only get one chance at this. We'll need to wrap up the purse and other loose ends when we've seen what the pathologist and mechanic had to say. I'll see you all on Tuesday."

CHAPTER EIGHTEEN

Molly and I eat that night at Peace and Loaf, a classy modern restaurant on Jesmond Road only a ten-minute stroll from my flat on (trust me, friends) Otterburn Terrace. It's not the Quayside, which is usually where we head in order to enjoy the bridges, the lights and the water of Tyne rolling by, but mine host is a one-time MasterChef finalist, and his Peace and Loaf (I have no idea where the name originated) is a memorable gastronomic experience. The decor is a crisp blend of polished wood, glass, brick and metal, and the dishes—and extras—are works of art.

Molly has expressed a wish to go to Otterburn tomorrow. She has passed through the village before but wants to familiarise herself with the various buildings she's been hearing so much about, the burn and bridge, Elishaw, and most of all Wolf's Nick. The roads, except for the verges, are now clear of snow, and she has offered the use of her car—provided I drive so she can enjoy the sights. I don't know what it is about my beloved Triumph TR6 that seems so off-putting to other people, but as Molly has a four-wheel drive BMW X3, who am I to argue?

"So what did you think of our up-and-coming barrister-to-be?" I ask her. "Did he impress as much in full glorious Technicolor?"

"If he will only learn not to rush in where angels fear to tread, he'll be formidable," she says. "But oh dear, the impatience, the loquacity. Good practice for him, but I think the others, except Bradon, are rather in awe. They may also be getting a little tired of him, Frances especially."

"They had some warning of the way he was thinking. He talked of a possible sex angle a week ago in Otterburn."

"By her standards, Frances seemed a trifle subdued today," Molly says. "Has he upset her in some way?"

"No. I think Frances has upset herself. She made her feelings, which basically amount to an unshakeable belief in Evelyn's story, perfectly clear last Tuesday. She may now be regretting it; not her feelings, but the way she came out in the open and pretty well dismissed any further analysis. I think since then she's been trying to atone."

Molly sighs. "It's never easy not to take sides, but they do need to step back and detach themselves. It's understandable they should be in Evie's corner. The presumption of innocence may be the bedrock of democratic justice but in this type of exercise they must leave themselves open to seeing both sides of the argument."

"The problem we have here is that there are very few grounds for seeing the *other* side of the argument. The police produced nothing to support their own theory that Evelyn was a fraudster and/or in some way unstable. They seem to have engineered a list of witnesses to address loose threads in Evelyn's story and persuaded the coroner they were righteous in their beliefs. We shall see what the students make of it next week but it makes it difficult for any one of them, if they so wished — or for you or I — to act as devil's advocate. All we can do is pick at the fabric of Evelyn's story and see if anything falls out. The police, apart from an abortive sally at a supposed insurance payout which they seem not to have pursued, didn't leave any fabric to pick at in theirs. Anyway, I've had my fill of it for one day. Let's talk about other things."

Molly gazes out of the venetian blinds and takes a sip of wine. "I'm looking forward to tomorrow," she says, and then smiles, "and tonight."

We set off at eight in the morning — a Saturday, not quite the full-on rush hour of a weekday — and are out of the city in minutes. It is a bright, crisp morning, not dissimilar to Friday past, but we begin to get traces of mist on our left in the trees of the Darras Hall estate. I tell Molly the residents won't like it; this is arguably the most exclusive housing development on Tyneside and (the last I heard) accommodates such legends as the former 'Magpies' stars, Shearer and Beardsley. They'll be unhappy with anything as confining as fog; it may threaten today's game and all those nice Jaguars will be going to waste. She tells me not to worry; they'll have indoor pools and hot tubs or saunas.

As we approach Belsay I ask Molly to keep an eye open for places where Evelyn may have turned, having gone 'through' the village. I'm wondering if we've been wrong in our assumption that the Hall/Castle entrance would have been the logical place. There are turn-offs both to right and left about a mile this side of it which would have been possible, but I'm inclined to stick with our first instinct. Neither would add greatly to our (or Bradon's) timings; perhaps two or three minutes. Also, the sense I get in reading Evelyn's statement is that the conversation she'd had with Bowler at Belsay was a quick exchange. He would not have allowed too long a gap to develop between grumbling about lack of buses and telling her to turn. *Why* he should have done so is another matter.

In any case, it is something of a relief to me that there is no longer any need to check distances or the speedometer. I can behave like a normal 50 mph driver and still get overtaken by boy racers and motorbikes. As we motor along the air is fresh and crystalline, and there is no more hint we could have problems with mist.

I point out Ferney Chesters to Molly, and the Capheaton junction, then the place near Kirkharle where Kirsopp-Reed thought he may have seen one of Robert Tait's buses, and then we skirt Kirkwhelpington. A little less than a mile later I pull into the same lay-by at Knowesgate where I'd stopped with the team. I tell Molly we are very close to Wolf's Nick and point up the hill to the change in the landscape from pasture to moorland. I am hoping she might be able to see things we missed, or ask questions we did not ask. Given the emptiness of the landscape we're approaching it's hard to believe we missed anything obvious, but I am sure if anyone can shed any new light on the case Molly may be able to.

"This crossroads up ahead?" she says. "That's presumably the road leading left to Hawick Farm and eventually to Redesmouth. The way the farmer, William Herdman, would have gone?" She points west.

"Yes."

"Oh, well. I suppose Herdman would have been tucked up in bed before Bowler had walked past, if he'd been heading for a Hexham train."

"Half a mile beyond the top of the rise," I tell her, "there's a lay-by where Peter directed us; a gated track leading off to the right, towards Wolf Crag. You'll get a good view of where it all happened."

Molly purses her lips and nods. I start the car again. The Beemer purrs up the hill and I point out Harwood Forest on the skyline to our right, flanked by the drover's road which the shepherd Sidney Henderson would have walked along when he saw the burning car. If there were a few cars on the A696 that night, there would have been none at all to disturb him on the old track. After a minute I pull over and cut the engine. The moss is bathed in golden light this morning. The grasses are glistening, but at this time of year are wisps of straw, the heather out of bloom, russet. The same kestrel is quartering the moor; his personal hunting-ground. On the skyline in front of us, above the dark belt of trees around Ottercops Farm, a brief flash of silver glints like a newly-minted coin from one of the two taller telecommunications masts.

Molly picks up binoculars and takes in the scene from Wolf Crag behind us, across the bowl of Todcrag Moss to the dark line of conifers winding up the contours ahead to our right, and finally the bend in the road as it curves towards the farmhouse in the distance.

She puts down her binoculars and turns to me.

"Why the moor?" she asks.

"Say again?"

"As Sven asked, why did Bowler choose to drive onto moorland, whether or not he thought it was firm, when there are lanes leading off right and left? Not many, I grant you, but most if not all would have existed then. There could even have been more, leading to old sheepfolds and shepherds' huts. And this gate we're beside doesn't look too old."

"She may have managed to yank the wheel," I reply. "The motor engineer's report seems to suggest the Hudson could have been out of control for some way before it levelled-off. He talks of scrapes under the running board where it ran over boulders."

"No; only the last bit of that makes sense. According to the sequence she described they pulled up, he offered her a cigarette, hit her then threw her into the back. She couldn't have yanked the wheel from behind. And if she had, I think she would have said so in her own defence when she talked with her mother. She was stunned, she was vaguely aware of him pouring something on her from a container in his pocket, he set it alight, and the next thing she knew they were jolting over the moor. The interview was not conducted at all logically, and at one point it could be inferred that he had attempted to rape her first in the back of the car while they were parked on the road. But still, why the moor?"

"He panicked. He had to get as far out of sight as possible."

"There is a good chance he panicked, and he surely wasn't thinking straight. And if she was already alight he would have been very keen to get off the road, and quickly." Molly gets out of the car and I follow her.

"Maybe in the dark he didn't see what a dip it was down there," I suggest. "Vehicles were infrequent but they'd passed one or two, and you're right, he wouldn't have risked having any witnesses. Sven could also have been right. The moor may have looked more negotiable than it turned out to be. Moonlight glinting on hard frosty ground?"

"Yes, but you can also see why the police might have been dubious. If you're going to assault someone, there are more secluded places along this road to do it—provided some tree belts existed then and we know some did not. But there again, if you planned to set a car alight and claim the insurance, there are a lot better places to do that too."

"Perhaps it was because he was unused to the controls, and skidded a bit. Or hit ice. Maybe she nudged him enough to cause a skid."

"Those are possibilities, but again, she couldn't have nudged him, could she? If she was in the back, lying semi-conscious or worse? Still, there could have been a patch of ice. We're high enough here for the temperature to have dropped since Belsay. You need to get them thinking about the sequence of those five minutes. The five minutes between pulling up on the road and the car being ablaze on the moor."

"I wonder how much of what we're seeing now has changed since."

"Not all that much, I guess. The plantation winding up the hill isn't shown on photos, and neither are the tree belts around Ottercops Farm. The fencing is newish. Some snow poles have gone. There are signs of irrigation ditches, but when they would have been cut...?" Molly shrugs. "Except for the tree-planting, the moor itself won't be much changed."

"Maybe the Forestry Commission were working here at some point in the past, trying to prepare the ground for tree-planting."

Molly echoes something I had thought at first sight of the place. "It makes you wonder whether people who walk or work on this land ever imagine today the horror that took place all those years ago. Would that be a burn running through the dip over there?"

"Ottercops Burn. But the Hudson lurched to a halt and stalled in a ditch before it got there." I point out as near as I can the exact spot.

"Yes…it's hard to imagine now, especially on a fine day and so long ago." Molly shrugs. "I'm still perplexed, but inclined to think that driving onto the moor was a miscalculation. What had he to gain? The car was still in full view of the road. If he'd wanted to have his way with her, a lane would have seemed a more normal lover's tryst to any passer-by. And how did the *police* rationalise it, when it came to their theory that she intended to set her car alight? It's nonsense. She could have let it run over a crag or into a lough. She could have driven off the road along one of the tracks. Maybe Bowler was drunker than she thought. Or a serial killer, and his comfort zone was lonely fells and unsophisticated police forces."

"You're beginning to sound like one of Goodman's theories. A serial fire-bug or the like." It's not impossible, but it doesn't feel right.

She laughs. "I wonder what Peter will make of *them*. Competition for him. But no, the only thing that makes me think of a serial explanation is that no one was ever nailed for this specific crime."

We ease into in the BMW again. I pull onto the A696 and head for Otterburn, pointing out Blaxter and Raylees on the way, the River Rede silvery in the sunlight like a snail's trail. Gloom descends as I pull into the Percy Arms forecourt. With an uneven coating of left-over snow and ice, it looks even less inviting. I imagine the ground on this side of the building, shaded and north-facing, will take a long time to thaw out.

Molly says, "If we were hoping for coffee, I think we're out of luck."

"It's a grim place," I tell her. "But I had in mind to try Otterburn Castle for coffee. Under these trees by the burn, or slightly different trees, is where Evelyn supposedly picked Bowler up for the second time."

Molly stands in a corner of the forecourt near the low stone bridge with its sturdy balustrade sides, looking down on the water and then back along the road. "Miss Carruthers would have been cycling towards him the way we've come?"

"Yes, and Miss Ferry would have gone in and out of that door to collect her sausages." I point to what used to be the hotel's main entrance.

Although the burn below us, aided by a weir upstream, is flowing steadily here, there is still the smell of mildew and decay in the still air. The hotel building looks like something that would have appealed to

Hitchcock. Wasn't there a time when local authorities tried to protect civic amenities, or is my memory playing tricks? They seem barely able to maintain their own school yards and playing fields and car parks these days, let alone sweep up fallen leaves.

"All perfectly logical," Molly says. "This hard-standing may have been cobbled then but Evelyn could easily have pulled over to pick him up. It's a dark enough corner even in broad daylight." She turns around. "And where exactly is the Foster house, The Kennels, from here?"

I point up the road. "Just past the church and around the curve, this side of the road. The garage is opposite, on the same side as the church."

"So he would not have seen her until the car reappeared, and she would not have seen him until she was halfway here. Plus, it was dark."

We cross the road into the sunshine and walk into the grounds of Otterburn Tower-cum-Castle. We are the only ones for coffee in the oak-panelled room, but there is a roaring log fire that cheers us.

"Nice temporary quarters for the police," Molly comments.

"Not only the police," I tell her. "George Phillipson moved in here for a while after Evelyn's death. He stopped working at Foster's."

"He did? What happened to cause that rift?"

"I don't know. Maybe it wasn't a rift so much as associations and memories becoming too much for him."

"I can understand that," she says. "I hope he wasn't blamed for not being there that night when he was wanted."

"Or maybe there were a lot of repairs and bits and pieces of joinery to do when the police had gone. Maybe they wrecked a few things and bequeathed him a project to get his teeth into."

She smiles. "That's a nicer reason, I think. I hope so."

"The owner, Mrs Pease, didn't spend much time here but she might have expected her house to have undergone some changes while the police were using it. They've never been noted for good housekeeping."

"She was the widow of Howard Pease, the author, wasn't she?"

"Well, yes, but not to be confused with a Californian writer of the same name. Our Howard Pease collected old books and spooky yarns. He wrote *Border Ghost Stories* just after the Great War. I imagine he took great delight in living in a house once owned by Mad Jack Hall, who among other things was a Justice of the Peace. Mad, or Crazy, Jack, aka Jock, was from a family of Reivers, a so-called English highland clan who had acquired Otterburn Tower in Cromwell's day. He was also a notable Scottish Jacobite. He joined his neighbour Jamie Radcliffe, the Earl of Derwentwater, in the 1715 uprising but was captured and hanged on Tyburn Hill a year later. He seems to have been well-regarded, so it dismayed most people around here. I think you could say he was a local character of some standing. I'll show you his initials carved on a lintel here before we go. You'll also see Howard Pease's memorial headstone, with his wife Marna, standing against the east wall of the churchyard."

"You do know how to treat a girl, don't you?"

I had phoned earlier in the week to get us access to the Village Memorial Hall, which in preparation for next week's sessions with the students is to plug a gap in my knowledge. We are shown in by a kindly Parish Councillor who leaves us to it while he goes to pick up shopping at the Border Reiver. Opened in 1923 by the Duke of Northumberland, the Memorial Hall made headlines eight years later as the venue for Evelyn Foster's inquest. Today, it is used by toddler and pre-school groups, occasional social and fund-raising activities, and the Parish Council itself for meetings. Goodman describes it as 'utilitarian… (its walls supporting) a timbered ceiling sloping from the centre…an uncomplicated oblong 30ft by 90…with a rudimentary stage.' It does not appear to have changed radically, except for the extension built towards the Percy Arms. Another door leads out to the rear yard. During the inquest it was used once or twice by the Foster family to escape the attentions of the media.

I picture the scene described by Goodman and Symons: a chair and trestle table covered with black cloth in front of the stage for the use of H.M. Coroner; acetylene lamps flickering in the early February gloom; an anteroom behind the stage where the jury could leave their coats and eventually reach their verdict; nine chairs for jury members set against the east (Percy Arms) wall; a chair for witnesses opposite and across the coroner's table; more chairs for the coroner's officer and policemen; and the remainder filled with rows of seats for spectators and reporters (the Hall, built via public subscription, was designed to hold seating for 240).

Nothing could be simpler. We wait until our friendly Councillor returns with his shopping, thank him and make our way up the street.

I point out to Molly where the Post Office used to be, and the Co-op and bothy. We view the headstones in the churchyard, including those of Howard and Marna Pease and the Foster family (Peter's rose has gone, I hope blown by the wind rather than purloined), and then the garage and The Kennels. My mind has become inured to The Kennels, but Molly is as horror-stricken by the house as we all were a week ago.

She looks back towards the bridge and the trees around the Tower. Almost the full length of Otterburn is visible, at least the northern side of the street, the church steeple looming over everything else.

"*Why* did he want to come back?" she asks, in an echo of a thought I'd had earlier. "What was in his head at that point, I wonder? Bowler, I mean."

"He was lying. It was a ruse."

"There seems to be no other conceivable explanation," Molly says. "In which case Peter was on the right lines; he wanted to get back to the moors. Maybe he intended to rape and leave her there, then take the Hudson as far as Newcastle and dump it. If she did manage to yank the wheel or they somehow skidded or lurched off the road, he would have become even angrier, wouldn't he? His means of escape was mired in the moss. So he was screwed twice over, by her monthly period, which he didn't like at all, and by being stuck. So, in a rage about one or both, he burned the lot. And whatever its cause, he was certainly in a rage."

She looks at me. "One evening this week I did some reading into fire-setting. What I found is inconclusive. Goodman cites a book written in 1951 in the USA by Lewis and Yarnell, who coined the phrase 'fire-bug.' It suggests that adult male pyromaniacs—implying a repeated pattern of fire-setting—will sometimes admit to some form of sexual thwarting just before their fire-setting. For ninety-two in a sample of 1145 arsonists, the motive was revenge against women who spurned them. It's not a big total but it's there. Davis and Lauber in 1999 said arson could act as a sexual substitute, and pyromaniacs would often admit a link between sexual excitement and arson. Freud himself thought that fire had a special symbolic relationship with the male sex urge. Other studies tend to play down that link. Some are more concerned with child arson, maybe linked to abuse. And, of course, arson is often connected to property crime, in which people are accidentally or deliberately killed; the Foster case in Shropshire in 2008 and the Philpotts in Derby in 2012 being two prime examples. You'll recall a young girl in 2009 in Arbroath, Jessica McCagh, was doused in petrol by her boyfriend, set alight and killed?"

"I do remember that case," I tell her. "But—"

"I got interested in it all," she smiles. "Did you know that arson is the biggest single cause of fires in the UK? There are 3,000-4,000 every week, and they account for a death every five days. And here's something which really took me by surprise: arsonists are among Britain's biggest serial killers. In 1980, a Mancunian called Peter Dinsdale—I'd almost forgotten about him—admitted killing twenty-six people in fires. That's exactly as many as Peter Sutcliffe, Ian Brady, Myra Hindley and John Christie, four household names in serial killing, combined. And if we're looking for connections between arson, serial murder, abuse and sexual frustration, we need only look a little further afield to Germany and the name Peter Kürten, executed for his crimes in Cologne. Coincidentally, he was guillotined in 1931, only six months after Evie died."

"That's useful, Molly, but it's treading close to a line I don't want to cross. Assessing Evelyn's innocence is one thing, tracking an arsonist and prosecuting a long-ago crime by someone else is another. It's tempting, but I think we can forget about pointing any finger of blame."

She nods. "Fair comment, but I think it bears looking into. You'll remember I found only the two cases during the entire decades of the 20s and 30s which bore any resemblance to Evie's death. We've talked about *Rouse* and *Brown,* and no doubt you'll be talking about them with your troops. One or two others, like *Fox,* involved arson, but the nature of the crimes was different. Sidney Fox's was a rare beast; matricide. In 1929, he killed his mother in a Margate hotel in order to claim insurance, and then tried to burn the room. In 1936, a well-to-do lady called Laura Mordaunt-Chapman was found lying in her bedroom doorway in Twickenham, stabbed 46 times and also charred. But Alfred Rouse, who in January 1931 was already under lock and key for his Northants murder, and Ernest Brown, stand out from all the rest. Evelyn's killer *could* have been some other Rouse imitator of the day, someone unknown who confined himself to one killing, but I don't think so. I think more likely a recidivist."

From which you will gather, friends, *viz-à-viz* the Northumberland Constabulary's theory versus Evelyn's innocence, that Molly's mind is made up.

She smiles, and changes tack again. "I'm thinking too about why Bowler said he wanted to return to Otterburn. There may just be another explanation. He seems not to have known anyone in the village, so we can rule that out, but he may have spent the southward journey stewing over his rejection at Elishaw and decided to come back to make an issue of it. A revenge mission may have been in keeping with his mood as expounded by Peter, but how would he have known where his target or targets had gone after they left him? And it wouldn't explain why he should change his mind and attack Evelyn, which by elimination, almost by default, reverts to being his primary motive for turning back. Don't you agree?" She sighs. "But you're right; however it was, he was lying."

"Let's enjoy a bite of lunch," I suggest. "The Redesdale Arms is just up the road. In Evelyn's day it was run by a splendid local character called Ben Prior, but the new people aren't trying to compete with that colourful bit of history and seem very nice. And you have yet to see Elishaw."

"And Troughend," she smiles. "I need to be able to look your Mr Maxwell in the eye and tell him where he might be wrong."

Over our bar meal she tells me she has a simple question she would like me to ask the others on Tuesday. It turns out to be so simple we spend an hour discussing it.

CHAPTER NINETEEN

Newcastle Law School: the present day, 3 February
Concerning 6 January–5 February 1931

Revitalised by the weekend break, I welcome the team to our usual venue on Tuesday morning. I tell them we will begin the week's sessions by looking at the evidence of the motor engineer who inspected the Hudson Super-Six on the moor, followed by the local doctor who attended Evelyn and the pathologist who examined her corpse. All were witnesses who were heard on Day Three of the inquest, 5 February 1931 (there had been a one-day break when the coroner had to deal with other business at Whitley Bay Police Court). I explain that, for the doctor, we will be covering familiar ground but felt it was sensible for us to take the medical evidence collectively. In 1931, Dr McEachran, Professor McDonald and William Jennings had been the last group of witnesses to appear prior to the coroner's summing up and the jury's deliberations.

There is some uncalled-for amusement before we start because in travelling to Otterburn from Morpeth on the morning of Day Three the police contingent, led by Captain Fullarton James, had hit a patch of ice and run off the road; some reports suggested headfirst into a snowdrift. They succeeded in manoeuvring their car back onto *terra firma*, escaped unscathed and were not badly delayed, but the point which was causing my team most hilarity was that this incident had occurred near Wolf's Nick. If nothing else, it suggests that Molly and I may not have been altogether wrong on Saturday in speculating about patches of ice forming along that exposed stretch of the road.

"Molly isn't joining us today?" asks Frances.

"No. She has returned to Durham, but sends her best wishes. We visited Otterburn on Saturday, and she posed a question she would like us to think over and discuss. It was a hypothetical question, one I do not recall being asked in any of the literature we've seen. It was this:

What would have happened if the bus crew had not *found Evelyn that night?*

"In other words, what if the bus crew had behaved like Walter Smith Beattie some time before? What if they had driven on, leaving Evelyn and her car to be found by a shepherd or passer-by in the early morning?"

No one speaks for a minute or so.

"We would have no statement from her about the latter part of the evening," Frances says, realisation dawning. "Goodness, she'd have…"

"Not a shepherd," Sven says. "Search parties would have been out overnight. If a burned and frozen body had been found on a fell near a burned car, the police may have assumed a fatal accident. And except for animals, the crime scene would have had a chance to survive intact."

I hold up my hand.

"Think it through. It raises some interesting points. But first, let's turn to Mr Jennings, whose statement was actually the last to be taken."

William Jennings' Tale (ID3)

Jennings was a motor engineer based at Morpeth, and in his work on the Foster case (but not at the inquest) he was accompanied by a colleague from Benton, Duncan Hodgson. Jennings had worked for the police before and his premises were close to their Morpeth HQ. He testified that at 10.30 am on 8 January 1931 he had visited 'Wolf's Jaw' (*sic*) to inspect the scene. He had started with an examination of the car's tracks after it had left the road.

The first sign of the tyre tracks was on the right-hand side of the road, facing north at an angle of 45° to the verge. The car had been in right-hand lock, and sandstone boulders near the verge showed marks made by contact with the undercarriage. From 2′ down the (4′6″) embankment the wheel marks took an erratic course for 12 yards, after which they straightened for a similar distance and then veered left as the front wheels entered a ditch. At this point, with the car sunk a few inches into the ditch, the steering had come into left lock and began to take a semicircular route for about another 30 yards. The car had come to rest in a dry shallow gutter. From the embankment to its place of rest it had travelled slowly; no more than 10 mph. In sequence, as indicated by the marks on the boulders, the front offside wheel was the first to clear the embankment, followed by the nearside front wheel and the two rear wheels. Had the car been travelling faster it may have turned turtle or nosedived.

Jennings concluded that car had been out of control for its first 12 yards, then 'under a certain amount of control.' He did not think it could have negotiated the ditch of its own volition with the throttle in the idling position, but given the relatively level hard ground it may have done so subsequently. It had stopped in low gear with the engine on and the handbrake off. He thought 'the person at the wheel had lost interest in driving before the car stopped.' There were no signs along its track that it had been on fire before that point.

Jennings then went to Foster's Garage to inspect the car itself. He found it had been in good condition, although now bearing marks beneath its chassis caused by the sandstones. There was no damage that could have caused it to ignite spontaneously. The car was 'wrecked by fire' and all the combustible materials, including the rear tyres, spare tyre and luggage box were reduced to ashes. There was no trace of where the fire might have originated exactly, but it was not near the front. The engine valves, ignition timing, carburettor, fan belt, spark plugs, front tyres and radiator were in perfect order or untouched by fire. Frayed wires or loose connections could be eliminated as a cause.

The car's fuel system was of the Auto-Vac type, with the petrol tank at the extreme rear and the Auto-Vac feed tank in front of the dash. Petrol was conveyed between the two, thence to the carburettor, by strong copper piping. There was evidence of soldered joints having been melted, the Auto-Vac had burst its top, and solder had melted from joints in the petrol tank, but it was otherwise intact with its filler cap in place. The exhaust pipe and joints were intact, but the tail lamp was destroyed. An inspection of the 2-gallon petrol can revealed that both the cap and neck had been separated before the fire.

The fire had been most intense at the rear of the car and its back springs had bent downwards about 4", suggesting a considerable quantity of petrol in the tank. Jennings concluded his statement by saying that some outside agency had been the cause of the fire, 'but whether inflammable liquid or other material has been the medium, there is no evidence to show.'

During questioning, and among other measurement he had taken of the Hudson, Jennings said its total length was 15' and total width 6'. The width of the front seat was 45", its depth 18"; the rear seat width was 47", its depth 20". The interior measured 46" floor to ceiling, with 21" clearance from the top of the seat. He said that it would be 'very difficult' for a passenger to drive without being behind the wheel if the driver acquiesced, and 'almost impossible' if the driver resisted. But he agreed that the left-hand side of the steering wheel was almost central in the car. (The driving problems were demonstrated by Jennings to the jury towards the end of the inquest, with the help of a similar model Hudson Super-Six in the Percy Arms courtyard).

"A roomy car," Peter immediately says. "More so than many modern cars. And nothing in the dimensions to invalidate my suggestion that a reasonably virile man could have bundled a smallish young woman into the back seat from the front. The fire was concentrated in the rear, where we believe Evelyn was located. If it had been started *on* her, then of course there would have been no trace of an origin point on the car itself. Jennings is more or less saying that while the car began its course out of control it was brought under control after twelve yards or so. Someone was at the wheel. Then, almost at its final resting place, trundling along under its own steam, Bowler turned his attention to Evelyn. He 'lost interest in driving.' She had started stirring again in the back."

"I seem to recall reading," Bradon says, "that the car may have gone over the verge at right angles. Or that 45° may have *been* a right angle."

"Dixon," Peter says. "At best, he may have been taking into account the curve of the road. At worst, he inferred it had been manoeuvred almost fussily to face the verge, of which there is no reported evidence. And let's not forget Russell, who said he had found tyre marks cutting west to east *across* the road at an angle of 45° before hitting the verge. He seems to have had better eyesight than Jennings, who only picked the tyre tracks up on the east side verge. But the Inspector did have a day's head start, and Jennings seems to have told the press on the site, although not the inquest, that the car *did* in fact cross the road at an angle."

"So there's nothing in his evidence to offer any new slant?" I ask.

"Joseph Foster kind of objected to this guy's presence, didn't he?" Bradon asks. "Would that have been professional pride, that someone should be considered to know the car better than he, or would he have thought Jennings a bit too cosy with the Morpeth cops?"

"Let's assume the former," I suggest. "Jennings seems to have done a thorough job—although that may have been due as much to his colleague Hodgson, who was not called, as himself. He was cagey about *how* the fire might have started but if it started *on* Evelyn it all appears to fit. The flames seem to have eaten everything inside the car and to the rear, only stopping when they hit metalwork beyond the dashboard."

"I have some concern about the gas tank," Bradon says. "Jennings says it still had a lot of gas in it. It couldn't have been entirely full, but it sure hadn't exploded like Evelyn thought. So, what exploded? Was that the springs giving way? I mean, fires aren't silent things, are they? Was it wood splintering? A window blowing out? A tyre? The luggage box bursting? Also, Jennings, Foster *and* Goodman say the gas tank held 15 or 15.5 gallons. The specs I've read for a Super-Six say 18.75. And according to something else I read, the conclusion was reached that if the tank was still full the car couldn't have gone very far, supporting the cops' theory that Evelyn didn't get beyond Wolf's Nick."

"Dixon again," Peter says. "With another not too robust conclusion. If she filled up with fuel before leaving, an extra trip of 23 miles, Wolf's Nick to Belsay and back, would barely have registered, whether it held 15 or 18 gallons. The car's fuel consumption is given as 20-22 mpg, better than the average in those days of 14-15 mpg. But whichever is correct, the level of petrol in the tank would have dropped, what?—an inch or less? Without syphoning all the gas out, which wasn't done, we have to assume from Jennings that it was still nearly full. He said the weight of it had bent the springs."

"Another not too robust conclusion?" I ask him. "Explain."

"Well, look at them," he replies. "Robert Dixon repeats several times that the road conditions were hazardous, the road itself twisted and steep with sharp corners. There may have been three or four bends between Raylees and Ottercops, as there are today, one of them a sharp corner, but elsewhere they were not too problematical. There is one steep hill and the night was frosty, granted, but not of the Cairngorms or *Ice Road Truckers* variety. In these respects, he exaggerates. But he does much worse later. He asserts that the inspection of the Hudson showed it had been set alight where it stood on the moor. It did not; this was Russell and Jennings' interpretation, and we shall come to it. He states, as we have noted previously, that Evelyn could not have driven beyond Ferney Chesters, and that 16 mph was 'about normal' given the speeds of other road users that night. We have seen it was not; it was significantly higher, and Dixon himself must have forgotten his own calculation of Evelyn's speed on her round trip to Birdhopecraig. Jennings, as we've just seen, opined that it was 'almost impossible' for a passenger to drive without being behind the wheel. It was a qualified opinion, but Dixon presents it as 'impossible' without qualification. Worse than any of these, however, and I will read it out in full, is his assessment of the case generally: 'Anyone studying the case is now left with the belief that the statement of Evelyn Foster was nothing more than pure fabrication from the start. If this was a court of law, and Evelyn Foster was on trial, then she would be deemed as guilty from the outset before the trial had even started.' That is his opinion. So much for justice, British or otherwise."

"Frances?" I ask. "Anything to add?" She looks disengaged.

"Oh, I'm just listening and learning. I agree with Peter, but I'm thinking more about the implications of Molly's question."

"We'll come to that," I tell her. "Meantime, Dr McEachran seemed sure Evelyn said the tank had exploded. Let's move on to him."

Dr Duncan McEachran's Tale (ID3)

McEachran was a GP, a graduate of Edinburgh University and employed in the Bellingham practice. When Mrs Kirk, the wife of his senior partner, took a call from Otterburn around 10.45 pm, she said the caller had described a case of severe burning and that two doctors would be needed. Kirk was ill, so McEachran volunteered to go alone and see if he could pick up another doctor en route. He set out with Shanks and they arrived at The Kennels at 11.30 pm.

When McEachran entered Evelyn's room, he found Mrs Foster, Mrs Jennings, Nurse Lawson and one of Evelyn's sisters (Dorothy) present. (Her youngest sister Margaret and sister-in-law Mary were not then in the room, perhaps being too shaken by the sight of Evelyn's injuries.) His patient was in 'extreme shock'; her hands, abdomen and face were excessively burned. He proceeded to treat her, and Dr Miller arrived while he was dressing the burns. As soon as Evelyn was as comfortable as he could make her, McEachran went downstairs and informed her parents in the kitchen, and Fergusson and Shanks in the lobby, that there was no hope of a recovery. He returned to the bedroom and asked Miller to go down and comfort her parents. Miller returned minutes later with Shanks and Fergusson, and the police immediately began to take a statement, he thought around '12.30 or 12.45 am'. Present in the room were Evelyn, Mrs Foster, the two doctors, the district nurse and the two policemen. McEachran recalled that Mrs Foster, prompted by the police, put the questions to Evelyn, her answers being written down by Fergusson.

He recalled Evelyn's statement as follows:

She had passed a car driven by a woman at or near Elishaw, out of which a man appeared and asked for a lift into Otterburn to catch a bus or car to Newcastle. She agreed, took him as far as the garage, and arranged that if he was unable to find a conveyance she would drive him to Ponteland. She filled up with petrol, left the garage and met him at the bridge. He sat in front with her. Evelyn did not make it clear if he had interfered with her going south but at Belsay he demanded she return him to Otterburn. She was questioned why she did not leave the man there or phone her father for advice, but gave no clear reason for not doing so. On the way back, the man tried to persuade her to hand the wheel over, explaining he could drive. She refused and he became annoyed. He hit her on the eye, bundled her into the back of the car, took something from his pocket and threw it at her. She thought she must have been unconscious for she was awakened by the bumping of the car. She seemed unable to explain how the car went on fire but managed to fall out and crawl away. Whilst lying on the fell she heard the petrol tank explode (McEachran stressed he had no doubt about this). She also said she heard a car approach, slow up, and then proceed on its way. She heard whistling, but was unclear whether this was when that car was there or not. The bus came soon afterwards and she was brought home. McEachran heard Mrs Foster ask her daughter if the man had done anything to her, implying had she been indecently attacked, to which the reply 'appeared to be in the affirmative.'

McEachran said his recollection of the precise words used was hazy, but this was a faithful rendition of what he had heard. When the police left, he remained with his patient until 5.30 am except for a two-minute period when he went downstairs to ask Gordon Foster to go to Bellingham for 'a special drug.' About an hour after the police left, Evelyn lapsed into unconsciousness and did not regain consciousness in his presence. She was perfectly quiet. When he left he expected death to occur at any minute; Dr Miller had gone at 4.30 am with Proud and only Mrs Foster and Nurse Lawson remained in the room with his patient when McEachran departed. At that point it was his opinion she would not regain consciousness before she died. During the time from his arrival until she lapsed into unconsciousness McEachran was certain she fully understood the questions being put to her and her replies were 'lucid and sensible.' He added that she had described the man as wearing a hard hat; a dark, probably blue, overcoat; and as having no definite accent, not Scottish and not quite Tyneside. He was plausibly spoken and a complete stranger.

On 8 January McEachran assisted Prof McDonald in the post mortem.

"Interesting to get another—shall we say lucid—perspective," Peter says. "But as far as McEachran is concerned we are short of information on the timings of Bowler's actions or where they occurred. It *sounds* as if his main attack was on the roadside before the car toppled onto the moor, that she became unconscious when she landed in the back, and she *may* have been alight to some degree as it travelled over the ground, but again we can't be sure. And he gave her morphine sometime between 1.00 and 2.00 am, brought from Bellingham by Gordon. The doc was called out to a very nasty situation, and seems to have coped to the best of his ability, which is a great deal more than can be said for the police."

Frances points out, "He would have been more concerned with his patient than with helping the police."

I recall something Molly had suggested. "We may be short on timings, Peter, and the sequence McEachran describes could, as he says, be wanting in some respects, but they do give an indication of what may have occurred between Belsay and Wolf's Nick. When we come to piece all this together it would be as well to remember his input."

"No problem," Peter says. "Not even the police could have avoided fielding him as a witness." He is continuing to drive every stake he can lay his hands on into the heart of the Northumberland Constabulary.

"I'm intrigued by something," Sven says. "It almost sounds from the doctor's interpretation that there could have been gaps in the sequence whereby Evelyn was first struck by Bowler's fist, then bundled into the rear seat, and finally assaulted and set alight at Wolf's Nick. His statement almost suggests that while Bowler may have demanded the wheel at Belsay, and got annoyed at her refusal, there could have been a hiatus, and a second stage assault, before he bundled her into the back. It would mean, wouldn't it, that he could have driven normally to Wolf's Nick? It would also mean that Evelyn, stunned by being thrown, would have spent some miles in a daze until they got there."

"That is good thinking, Sven," says Peter. "It's a possibility. Why should these snippets of information from Evelyn, given the state she was in when she was interviewed, be taken as a perfect continuum?"

"Why indeed?" I ask. "And I must say it's a comfort to have you all thinking these details through, whether or not there are perfect answers. But let's spend a little time on Molly's question," I suggest. "Frances?"

At first it seems she is neither listening nor aware of us, lost in a universe inside her own head.

Then she takes a sip of water and says, "It's an interesting question. I think the main impact of finding Evelyn dead might have been on the way the police conducted themselves, and on the press and local people. With no input from Evelyn at all, everyone's response would have been different. There would have been, as Sven said earlier, a search launched for her had she not returned by, say, 11.00 pm. Her parents would have been alarmed. Fergusson, I'm sure, would have been first to be informed she'd gone missing, and there would still have been a small glow from the fire after midnight to help any searchers. But let's say, for the sake of argument, the search was unsuccessful and she was only found dead at Wolf's Nick when it got light. As the case stands, it's clear to me that the police, somehow and at some point, developed an irrational dislike of Evelyn Foster. I mean Evelyn as a person, nothing to do with Scotland Yard sensitivities or media pressure. What that was rooted in, except an early failure to find a third party to confirm any part of her story, I have no idea. Maybe it was prejudice against a young woman who was ahead of her time and was making a successful business for herself. A woman's place in those days, after all, even after their Great War contributions, the Roaring Twenties, working-class unrest and the pressures that placed on families, was in the home. This may have got under the skin of the Chief Constable, stuck as he was in the Dark Ages. Fullarton James would not have been a man to dwell on cultural change, but nevertheless imposed his own ideas of corporate culture on his Constabulary."

"I think he imposed rules and regulations, Frances," Sven smiles. "I don't think he'd have known about corporate culture."

"It would have amounted to the same thing," she says sharply.

"Granted," Sven says. I think he'd been trying to be fair-minded.

"If Evelyn had been found dead," Frances continues, "an irritant would have been removed, or would never have been felt in the first place. She would have died silently, so arguments about her honesty would be moot. The police would still have had to be seen making earnest efforts to establish whether her death was murder, accident or suicide, but the pressures on them from all quarters would be reduced. Hopefully, within an hour or two of her body being discovered, the crime scene, as Sven said, would have been secured—although what happened in actuality sheds doubt on that premise. Hopefully too, an uncontam-inated, or less contaminated, search would have been carried out at the scene—depending who found it—and it would have been much later still, if ever, that the thought of launching a manhunt would have crossed anyone's mind. Might fingerprints have been taken? Doubtful. Might scattered pieces of clothing, including underclothing, have hinted at someone else's involvement? Possibly. But the problem is: who among the police would be the first to know and how would they handle it? And the answer, of course, is Fergusson, who would have phoned Shanks, and one or both of them would have been sufficiently insensitive to ask the Fosters to take them to the scene in one of their cars, whether or not the body had been identified. Those two, hearing that Evelyn had picked up a passenger to take to Ponteland, may even have jumped to the conclusion that this was a simple, tragic accident and that Bowler had been delivered by Evelyn to his destination. Who was to think otherwise, without Evelyn's tale? She had picked up a seemingly respectable man— her mother knew that much—and had taken him onwards. And as the fare would vary depending on the season and what would now be called unsocial hours, she had as usual asked her father to check how much to charge. On the way back, she had accidentally driven off the road."

"But how would the auto have been burned?" Bradon asks. "If there was nothing wrong with its wiring or fuel system?"

"There may not have been a proper inspection," Frances says. "Why would there be? For Fergusson and Shanks the attraction of a simple, tragic accident would have been a godsend. It would have meant no work for them to do, except of the paper variety. The doctors would not have been called out, other than to certify the death. Remove Evelyn's tale and, apart from Jennings' inspection and conclusion, airy-fairy as it was, the thing is dead in its tracks as a murder case. Of course, once the car was back in the garage, rumours of foul play may have kicked in. But it would have been too late. It would have needed real diligence to run with them. The Chief Constable's equilibrium would never have been disturbed. Not a single witness we have looked at categorically points to Evelyn having been south of Otterburn, let alone Wolf's Nick, with a fare. Not even John Robson, who at least saw the car. In the material we have seen, not one witness came forward later, even with all the publicity, to say they had seen *her*, let alone seen her with a passenger. None that we know about, anyway. What chance did Evelyn's tale stand against that? The possibility of suicide would have reared its head, it may even have been considered at an inquest, but that would have been be the worst, bad as it is, the Fosters would have needed to defend their daughter's name against."

"Why do you think Molly tabled the question?" I ask her.

"I imagine to bring the stark reality of these points out."

"That it stands or falls on Evelyn's word?"

"It comes down to a matter of belief. And we have yet to come in detail to the efforts of the police, their solicitor and the coroner to skew this case—I hope I'm not insulting your homeland in using this phrase, Bradon—every which way they could. I think we will find better cause to cast reasonable doubt on their innocence than they ever did on Evelyn's."

"Superb, Frances," Peter says. "Excuse me for asking the obvious, but did Evelyn carry a lighter or matches, or did anyone ever find either at the scene?"

CHAPTER TWENTY

Newcastle Law School: the present day, 3 February
Concerning 8 January-5 February 1931

We break for coffee. Peter's question, of course, has blown every other thought from our minds and we are wracking our brains for anything we may have read that might answer it. Could it possibly be that something so simple escaped the attention of the police? And ourselves? We might scour through every bit of paperwork we possess, but I suspect, in the best courtroom tradition, Peter has not asked a question to which he does not already know the answer. But before we delve further, we have arrived at the last and perhaps most eagerly anticipated of the witnesses:

The Pathologist's Tale (Part One) (ID3)
Professor Stuart McDonald of Newcastle University's Pathology Department performed the post mortem on Evelyn Foster's body at Foster's Garage at 12 noon on 8 January, assisted by Dr McEachran. His son, Dr Stuart McDonald Jr. and P.C. Fergusson were in attendance.

Prof McDonald was an imposing, bespectacled cigarette-smoker with a forceful personality and a reputation as a disciplinarian. He described the body as that of a well-developed but rather small young woman, 25-30 years of age. Her height was about 5', weight about 10 stones, and she had good muscular development. The trunk and limbs were bandaged and the bright yellow staining of picric acid showed through the surgical dressings. On removing the dressings, the body was found to be the seat of extensive burns, the most severe being on the front of its middle portion, i.e. the front and inner aspect of the upper part of both thighs and lower part of the abdomen. The burned area extended over the outer thighs and to a less extent the lower portion of the flanks on both sides. There was also extensive burning extending from just below the middle of the buttocks downwards. On the right side (of the thighs) the tissues had burst from the intensity of the heat, leaving deep fissures irregular in distribution and several inches in length. Underlying fat had been destroyed and muscles exposed. On the left side there was a similar area of destruction, roughly oval in shape and close to the groin. On the front of the thighs the skin on both sides was destroyed, leaving a dark parchmented surface. The degree of burning reduced in intensity downwards, but the superficial layer of the skin was extensively removed down to the middle of the legs. Upwards from the abdomen, burning had reached as high as the breasts, not quite so intense but with localised skin-peeling even there. The upper part of the chest, the neck to the point of the chin, and the back of the body showed no signs of burning. The right arm was burned from shoulder to hand, the left arm less so but the left hand was severely burned. The left foot was practically untouched. There was superficial burning of the face and the eyelids were swollen; the hair of the head had practically escaped the reach of the fire, but skin around the chin and mouth had been extensively removed.

The hair of the external genitals was almost entirely burned away. On separating the lips of the vulva some thin turbid fluid escaped which was kept for later analysis. Inside the right outer lip there was localised swelling and the surface appeared to be abraded. The hymen was roughly oval in shape and there was no laceration or sign of recent trauma. The whole of the genital and lower urinary organs were removed in a piece for subsequent dissection.

The surface of the body was examined for signs of external injury other than burning. Facial features, eyelids especially, were swollen and obscured by burns, but there was bluish discolouration about the root of the nose and upper part of the eyelids, and on dissection there seemed to be a slight amount of superficial bruising above the nose on the lower part of the forehead (part of which was removed for further examination). No external marks suggesting injury apart from burns were found on other parts of the body, but 'over the burned areas superficial injuries…could not possibly have been recognised.'

On internal examination, little of relevance or abnormality was found in the heart, lungs, liver, stomach, spleen or kidneys. There was no wound of the scalp and no evidence of superficial or deep bruising, or of injury in the skull bones. There were a few minute haemorrhages on the surface of the brain on both sides in its upper part.

The examination concluded that death was due to shock as a result of severe external burning. The distribution of the burns and their severity in certain places suggested that parts of clothing had contained an inflammable substance and that the burning had started in front and was most severe on the upper and inner aspects of the thighs, generally reducing in intensity upwards and downwards—although both hands and face were severely burned. The distribution of the burned areas suggested that the deceased had been seated during some period of the burning and that burning to the face, but not the upper chest, might be accounted for by a bending forward of the head. The pattern of burns outside their area of concentration suggested spots or splashes of inflammable liquid elsewhere in the clothing.

Further conclusions were deferred pending detailed examination of the genitourinary organs, the root of the nose and portions of forehead skin.

"I ask you," Peter says, "would this girl, *any* girl, have poured petrol into her lap as a means of setting her car alight and claiming insurance? What were these clowns thinking? Did any of them decide that police work was perhaps not after all their calling, and they'd be better used as cartoon writers? And where was Bates, for God's sake? Had he dropped off?"

"Before we get into any discussion, Peter," I suggest, "let's first look at what the additional examination and site visit revealed."

The Pathologist's Tale (Part Two) (ID3)
On dissection of the genitourinary organs, it was confirmed that the hymen showed no rupture or laceration and the vagina 'showed the appearance normally seen in a virgin.' The uterus was normal, and in a virgin state. On opening it there was found marked thickening and congestion of the lining membrane in its upper part, suggesting the presence of a monthly period. In

the left ovary and outer opening of the womb there were also indications of a menstrual period, including the recent discharge of a mature ovum (egg cell) from the left ovary. Inspection of fluids removed from external passages showed no evidence of spermatic fluid. McDonald concluded that there was no evidence of 'violation' (i.e. penetration), that the genital passages showed no evidence of injury or disease, and that at the time of death the deceased was in the first stage of a menstrual period.

Nothing else was found to add significantly to the post mortem results.

McDonald visited the scene of the incident on 15 January 1931. He had Superintendent Tough and Inspector Russell for company, plus College of Medicine colleagues Prof Briscoe and Dr Dunn (who were to subject certain exhibits and items of clothing to chemical analysis). He picked up several skin fragments, one quite large, near where the deceased had been found and where the front nearside wheel of the car had rested. On microscopic examination, one of these portions appeared to have come from the palm of a hand.

"So," Peter says, "am I right in thinking that the first person to wade into Professor McDonald with questions was the coroner?"

"You are," I reply, wondering what's coming.

"And he asked him first to confirm that there was no sign of bruising caused by blows or smacks to the face. No sign of bias there, then, and he got the answer, 'No.' Pressing on, Dodds asked, 'If it had been severe, could you have found it?' To which he received the Prof's wisdom that any severe injury would have left a mark, but: 'I pointed out in my report that anything superficial could not possibly be detected.' Not content with that, our coroner asked whether some trace might have been found if the girl was knocked out, to which he was told, 'One would reasonably have expected it.' Dodds then changed tack. He asked if there was evidence of injury or 'interference.' He was told not. The Prof must have been a touch bemused at this point, as he seems to have eliminated deep burning from being either injury or interference. To clarify matters, Dodds asked whether there was absolutely no sign of 'outrage.' He got the answer, 'None.' And so it went on, distortion piled on euphemism."

"However," Sven says, "it's another line of questioning which leads to the suspicion that the coroner may have been primed by the police. Out of the blue, after coming close to danger-point by having the Prof admit, given the pattern of burns, that the girl could have been sitting in the back seat, Dodds asked, 'If no burning took place in the way she alleged in the back of the car, and assuming the car was standing where she put it, and she threw some petrol into the back of the car and set fire to it, with her left leg probably on the running board, could the flames have come back on her?' He received the answer, 'I think that is possible.' Where," Sven asks with his crooked smile, "did a running board come into it?"

"Straight out of the coroner's head," Peter says. "He is a clever man.

He must be seen to have unimpeachable theories of his own. A spot of coaching from the police, those conniving so-and-sos, may have helped."

"But," Bradon says, "McDonald said he couldn't understand in that case why there should have been localisation, or concentration, of the burns. Who could, come to that? Dixon in his book introduces the concept of a 'straight edge' which might have been substituted for a seat, i.e. that the running board was a straight edge on which Evelyn sat to pour gas on herself. This, he suggests, was admitted as a possibility by the Prof and latched onto by Dodds. He's right, but it goes beyond what they said."

"So Evelyn, to add to her woes, is now a suicidal maniac," Peter says. "But hey, you can't keep a good man down for long. Here is Dodds again, now hell bent on bolstering the police theory: 'Assuming she herself had upset some petrol over the lower part of her clothing and then ignited the car, which had already been soaked with petrol, might that have caused localisation?' He was told it could. Dodds persisted, 'Is it not a possible solution, assuming she put the petrol on?' Again, 'Yes.' And to cap this exchange for good and all, Dodds asked, 'And if she had taken the petrol tin and poured petrol over herself in that way, is it possible that she might have got those extra splashes on the top above the breast?' The Prof answered, 'Yes.' *Quod erat demonstrandum*, as they say."

"Frances?" I ask. I find I am having to make sure she stays with us. Believing something to her own satisfaction is not the same as proving it beyond reasonable doubt to others. I make a mental note to have a quiet word with her when we've finished here.

As if she reads my thoughts, Frances smiles and says, "You'd have thought there'd have been some damage to her lungs, wouldn't you? But that's just me speaking out of ignorance. Maybe there were no traces of smoke or fumes, or the Prof skated over them. But that aside, the coroner made Smirk's life easy for him, didn't he? Smirk needed only to tidy up loose ends. He asked whether the deceased was 'outraged'; that archaic word again. McDonald said not. Smirk asked if she was 'absolutely' a virgin, as if there are degrees of virginity. McDonald said he had found nothing to the contrary. Goodman finds this strange as, given the extent of burning, McDonald's opinion was based mainly on the appearance of the vagina. Smirk asked if there was any evidence of the girl having been knocked about or 'nipped' as her mother had suggested. Without asking what nipping might have meant, McDonald said there was no such evidence." Frances raises her eyes heavenwards. "Ever get the feeling the cards were being stacked up against you, Evie?" she asks the ceiling.

"And here," says Peter, "in all his soporific glory, is Bates. Did he ask McDonald the simple question, 'Was she raped?' Did he follow-up with the equally simple question, 'If not, are you ruling out *any* kind of assault?' Did he ask, 'Are we all clear about what we mean by the words interfered with or outraged?' No: he asked none of these things. He did not ask if blows had to be of the sledgehammer variety to be discerned. He did not ask if Evelyn, rather than being knocked out by heavy blows, might have fainted from shock at having received some rather lighter blows and being thrown into the back of the car. He did not ask about the bluish discolouration around the nose or the swelling around the eyes. He did not ask if Evelyn's left hand could have been burned in trying to beat out the flames or holding her abdomen. He did not ask if there might, just might, have been trace evidence under Evelyn's fingernails, evidence she may have put up a struggle, or whether this pathologist had bothered to look. He did not ask if the police had seemed in any way embarrassed to have fallen upon several bits of skin, undetected by them previously, nine days after the event. He did not ask about the blessed footprint, of which a mould had been taken, or about the 10 by 8 feet area of turf which had been carted away. He did not ask McDonald to explain his belief that Evelyn had been sitting down at some point in the burning. He did not ask whether the concentration of the burns in the girl's lap suggested someone might have poured petrol there. He did not ask if petrol could have pooled in the tweed skirt Evelyn was wearing. He did not ask whether McDonald thought the *absence* of burns on some parts of her body, such as her back, could be as significant as their *presence* on others. He did nothing to counter the coroner's scenario that Evelyn had stood, one foot on the running board, repealed the law of gravity and managed somehow to throw as much petrol over her lap as over the car. He did not ask McDonald if there had been any suggestion in her musculature that Evelyn was a double-jointed contortionist. He did not ask—no one did, yet—if the piece of white wadding found at the scene might have been part of a sanitary towel. He did not ask why, if so, Evelyn would have felt its disposal to be of higher priority than her burning to death. Instead of all these questions and a dozen others, he zeroed in on the surreal and asked questions which an inattentive five year-old might have drummed up if he had first imbibed a pint of whisky. Bates asked whether, if Evelyn had taken the petrol can from the luggage box, poured it over the car and herself and put the petrol can back, the petrol might have evaporated before she returned to the car. He asked whether there was any evidence to suggest Evelyn had been gagged with her scarf to stop her—this is in the middle of a desolate fell—crying out for help. And not content with this ludicrous piece of kite-flying, he asked if there had been any marks on Evelyn's neck to indicate that pressure had been applied there. A juror, Reverend Brierley, tried to help out by asking if there had been any facial discolouration on Evelyn, but McDonald told him he had found none and—unchallenged as to the presence of extensive burns or what he had said earlier about a bluish discolouration—he would have expected it still to be there when he examined the body. At the end of this exchange, one couldn't have blamed McDonald for turning to the coroner and asking if he was sure Bates came from planet earth. Or the Rev Brierley asking his assembled congregation if *anyone* present was sure they were still on planet earth."

After this diatribe, everyone of course is cracking up. You could accuse Peter Maxwell of many things, but never of lacking eloquence. Words flow out of him as easily as water over rocks. The best of this deluge of words, of course, is that every one of them is justified.

"I think we are inevitably straying into areas of the inquest itself," I tell them once the buzz has died down. "You are all making some valid and pertinent observations, but we can leave most of them for another day. We still have work to do, but not quite the same work. We are coming close to the end of this story and I would like us all to think carefully about all the evidence we have been able to access so far. We are done with the witnesses and other statements, except for the analysis by McDonald's colleagues of Evelyn's pieces of clothing and other items found at the scene. As Peter has suggested, we also need to see if we can find any reference to Evelyn carrying a lighter or matches. In the interests of thoroughness we have to look at these things next and at the conduct of the inquest itself. But more importantly, we need to look at everything, as far as we can, through more clinical eyes, and avoid sounding-off at perceived faults. Remember, this event occurred a long time ago in a very different world, and we have to make allowances for that. An example of the different world was Evelyn's funeral, and we can spend, in passing, a little time on that when we meet again on Friday."

"Fair enough," Peter says. "But don't you think it strange, Matthew, that not one of the policemen in their direct evidence, or any other witness for that matter, floated the idea that this death may have been the result of an attempted *insurance fraud*? The coroner edged very close once or twice, and we have still to discuss the rest, but wasn't it unusual, even in those days, for what amounted to a prosecution theory to lie in shadow and then be floated without evidence and with no challenge? We have seen how inept Bates was, but for a coroner—effectively a judge—to be a willing party must have been outside normal practice. And apart from fielding witnesses whom they hoped might shed doubt on Evelyn's claim that she had driven as far as Belsay, none of them has begun to address that point directly either. It seems all to have been conducted by nudges and winks and spurious implications. Not that most of them stand up to any real scrutiny, or are we all guilty of missing something here?"

For Peter, this is about as mild as it gets. I make a note on my pad.

"I think we will find the Chief Constable may not have been entirely sold on the insurance fraud theory," I tell them. "Although he seems to have been sold on the idea she hadn't driven beyond Wolf's Nick. And again, if *he* wasn't keen on something, there is nothing to suggest any of his officers might have tried to argue the point. But that aside, I'm sorry to say I've been derelict in my duties. We need to include some discussion of the role of a 1930s coroner in our next session. It may help when we come to look at the conduct of the inquest."

CHAPTER TWENTY-ONE

Newcastle Law School: the present day, 4-5 February
Concerning Evelyn's funeral and the forthcoming inquest

The Funeral

Evelyn Foster's funeral is not part of our investigation, nor was it of the Northumberland Constabulary's. The latter, however, had a presence in it—which may or may not have helped their community relations. The former, more than I believe we have done so far, need to grasp the period of history and the social environment in which this crime took place. If anyone should doubt what I'm saying, I can do no better than refer them chronologically to the books of Dickens, Chandler and James Lee Burke. I would add William Shakespeare, but that may be overcooking it.

With this in mind, I offer a short essay:

The funeral took place on Sunday 11 January 1931. It was a dreich day, a day of rain and sleet and mist, and it got no better by 2.00 pm, when the coffin began its journey from The Kennels. It was carried a hundred yards down the main road—open fields on both sides, mature trees to the right—to the Church of St John the Evangelist.

People, hundreds of them, lined both sides of the street, many not to attend the service but to be able to say later, 'I was there.' After four days, Evelyn's death had achieved such notoriety that being there became more of an after-dinner conversation piece than Pope Pius XI's New Year ban on artificial birth control. Many people came to the village on foot from the hamlets or farms of the area, cold and soaked, stamping their feet and rubbing their hands for warmth as they stood for a miserable purpose in miserable conditions. Some came on horseback, some in horse-drawn wagons, some in cars or buses. But none arrived in a Foster's bus; Joseph had given his employees the day off so they could pay their respects. He was touched that every able-bodied person from the village had turned up, but was not so sure about many of the hangers-on and all of the journalists. He wished the journalists would stop going around pestering people for stories that led to nothing, and concentrate their minds and pens on helping the police find who had killed his daughter.

The Dowager Lady Redesdale arrived in her brougham, its horse decked in black finery. Joseph took heart at seeing her. Lady Redesdale's appearances at christenings, marriages and funerals in the village were rare, and he felt not only honoured by her presence but also hopeful it might inspire in the police the thought that catching the man responsible for Evelyn's death should be pursued with the utmost vigour. This was Northumbrian royalty after all, only one rung below Henry Percy, the Duke himself, showing its respects, offering its support.

Four Foster employees carried the coffin to the church at two o'clock, seen out of the house by Joseph Foster and his remaining close family, and led by Hedley Ord, the village carpenter and undertaker. After them came a massive crocodile of friends and neighbours and lookers-on, fifteen abreast across the street, filling the length of it from house to church. George Phillipson was amongst them. P.C. Fergusson, swarthy and ill-at-ease under his cap, took up position near the lych-gate. The Reverend Joseph Brierley, Vicar of Otterburn, a juror bound over on his own recognisance of £10 three days before, was to conduct the service. Accompanied by the Reverend Frank Wright, Vicar of Horsley, he met the cortege at the entrance to the church. Behind them stood George MacDougall, head gardener at the Tower and the Vicar's Churchwarden, also a juror bound over in the sum of £10 and the elected jury foreman.

The small early Victorian church could not hope to accommodate so many people. Crowds stood outside in the rain, water splashing in the churchyard, on gravestones and on the road below. When Mary Ferry, the schoolmistress and church organist, struck up with *Rock of Ages* people began to weep. It felt, said one spectator afterwards, as though everyone there, the whole village of Otterburn, was held in a cocoon separate from everything happening in the rest of the world.

The rain intensified as the coffin was borne out. A few umbrellas were flung up to protect some of the women. Others wore shawls or headscarves. The men were respectfully bare-headed, three or four trilby hats to be seen, only two bowlers. At the graveside, a yard or two inside the lych-gate, Joseph Foster, grey head bowed and handkerchief to his face, stood with his wife on one side of the tall figure of Reverend Brierley, the Vicar's brilliant white surplice in marked contrast to the blacks and greys and sodden earth surrounding him. Joseph's son Gordon, his wife Mary and Evelyn's two sisters stood on the Vicar's other side. They were all numb with cold and grief, and stood with heads bowed and grim tear- and rain-washed faces. They stood until the grave was filled and the last flowers were laid and then turned away, Mrs Foster sobbing as she walked back along the street to the house, supported by her husband and son, her eyes fixed downwards on the slick tarmac, a silent crowd on either side.

Slowly, just as silently, the crowd began to melt away. More wreaths and flowers and were heaped on the grave as people made their way home or to their vehicles or to the Percy Arms. Many of them had come a long way, and with varying degrees of difficulty, just to be there.

The *Newcastle Daily Journal* was to report it thus:

The funeral yesterday was one of the saddest ceremonies, but even in the midst of their grief the parents and relatives of the dead girl must have found some little solace in the great outgoing of sympathy from their own folk of the villages and dales.

A few policemen in plain clothes mingled with the crowd. They looked uncomfortable in their suits and were soon identified as police by other spectators. They became false mourners. Someone, tongue in cheek, reported one to another for what was perceived as strange behaviour. If they were present on the basis that a murderer is always drawn to return to the scene of his crime, or in this case his victim's funeral, they were to leave empty-handed. The few unconfirmed 'sightings' in the churchyard and on the street, like so many before, came to nought.

A man was seen loitering near the gates of the church. He seemed to fit Evelyn's description in most ways, except he had a distinct Tyneside accent. According to *The Evening World*, he asked two youths where he could find a lift to Newcastle, but before they could answer, heard footsteps. He asked the youths, 'Is that a policeman coming?' and then turned tail and vanished into the gloom. Another stranger was seen by a boy on a bicycle. He took offence at the boy's curiosity, yelled, 'What are you looking at me for?' and likewise disappeared up the road.

The Fosters had received hundreds of letters of sympathy in the past few days—at least the great majority had been written with that sentiment. But some were vicious, forerunners of today's online abuse, accusing members of the family of conspiring with the murderer, in one or two cases suggesting an insurance payout as the motive. Madeleine McCann's parents will know the feeling. Gordon Foster had assumed the role of censor, allowing his parents to see only genuine messages of sympathy, passing all the others to the police. Their content may even have sown the seeds of the police theory that insurance fraud was at the bottom of this business which was now causing them so much hassle.

I do not know, can only imagine, what the atmosphere in The Kennels must have been like that evening. I do not believe there would have been any relief that the day was over, only four days after the death of a daughter and sister. This house, this village, had been the Fosters' home, their safe harbour, since 1901, before the three girls were born; Evelyn had arrived within months of their moving in. By an accident of their ages, Joseph and his offspring had escaped being called-up to serve in the Great War, but the family had played their part, then and now, transporting soldiers and heavy equipment to and from the camp. Otterburn had lost nine of its sons in those four deadly years.

Now, it was a home with a hole in it. Mrs Foster and her two remaining daughters tidied up the furniture, putting back in place the chairs on which Evelyn's coffin had finally rested, lighting the fire, making a pot of tea. The day before Evelyn died all the sprigs of holly had been taken down from the mantelpiece and around pictures on the walls; the Christmas decorations packed away. Even then, on Twelfth Night, the house had seemed bare without them. Dorothy found her mother sitting on the bed in Evelyn's room, staring at nothing. She took her back down the stairs. Her father and brother were in the kitchen, talking desultorily about who they'd seen in the street, what the police would do next, now their traffic duties of the day were over; about maybe walking down to the Percy Arms later when things had quietened down.

Rule No. 1: Life must go on. There was a business to run, and the family would get back to it tomorrow.

The Coroner

In many respects the inquest proceedings in the War Memorial Hall at Otterburn resembled a posthumous trial for fraud more than a genuine investigation into what had happened and why. At the 'seat' of the problem, to use Professor McDonald's word, lay the scope of the coroner's powers. In any case of sudden, unexplained or unnatural death, it was and still is the coroner's duty to ascertain if there has been foul play. His (or, in today's world, her) verdict was crucial in either closing a case or leaving it open for further investigation. It was a considerable power, only regulated by successive enactments and amendments of the Coroners Rules. As one example, involving a death almost three years to the day before Evelyn Foster's death, Coroner Maurice Carter had refused to accept an open verdict by his jury in the case of Mr Harry Pace, a sheep farmer in Forest of Dean. His wife, Mrs Beatrice Pace, with a long history both as a recipient of domestic violence and of ministering to her husband, was suspected of having poisoned him with arsenic, heavy traces of which were found in his liver and kidneys. Following Coroner Carter's intervention Mrs Pace was arrested. I do not intend to go into the details of this case, which you can find out for yourselves. Suffice it to say they were tortuous and led to an outpouring of public sympathy for Mrs Pace. The judge at her trial ruled there was insufficient evidence. He directed the jury to return a Not Guilty verdict.

Mrs Pace's father (we shall see more of this reaction) wrote an angry letter to the Home Secretary of the day complaining at the treatment his daughter had received at the hands of British justice.

As another example of inquest proceedings in that era — in fact a classic case of trial by coroner — Alfred Oliver was robbed and murdered in his Reading tobacconist's shop on 22 June 1929. The inquest opened on

25 June with Coroner John Martin, a friend of the deceased who had been moved to write a letter of condolence to his wife, presiding. After another almost impenetrable police investigation, Philip Yale Drew, a flamboyant New England travelling actor and heavy drinker, finally fell under the police spotlight. He had been interviewed before, but now the police felt sufficiently confident that the inquest could be re-opened. Before long it assumed the aspect of a murder trial. Amongst other things, including a somewhat biased selection of witnesses (!), the mislaying of a crucial statement and the shelving by the police of more credible theories, Drew was asked several times by the coroner to stand up and be identified in court, even though other witnesses were present and were still to give evidence. Drew was subjected to a process in which the police knew they had insufficient evidence to press charges; that if their man came to trial he would be acquitted. In fact, he was acquitted in all but name, since the inquest jury returned a verdict of 'wilful murder against person or persons unknown.' But Drew was to say later that he wished he *had* been sent for trial; he would have stood a better chance of 'escaping the shadow cast over me ever since.'

Why should he have said so?

In his court, Coroner Dodds—and any other coroner in the land at that time in history—could act as both judge and prosecuting counsel, although in this case Smirk partly filled that role. The 'defence', however, had far fewer rights. Inquests were not bound by the same rules of evidence that applied in criminal courts. The coroner's word, almost literally, was law. He could admit hearsay evidence, could call on anyone he chose (or vice versa), and could ask a witness questions, including incriminating and leading questions (c.f. our Coroner Dodds), that no judge or policeman would be empowered to ask. The witness's replies could then be used in any criminal proceedings that followed.

The Coroners (Amendment) Act of 1926 attempted to address this problem, at the same time eliminating some already obsolete powers, such as safeguarding the king's property (treasure trove excepted*) and serving as a counterbalance to the powerful office of sheriff, both responsibilities being historically part of a coroner's job description. The 1926 Act established qualifications for holding the office, requiring a coroner to be a barrister, solicitor and/or qualified medical practitioner. It also stipulated that a coroner was obliged to adjourn an inquest once criminal proceedings were underway, *provided* an arrest had been made.

Enter the law of unintended consequences.

In effect, this provision created the anomaly that someone like Drew who was suspected of murder, but not charged, had less legal protection than someone who had been charged. It meant, among other things, that the police could defer any arrest until the inquest had done most of their job for them. The Royal Commission on Police Powers and Procedures in 1929 had concluded that a person in custody should not be questioned at all (although it did not go so far as to prohibit voluntary statements of the 'unburdening of the soul' kind, which left a grey area to be filled by the kind of mild but repetitive questioning which might induce a confession). The liberty allowed by coroner's inquiries became an attractive option to the police as a means of avoiding these pitfalls. I imagine it was inevitable that the police would tell the coroner beforehand which areas they would most like explored, which questions they would most like answers to.

Our coroner for the Foster inquest, Mr Philip Mark Dodds, a myopic little man with a toothbrush moustache, had practised as a solicitor before his appointment to the Coroner's Office. In outward appearance, down to the moustache, he could have been police solicitor Smirk's elder brother. As was normal, he was appointed by the Northumberland County Council (until 1926, the sole qualification was that a coroner should be a landholder) and was an independent judicial officer.

The following clarification is mainly for Bradon's benefit (I hope!) since the role of 'coroners' and 'medical examiners' is different in US States and counties. In the USA, a coroner is an elected local official, usually with a term of 2-4 years, and need not be qualified in law or medicine:

As with all coroners, when a death is of a nature to warrant being reported, Mr Dodds' duties were to gather all the relevant information surrounding it in order to make a decision about its cause. If there were questions about that cause he would arrange for a post mortem to be carried out. If the post mortem showed the death *not* to be due to natural causes he would hold an inquest to find out the cause and also provide the particulars needed for the death registration. It was, and is, not the coroner's responsibility to identify the person(s) responsible for the death. That sometimes came almost by accident, but it was not the purpose.

The four main questions to be answered at an inquest are: *who* was the deceased (which in our case was done on 8 January 1931**) and *how*, *when* and *where* did they meet their death?

Prior to 1926 (the Coroners Amendment Act) all inquests were held with a jury. After 1926, although a jury could be called, and if so would comprise seven to eleven members, the majority of cases were heard in public without one. If the proceedings were of public interest they were reported in local and sometimes national media. Similarly to a magistrate, a coroner could insist that witnesses attend an inquest to give evidence. Coroner's juries are now rare but inquests, unless the 'national interest' is at risk, are open to the public. There are superficial similarities with the role of grand juries in the USA, virtually the only country in the world which still retains them (they ceased to function in England and Wales in 1933, except for offences relating to officials overseas, and were abolished entirely in 1948).

Note 1*: an abiding part of a coroner's duties is in treasure trove cases, dating from the ancient duty of the coroner to protect the property of the Crown (*coroune* = *crown*).

Note 2**: few local people were present on 8 January. This may have been because the proceedings were brief and formal, or because there was reticence about intruding on the Foster family's private grief.

I email this to everyone so they have it before our Friday meeting. I receive four acknowledgements and an additional note from Peter:

Nice description of the funeral, maestro. Are you telling us there were shorter straws for Evelyn to draw than Dodds??!!

CHAPTER TWENTY-TWO

Newcastle Law School: the present day, 6 February
Concerning 2-5 February 1931

"Good morning, everyone," I say when we're all seated. "As a treat today, we have blueberry muffins." I point over to the coffee table. "They are something of a celebration, as we should by close of play have completed our review of all the material. That's not to say we'll have completed our work, because next week we need to wrap things up with our final analysis and conclusions."

"What do we get then?" Peter asks with a smile. "*Two* blueberry muffins?"

"I think I might stretch to a bottle or two," I tell him. "You'll need to think of something else for Bradon."

"A quart of huckleberry ice cream would be real nice," Bradon says.

I hate to think how we are going to get huckleberries, let alone huckleberry ice cream, shipped to the UK, but that's for another day. I'm grateful Frances realises that I'm temporarily stumped.

"It was a useful note you sent us," she says. "But where do we start with the inquest? We've covered most of the statements already."

"At the beginning," I tell her. "And please remember, in addition to the Dodds-Smirk-Bates triumvirate and what they asked, we have the contributions of the jurors, chemical analyses and so on. The fact that both the police and Fosters had counsel present made this inquest unusual. It gave the proceedings an adversarial character from the outset."

She smiles. "I think I already feel an urgent appointment coming on before we get to the chemistry. My hair is in a dreadful state."

It looks as healthy and immaculate as ever. Why, my friends, do so many of us dislike chemistry so much, when we are all made of it? I may spring it on them halfway through, when no one is looking.

"Please remember also," I tell them, "that while the inquest was underway the police were continuing with their enquiries. We've seen some of their representatives appear in the Memorial Hall but foot soldiers were still occasionally searching the hills, questioning shepherds and real soldiers, and doing their best in the chambers of Otterburn Tower to find clues in all the paperwork that might reinforce their theory that the case was one of fraud, or throw up anything new at all."

"And if they failed," Peter says, "Fullarton James would have had them court-martialled and shot at dawn in the stable block."

"Speaking of our Chief Constable," I say when the chortles have subsided, "he was there promptly that first morning, Monday 2 February, seated ramrod-straight in his seat, his hat, baton and gloves on his lap, waiting for the coroner to appear. Which Mr Dodds did, bang on the stroke of nine, and the first words he uttered were directed at the jury. They were not, he told them, to accept statements made by Evelyn Foster, either when she returned from Rochester or later from Wolf's Nick, as evidence of fact. The jurors would have to take them as part of the inquiry, yes, but judge for themselves whether other evidence, direct or circumstantial, confirmed them. This in effect was a direction to doubt Evelyn's story before it was presented, and it's a debatable point whether it should have been said at all, or said when it was."

"Let's give him that small battle," Peter says. "No legal reason why he shouldn't say it. I guess it coloured things a little and some of the jury would already be looking at him and thinking…what's the phrase…?"

"Up yours?" Bradon suggests.

"Exactly, Bradon. But what I think was *very* wrong about Dodds and the presentation of Evelyn's story was that here was the only chance to hear the victim's voice from beyond the grave and it was left to her mother to do it. The doctor apart, no one else adds anything much to her mother's evidence about Evelyn's last hours—not even the police, and it was after all, in large part the results of *their* interview that Mrs Foster was relating. The District Nurse, the neighbour, Evelyn's sisters and sister-in-law, were not called. Does anyone else find that strange?"

"No," Frances says. "They were women."

"Yes," Bradon says, smiling at her. "But it may have been simple psychology. If any cop, especially the senior cop Shanks who was at the interview, had testified, it would have given Mrs Foster's words added force, wouldn't it? Shanks wasn't even on the witness list, and maybe that was the reason. Fergusson barely mentioned the interview, and Bates sure didn't question him about it."

"I think that makes very good sense, Bradon," Frances says. "As far as the police were concerned Evelyn had manufactured her own murder, and the more Heath Robinson her product could be shown to be, the better. They couldn't avoid calling Mrs Foster to the witness stand but made sure her evidence, already subjected to a heavy caveat by Dodds, stood alone and unsupported. Apart from McEachran, no other person present at that last interview was asked about it. Not even Dr Miller, who at least had his gender going for him. They vanished from the frame as completely as Shanks, and Fergusson strayed no further than the fact it had happened. Other than that, of course, Mrs Foster made a very good witness, which must have upset the police dreadfully. Her memory was crystal clear, she used Evelyn's precise words when she could, she stood up to Dodds and Smirk, and if she was unsure about a detail she said so."

I look at Sven, who is stirring, and raise my eyebrows.

"I agree," he says. "When Dodds asked her mother if Evelyn had any worries — this no doubt to sow the seed that she'd lost her senses — she answered clearly that as far as she knew she had none. When the police solicitor Smirk asked if Evelyn had actually called at the Percy Arms to pick up her fare — as if Mrs Foster could have known what was happening in the darkness three hundred yards away — she took the wind out of his sails by simply answering, 'No.' When Smirk asked whether her daughter Margaret had seen George Phillipson in the village earlier, Mrs Foster readily agreed. When he persisted in his attempt to show Evelyn had broken a promise to her mother in not calling on Phillipson, Mrs Foster said, 'I've thought since then that my daughter would not have cared to go to his lodgings.' That would have impressed the jury, who would have known exactly what those lodgings were like, but it left Smirk high and dry. He could hardly then ask *why* Evelyn wouldn't have cared to go, as he would be sure to get an answer that would accord with every juror's opinion."

"Given that the last of Mrs Foster's contributions was to identify remnants of Evelyn's clothing," I tell them, "this might be a good time for us to introduce them, and the analyses which followed."

Frances groans and mutters, "False prophet."

The questioning of Mrs Foster (ID1)

After giving her statement, which most neutral observers agreed was performed with dignity and without guile, Mrs Foster faced questions. First in line was the coroner. She told him that all three Foster girls had received routine medical check-ups on 21 December in Bellingham, attended by Dr Kerr. Evelyn's examination had not been completed 'owing to her courses.' She had been quite regular in her courses and her behaviour was not unusual during them. She wasn't sure whether Evelyn had been 'unwell' on 6 January.

When his turn came, Smirk reminded Mrs Foster that Evelyn had planned to pick the man up at the Inn. Mrs Foster agreed. After probing unsuccessfully at Evelyn's failure to pick up George Phillipson, Smirk asked if the answers Evelyn had given to questions in her interview were voluntary. Mrs Foster replied that she had asked the questions and her daughter had made the statements herself. Smirk then returned to Evelyn's description of the car from which 'the man' had emerged at Elishaw. Mrs Foster replied that Evelyn had said it was a dark-coloured closed car but she could not recall the number. She had described the man as wearing a dark overcoat and bowler hat. He was dark-haired, but she couldn't say what colour his eyes were. She had worn a felt hat when she left the house but not when she returned.

Bates asked Mrs Foster if Evelyn had said if the man wore glasses.

In answer to a question by a juror, Mrs Foster said Evelyn was 'quite as usual. She was not anxious to take the hire.'

After questioning Mrs Foster about Evelyn's identification of Kirsopp-Reed's car, her description of the journey back to Wolf's Nick, and the way in which the man had assaulted her, the coroner asked if Mrs Foster could identify pieces of clothing Evelyn had been wearing when she left the house, all somewhat charred. Mrs Foster nodded. These items included: shoes; a checked skirt and bodice; a jumper; corsets; a camisole; a vest; stockings; a brown scarf; and pieces of tweed cloth and other material. When she saw them Mrs Foster broke down in tears and her testimony ended.

"If this whole thing was not so serious," Peter says, "Bates would be a joke. *Glasses?* Why not braces or a cravat? Matching socks?"

"Let's do the chemistry bit, Peter," says Frances. "Get it over with."

"As you wish, Frances," I say. "I'm sure the various tests, not just chemical, which were carried out by Professors McDonald and Briscoe and Dr Dunn, should not prove too much to bear. I'm no chemist either, but most seem basic and again we have to remember this is not a modern episode of *CSI*. I've done my best to summarise. Let's take a look:"

Item	Analysis/comment
1 Pair, brown leather shoes	No signs of recent burning. Grass/heather traces.
2 Portion of check skirt	Remnant, 15"x19". Variously burned/charred.
3 Portion of bodice	Front burnt away, back intact: minor charring.
4 Part of woollen jumper	Front burnt away. Lower back/right sleeve burnt.
5 Part of lady's corsets	Front burnt away. Back mostly untouched.
6 Part, bust bodice/camisole	Front badly burnt. Back almost untouched.
7 Part of white knitted vest	Front extensively burnt. Lower 6" of back burnt.
8 Pair brown silk stockings	Upper parts extensively burnt, with greasy stains.
9 Lady's cotton mix scarf	*Found near car. Minor burns, largely complete.
10 Pieces brown tweed cloth	*Parts of coat and skirt. All badly charred.
11 Piece wadding & material	*Charred at edges/saturated with oily substance.
12 Piece of burned linen	*Probably lining; badly burned.
13 Buckles of suspenders	*Inside front attachments? Much burned.
	*All found nearside, near front door/footboard
14 Piece of white cotton tape	3 yards. Much weathered. No sign of burning/oil.
15 Green glass bottle, 3-gill	Containing 1 teaspoonful of (lemonade/sherbet)?
16 Cone-shaped material	Burned. Found in well of back seat.
17 Piece of scorched heather	Found in first ditch. Withered: no scorching.
18 Grass in two bottles	Bloodstained? To be examined later.
19 Door handle	Bloodstained? To be examined later.
20 Piece of mudguard	Bloodstained? To be examined later.

"We will see the rest before we comment," I tell them. "For the moment, the twenty items listed correspond to those given as an addendum to Russell's statement, except the suspender parts have been added and he describes item 11 as a 'piece of wadding and dress material with elastic attached.' I'm sure Frances will be glad to hear we do not need to dwell on the ultra-violet tests, since of the four items analysed—numbers 6, 8, 10 and 11—only the last three showed a distinct blue fluorescence. Similarly, after control experiments were done using filter paper, only Castrol oil, Vaseline and paraffin wax showed strong blue fluorescence. Human fat showed none. Items 17-20 were tested by McDonald for blood using a benzidine test. Only the piece of mudguard came up positive—that is, showed any blue colouring—but further confirmatory and spectroscopic tests revealed no blood. McDonald concluded there was none on any of the exhibits. Russell seems not to have believed him."

"And I doubt if any of it really matters," Peter says. "McDonald would have drawn attention to it if it had. These were add-ons to his statement, just so everyone would know he had left no stone unturned."

"So find something significant, Peter, if you can," I challenge him. "Gil Grissom would take real offence at what you just said."

"Who's Gil Grissom?"

"He is, or was, head honcho in *CSI* Las Vegas," Bradon says.

"What's...oh, never mind." Peter flicks hair from his forehead.

"McDonald," I tell them, "also carried out some experiments to show the effect on human tissue of the burning of cloth soaked in petrol."

"Don't tell me," Peter says. "It burned the skin and the fat layer."

I ignore the sarcasm. "It did. He found it burned fiercely for ten minutes, and was still smouldering three hours later. He passed the piece of cloth on to Dr Dunn for chemical analysis."

"For God's sake," Peter says. "Talk about using a sledgehammer."

"I see I'm losing you," I tell him, and look around. "If not all of you. Well, let's be as quick as possible with Dunn's chemical analysis."

"Oh, please," Frances says. "I've been so looking forward to it."

Sarcasm seems to be breaking out all over.

"Dr Dunn did the chemical analysis on items 8, 10 and 11; the stockings, the tweed cloth and what he describes as 'a small quantity of wadding with a fragment of textile material.' He concluded that the wadding was 'probably part of a sanitary towel', since a sanitary towel said by the police to have been obtained from Mrs Foster contained similar wadding. The edges were burned, the wadding was very oily and smelt like burned tallow. A grease-spot on filter paper from it showed blue fluorescence in ultra-violet light. However, unlike the stockings and tweed cloth, especially the piece from the skirt, no smell of petroleum could be detected."

"Hold on a minute," Peter says. "*There's* something of significance. The sanitary towel had been removed first and thrown away in anger, and then was scorched as the flames spread around the car. It wasn't doused in petrol like the other bits and pieces."

Sven nods. "That figures, Peter," he says. "And it's obvious *Evelyn* wouldn't have discarded it, unless it was burning."

"Anyway," I continue, "Dr Dunn took various measurements of the oil from his exhibits, such as fatty acids, their iodine value, their saponification value—which broadly means the conversion of a fat into soap—and melting points. His conclusion was that the oil present in exhibits 8, 10 and 11 was undoubtedly human fat."

"Fascinating," Frances says. "Do we know what IQ this chap had?"

"Dr Dunn also tested the liquid in the glass bottle (15). It was lime or lemon juice and contained no alcohol or inflammable properties. With the help of Joseph Foster at the garage, he concluded that the burned cone-shaped item (16) had been a tyre hammer."

"I wonder if Bowler was tempted to hit her with it?" Peter asks. "He couldn't have, of course. Our good Professor would have been wallowing in all the superficial bruising like a pig in muck."

"You will all, I'm sure," I tell them pointedly, "be delighted to know that our next summary note is the final one in the sequence."

"And a sterling job you did with them, my good fellow," Peter says. "Life will just not be the same without our twice-weekly dose."

"You can drop the sarcasm now, Peter. I am not Prof McDonald."

EF: clothing worn leaving home	How/where found afterwards
1 Pair of brown leather shoes	Worn when brought home
2 Checked tweed skirt and bodice	Partly worn by EF when brought home
3 Dark brown Otterburn tweed coat	Pieces found at scene and identified
4 Dark brown felt hat with ribbon	Never found
5 Navy blue or brown knickers	Part found at car/thought to be knickers
6 Cotton silk bra bodice/camisole	Partly worn by EF when brought home
7 Pink corsets with suspenders	Partly worn by EF when brought home
8 White vest or bodice	Partly worn by EF when brought home
9 Short brown cotton scarf	Found at scene of burned car
10 Pair of brown silk stockings	Partly worn by EF when brought home
11 Cinnamon/brown woollen jumper	Partly worn by EF when brought home
12 Mrs F unsure about sanitary towel	Wadding found at car/thought to be part

"Symons and Heslop both mention a glove being found, but Russell doesn't list one. A curiosity, or something more?" Sven asks.

"Oh please, surely not even the police would go as far as to hide a glove," Frances says. "I suppose it could have been rumour or journalistic licence but why should it crop up in the first place?"

"It's an odd one," Peter says. "No one mentions seeing it out there, not even the constables or Foster's men. A *man's* glove would have put a whole new complexion on the story. Where would the police have been then with their concoction? Strange how they knew about positive spin in those bygone days, though," he adds as we all head for the table.

"In what way?" Sven asks, picking up a muffin.

"A list of the bits of rags she was still wearing when she was brought home. Not the bits she *wasn't* wearing, except the felt hat, or the things she had with her."

"No wonder her mother broke down when she saw them," Frances says. "I mean, did she really have to be shown this stuff in public? These muffins are delicious, Matthew. Really fresh and moist."

"And glove or no glove, where did the hat go?" Bradon asks. "And most of her coat? And her purse with the cash in it?"

"Good questions, Bradon," Peter says. "And even better ones when you consider part of every other item was accounted for and *nothing* seems to have been totally destroyed in the fire. By simple deduction, if they weren't there and Evelyn wasn't wearing them when she was brought home, Bowler took them or the police lost them. Her coat was burned. Johnstone, don't forget, had to wrap her in *his* coat to carry her to the bus. And how did her scarf survive the blaze when her coat didn't?"

"Perhaps someone else took the missing items or part items," I suggest. "A souvenir hunter? Or a passing tramp?"

"We've already discarded the idea of a tramp," Frances says. "Haven't we? No tramp would have left money lying around."

"Besides which," Peter says, "those old boys had a kind of code, didn't they, like the American hobo? Am I right, Bradon? They depended on people's goodwill, so most of them—not all I grant you—would take care not to abuse it. My grandmother once told me she used to give one of them leftover food, a mug of tea, when he passed the house. And it's not likely a tramp would have taken much, except maybe the cash, while she was lying there and without reporting a burned car. It may happen in Oxford Street today, but Otterburn, then? It was more of a lifestyle choice then, wasn't it, and less an excuse for scrounging? Or it was simply a way of life they enjoyed. No roots, no responsibilities, the freedom of the road and all that. Some of those old boys were gentlemen, until the streets got too dangerous for them anymore. They live underground now, I guess, those that still exist, or in emergency hostels or night shelters. We shouldn't romanticise them, I suppose, but the rural tramp of old seems to have been a different individual from the urban tramp of today. They were a different breed in a different country." He looks at his notes. "And here's something else. Why were so many of those items found near the front nearside door? We still haven't answered that one, not to my satisfaction anyway. Any ideas? I think we'll find all these people have been obsessing about the wrong things. The car doors opening and closing, for instance. The petrol can and its accessories, as if petrol cans were the 1930s equivalent of UFOs and could appear and disappear, glow with an eerie light and change position at will. Because of that, other things were totally ignored, never mentioned. Given that the police were handed the where and when on a plate, this was a very superficial effort at establishing the *how* of Evelyn's death," he says disgustedly.

"And as Bradon said, what about her purse?" he adds. "How did it get to be on the ground at the nearside rear wheel? That's another detail we haven't properly answered yet. It's not listed by Russell, let alone by anyone else. It doesn't appear at all. Is that an error, or a case of mislaying evidence? The more we look at this, the worse it gets."

"The police took the purse," Frances says. "The last we heard of it was in Kirkwhelpington, at Sinton's police house."

"Right," Peter says. "So they forgot it or lost it. That may explain its absence from that list, but it doesn't explain why Proud found it where he said he did. Unlike the bits and pieces found near the front we know no one could have touched it after 1.00 am, and it's unlikely anyone saw it before. And we know two policemen handled it and two more may have done; Proud and Fergusson certainly, and Shanks and Sinton probably. What price fingerprints after that game of pass the parcel?"

"I shouldn't obsess about it, Peter," Sven tells him, grinning.

"No, Peter's right," I say. "It's another detail, another loose end or oversight, and we'll have more of those, I think."

"And we can dismiss the car doors," Peter persists. "Beattie saw the two offside doors open at 9.50 pm, Johnstone says they were open at 10.00, Fergusson and Proud say they were open at 1.00 am. They may have started opening and closing after that, because people couldn't leave them alone or couldn't tell open from closed, but it doesn't matter, does it? At 8.35 pm, Bowler was in the offside or driving seat, he got out and left the front offside door open. He opened the rear offside door to get to Evelyn, and left it open. Why would he have closed it? The draught would have helped the fire. What more do we need to know?"

I'm conscious of Bradon scribbling and smile to myself. It seems to be getting dark in the room so I switch on more lights to help him.

CHAPTER TWENTY-THREE

Newcastle Law School: the present day, 6 February
Concerning 2 February 1931 (Day One of the inquest)

"Let's continue to review what the witnesses were asked," I suggest when we are back around the table. "And as near as we can in the order they appeared at the inquest, which was somewhat different from my notes. That is, unless you wish to expand on your last comments, Peter?"

"No," he says. "Not yet. I'm mulling over a few things."

I wonder to myself whether this could spell trouble. But maybe I'm doing him an injustice. I walk over to open a window and let in some air.

"Very well," I resume. "Mrs Foster was finished at that point. She broke down and was given a glass of water by one of the policemen. The coroner reputedly—this is by no means certain—tried to persuade her to leave the room with the help of her neighbour, Mrs Jennings. She refused and sat down again between her husband and son."

"So what form did this persuasion take?" Bradon asks. "Was it an act of sympathy or unease at the stitch-up to come? She'd surely have wanted to hear what went down next. By then, she would have expected it wouldn't be anything good. But at least she might have felt the worst was over. Finally."

"I'm sure no armlocks were used," I smile at him. "But let's move on. Next up were Robson and Harrison, the two bus drivers apart from Johnstone who had cameo parts. Why they should have been next I've no idea. I can only assume availability may have affected the order."

"Robson is relevant because of the time he saw the Hudson at Raylees," Frances says. "I don't know how Harrison would have helped the police. We've discussed before how he could have seen, and been seen, in the Ferney Chesters area by Kirsopp-Reed, but that wouldn't have helped them. Quite the opposite, as Evelyn claimed she'd seen Kirsopp-Reed in the same neck of the woods and presumably the police were trying to suggest she'd never got beyond Wolf's Nick. On the other hand, Goodman thinks the police may have *wanted* the jury to think Harrison saw her, on grounds that, if he had, it would indicate she'd suffered a rush of blood to the head: that beyond Raylees she'd become reckless to the point of developing a death wish and had driven like a bat out of hell to Belsay and back in order to back up her story."

"So who sounds crazier?" Bradon asks. "The cops or Goodman?"

"Yes," Peter says, waking from his reverie. "There were, and still are, some jaw-dropping theories on offer."

"Anyway," I say, "both these bus drivers seem to have escaped with no questions asked. The next witness to be called was Joseph Foster and duplicity, as we've seen, was not in Joseph's armoury. Asked by Smirk about Evelyn's return from Rochester, Joseph could easily have claimed that people often popped down to the Percy Arms or, when it was open, the Co-op. Instead he readily agreed it was strange her passenger hadn't waited at the garage. Not for the last time, Smirk then trailed his own version of duplicity across the proceedings. Is everyone still with me?" I ask in case they are tempted to fall asleep.

I think they have been distracted by the sounds of an Atlantic storm passing overhead. It was forecast, but not this early in the day.

Sven says, "Smirk asked Joseph whether he was sure the man had not waited or come back to the garage. Smirk already knew the answer to that; he was underlining Bowler's odd behaviour, or the odd behaviour of Evelyn's creation. It was impossible for Joseph to have seen Bowler. Both Mrs Foster and Joseph himself had testified that Joseph was in The Kennels preparing a quotation for Evelyn. At that point in the evening, struggling as ever with his book-keeping, Joseph barely saw his daughter except when she passed through the house."

"And Bates asked no questions at all," Frances says.

"In these proceedings," Peter says, "Bates was as useful as a straw man. Worse, as straw men can't speak."

"Joseph was, however, asked some questions by the coroner," I remind them, raising my voice against the drumming on the roof and wondering if I should close the window. "Apart from enquiring when Joseph had first heard about Evelyn taking a man to Ponteland, Dodds began probing into Evelyn's finances, her role in the Foster's business, and some questions about the 2-gallon petrol can found at the scene."

"Questions about that petrol can were a red herring." Peter's voice is big enough to have no difficulty in being heard. "A rotten one at that, dragged across the case as if it had significance beyond its purpose. It had clearly been used as the agent for the fire: no one would dispute it. What more would anyone want to know? Dodds, to my mind, was trying to demonstrate a kind of spurious thoroughness. How had a Pratt's can suddenly become a Shell can? Because Evelyn had bought a replacement, what else? In the ten days since Joseph thought—*thought*—he'd last seen it, she'd sold the Pratt's can to a needy motorist. Or she may have laid it down somewhere to accommodate someone's luggage in the carrier and forgotten about it. Big deal. Was the can sealed? Well, it would quickly have become unsealed once Bowler laid his hands on it. This was all a smokescreen, nothing more. Even if Evelyn had used it herself it would have been empty with its top off. What was the point in all this?"

"I'm wondering about the sequence of questions asked of these first witnesses," Frances says, and she has the advantage of being a lyric soprano. "Dodds ended his questioning of Joseph by introducing the state of Evelyn's finances. As far as the police theory went, it was an opening salvo, their first opportunity to lay down a marker—except for an oblique attempt when Dodds had asked Mrs Foster if Evelyn had had any 'worries.' Up till then, nothing about finance or insurance or Evelyn's state of mind had appeared. Here, Joseph was being asked how much Evelyn had paid for the Hudson just over a year ago. He said, 'over £200' and was pressed by Dodds to find out an exact figure. He said he would do so. People have commented that it was strange he didn't have the answer at his fingertips, but why would he? Evelyn had her own bank account and even Bowler had spotted that she was an independent young woman. Stranger still, as Peter said a few days ago, is the fact that Dodds was asking these questions and not the police beforehand. Were they chary of breaking cover? Of exposing their hand?"

"You said 'sequence of questions,' Frances," I remind her.

"Yes. I'm comparing the questions asked by Dodds against those he might have asked if he intended impartially to get at the truth. For this purpose Smirk can be ignored as he was in the police's pocket and Bates, as Peter says, was worse than useless. But Robson and Harrison aside, Dodds to this point had seen only Evelyn's mother and father. He had asked not one single question about her family background, her character or personality, whether she tended to be level-headed or moody, her education, her home life, her social life, her dreams or ambitions or contributions to the community. Instead, he asked her mother if Evelyn had seemed sensible on the night she was questioned, whether she had these mythical business worries, and if Mrs Foster could identify items of Evelyn's clothing. When it came to her father, Dodds asked when he had first heard of Evelyn's trip to Ponteland, a raft of questions about petrol cans, and how much she had paid for her car. Does that sound to you like someone from the same professional stable as Atticus Finch?"

"Nailed the guy in one," Bradon says, who might arguably know better than any of us about the life and times of Atticus Finch.

"So let's see how things developed from there," I suggest. "Next up was our steam-roller driver Beach."

"What's the point?" Peter asks. "We've dealt with Beach." (Which he has). "We've dealt with all the questions Bates should have asked him but didn't. Beach thought he saw a car stopped at Elishaw Road Ends, then a second car went 'tearing' past him, possibly—I'm not going to belabour this again—no further than Troughend Hall. Then, within minutes, he saw what could well have been the first car, Evelyn's car, heading towards Otterburn. I was heavy-handed on Bates a couple of weeks ago, and don't regret it, but on reflection the coroner was as much to blame if, *if*, he cared a jot for finding out the truth. In my eyes they're both damned, and this is only the first morning of three days."

"We have to agree with Goodman here," Frances says. "He sums it up by saying that if the cars Beach saw were unconnected with the case, then it's an odd coincidence that on roads almost empty of traffic, those two cars reached and diverged from Elishaw at a time matching Evelyn's account. The one person in this ugly trio who could not be blamed for asking questions, or not asking them as the case may be, was Smirk. Any answers, or wrong answers, he got may have damaged the police theory."

"Also Townes, the Brownrigg Cottages gardener, should have been called next," Bradon says. "But he wasn't called at all. The cops would have been pushing it if he had been, since he virtually corroborates what Beach saw. He might even have stirred Bates into semi-action."

"Let's move on," Peter says, glancing upwards at the ceiling as if it might spring a leak. "We've already agreed, haven't we, that Evelyn's tale stacks up from Otterburn to Rochester and back?"

"Very well," I say. "In that case let's look again at the quarter-hour between 7.00 and 7.15 pm in Otterburn itself. It's a crucial quarter-hour, I think you'll agree, and is distinguished more by the witnesses who were *not* called as those who were."

"Thompson, Maughan and Luke all had contributions of some kind to make about those fifteen minutes," Sven says, looking at his notes. "Except they didn't gel. As did Sinclair, the juror; Misses Carruthers and Ferry, who weren't called; and the hotel staff, Tatham and Scott. I think we can forget Tatham and Scott, except for saying that the non-appearance of Evelyn in the hotel actually supports her story that she picked Bowler up at the bridge. The rest, as we've said before, is messy."

As he has been speaking the noise has abated as quickly as it arose.

"So summarise the mess for us, Sven, if you would," I tell him.

He looks again at his notes. "I'll try. Three witnesses—Thompson, Maughan and Luke—saw the Hudson at the garage, or rather at The Kennels, as the petrol pump was on that side. No one saw Evelyn, except Thompson thought he heard her voice and Maughan thought there was a woman in the car when it pulled up. He admitted under questioning that he could not have seen anyone in the back. Mrs Foster seems not to have seen the car, but she was indoors when Evelyn returned to say she had picked up her fare. Only George Phillipson, or so he said to *The Evening World*, saw the tail end of the Hudson a few minutes later heading out of the village. Ironically, he'd been in the garage asking if anyone knew Evelyn's whereabouts, and we don't know why he wasn't called as a witness either; he might at least have been able to speak to Evelyn's character and their relationship. Dixon suggests he may have been the man seen by Sinclair and the two ladies at the bridge, but it's unlikely if he was at the other end of the village. Besides, no one recognised this man. Sinclair, Miss Carruthers and Miss Ferry saw *someone* further down the street who could well have been Bowler; a stranger certainly. Maughan may have done so too, except he and Thompson both added those odd postscripts to their statements, each confirming he was 'satisfied' he had seen the other. Because of their similarity of wording, these notes, as Frances once said, have every appearance of having been prompted by the police. Other than that, Maughan's testimony is unreliable in several respects, not least because he seems to have changed his story overnight, and Thompson's timings were all over the place."

"So were Dr McEachran's, *in re* of the police interview," Peter points out, "and *he* was supposed to be a reliable witness." He looks round at each of us. "I'm saying most people's times have to be taken with a pinch of salt, larger or smaller as the case may be, along with what they saw or were told to say they saw. We can't take anything at face value."

"Up to a point we have to, Peter," I tell him. "Unless we see an outright untruth, that's where we have to draw the line. People can be wrong—as I suspect Kirsopp-Reed was in parts of his evidence—but that does not make them liars. In large part they were in unfamiliar territory, saying what they believed to be true, and if there were grey areas the coroner and family solicitor should have clarified them."

"Very simply," Frances says, "Thompson's times were out. He was earlier than he thought. If by his estimate it was after 7.20 pm when he saw the saloon at the garage, either there were two saloons, which no one else has mentioned, or the Hudson could not have been at Raylees."

Bradon says, "I see Mr Bates asked a question of Maughan, which seems to have been his first of the day. He asked Maughan if he would have been able to see anyone in the rear seats of the car. Maughan said, 'No.' Strike one for Bates. Then Smirk asked him to confirm it had been Thompson he met on the street which, rightly or wrongly, he did."

"Goodman makes a fair point here," Sven says. "He suggests the police and coroner would view Thompson and Maughan's evidence as being mutually corroborative, when in fact it was not. Goodman himself is wrong in suggesting Maughan left his house at 6.30 pm, but that may be because Goodman did not have full access to the inquest statements. Nevertheless, his thesis holds good. Times aside, Thompson saw a car *already* parked at the garage when he got there; Goodman suggests it must have been there for a while. So how could Maughan, walking to the garage from the opposite direction, have seen *Thompson* 35-40 yards before he reached the garage and *then* have seen the car pull up? Had he actually seen Thompson, or someone else? Maughan's memory seems badly clouded when he speaks of seeing Mr Blackham just before he saw 'another man.' Blackham later confirmed he had indeed met Maughan, but between the garage and the school."

Peter shifts impatiently. Frances groans.

"All we can say," I tell them, "is that in all these complexities Sven gave us a good summary of who might have seen both the Hudson and Bowler in Otterburn between 7.00 and 7.15. Maughan and Thompson may have seen Bowler too, but adding them to the three who almost certainly did may devalue their evidence rather than add weight to it. As things stand, neither Maughan nor Thompson, or for that matter Luke, were asked the questions they should have been asked. In any case, let's press on to the witnesses between Raylees and Belsay and back to Wolf's Nick. In the order they appeared on the first day of the inquest, they were Kirsopp-Reed, Henderson, Johnstone, Rutherford and Vasey. It was only on the second day that Kennedy, Herdman and Beattie appeared — which again seems an odd sequence, as they should have alternated respectively after Kirsopp-Reed and Henderson."

"Who would have decided the sequence?" Frances asks.

"Within reason, and the practicalities of people's availability, the coroner," I reply. "Who would also have the final decision, with the help of his office, on whom to call. Today, he would listen to representations made to him by properly interested persons, the test being whether a witness would provide relevant evidence."

"And back in 1931?"

"Much the same, but shall we say less structured. Remember that only five years before *this* inquest the coroner could have been a lay shopkeeper or sheep farmer, so there would have been some history born of habit and protocol about who was responsible for what."

"One more before lunch?" Bradon asks. "Kirsopp-Reed?"

"The coroner seems to have sat back after establishing that the car Kirsopp-Reed saw *may* have been Evelyn's," Sven says. "Perhaps he saw danger signals in pressing the issue. Again, Reed had changed tone from his original statement, when he was sure he'd have recognised it if it had been there to see. Smirk stepped in and pointed out that if Reed had seen a car at Ferney Chesters at 7.20, it could not have been the car Robson saw ten miles away at Raylees at 7.22. He asked Reed if he was sure of his times. Reed said he was, to within five minutes. As we've seen earlier, Smirk then tried to suggest Evelyn may have known Reed's movements that day from her brother Gordon. Bates, as with many other things, let this point fall through the slats by not asking Gordon if he'd actually told his sister, but even so she could not have known the exact time Reed would be going home. Still, Smirk's was a hollow victory. He missed seeing Harrison's sighting of what must have been Reed's car near Ferney Chesters, and therefore that Reed's timings could be questionable. Or maybe he didn't want to draw attention to this sighting. In any event, it should have been picked up by the coroner, casting some doubt on Reed's reliability as a witness. Evelyn's claim of seeing his car should then have been given more credence. But none of these things happened. Hey ho."

It seems a good summary from Sven—again. I say, "We'll break for lunch, I think. But please bear in mind in all this that it was Smirk's job, if he couldn't actually blow holes in a witness's testimony, to confuse the jurors or cast doubt in their minds. That is what he was being paid to do."

I walk to the window. The Robinson Library isn't under water and we won't need the RNLI. There is, as usual if the windows are slightly ajar, only the faintest of murmurs from traffic on the nearby motorways.

Over lunch in the Students' Union I'm interested to hear that Sven is planning to fly to Oslo the week after next, heading for the ski resort at Kongsberg about an hour's drive away. He says he can do it in four days and still have three good days skiing. He falls into discussion with Bradon, who is talking of places like Mill D and Willow Fork in Utah's Wasatch Mountains. I hear them laughing as Bradon says he stays strictly within the aspen belts and spends a lot of time before he sets out reading the Utah Avalanche Center's daily report. He tells Sven he hasn't died in an avalanche yet and aims to keep it that way. It sounds as though he may be tempted to join Sven in Kongsberg.

By two 'clock we are back in our home from home and turning our attention to the shepherd, Sidney Henderson. There is not a lot to discuss about Henderson, and certainly no controversy. From two miles distant he saw a fire ablaze at Wolf's Nick at 8.45 pm on 6 January and thought not much more about it, except it had diminished by 9.00 when he arrived at Harwood Gate and had almost disappeared when he returned at 11.00. Yet again he wasn't questioned, although one or two questions may have narrowed down the time the fire had started. Todcrag Moss is exposed along the whole stretch of road Henderson was walking.

The last witnesses of the first day were Cecil Johnstone, Tommy Rutherford and Thomas Vasey. For clarification, the coroner might have asked the first two about the state of Evelyn's face and clothing when they found her, and if they had touched or removed anything, but he didn't. Bates asked Johnstone how long the fire may have been burning. All he could say was the wheels were still alight and the interior glowing. For Smirk, there was little value to be had in questioning witnesses whom no one disputed had found Evelyn halfway between burned and frozen alive on the moor, but he zeroed in on the doors with Johnstone and the gears with Vasey. Johnstone told him the two offside doors were open when he and Rutherford arrived, the nearside doors were closed, and they were in that position when he and Vasey returned with the police at 1.00 am. Vasey told the coroner that he had thought on arrival the car was either in gear or the gear box had melted. Smirk tried to confuse things by asking that if the gear box wasn't melted, had he thought the car was not in gear? When a bewildered Vasey answered 'Yes', Bates made an effort to clarify things. Vasey told him he was not familiar with the gear positions at first but had made himself familiar. The car had been in low gear when they arrived and it was still in low gear he saw it in the garage.

That night, Joseph and Gordon Foster had their clash of wills about the advisability of continuing with Bates, whose questions on the first day they could count on the fingers of one hand. Gordon argued that a man who asked no questions actually caused damage, since the jury might infer from it that all was well. Joseph finally agreed to take Bates aside the next morning and tell him to pull his socks up, or whatever it took.

I must say at this point, my friends, that there have been times in this process when I have doubted my judgement in embarking on it. My doubts are not that my students won't in some way have benefitted, but where has it led? Will it be of any use at all in the wider context of justice?

The stories are legion of people in or under 'authority' believing they are righteous when they are not. A classic case is Adolf Eichmann, who had little defence at his trial other than he had followed orders, that he was obliged *'to obey the rules of war and of my flag.'* They are variations on the themes of conditioning and compliance, in this case a concept in which human beings may be brainwashed into a belief that anything they do is acceptable provided they have 'authority' to do it. Thus we have Eichmann, the loyal servant, the put-upon bureaucrat.

We are trained to obey authority figures from our infancy. Stanley Milgram, a Yale and Harvard University social psychologist, conducted a controversial experiment in the early 1960s to measure this propensity to obey. He instructed participants to perform verbal tests—giving fake electric shocks of increasing intensity (up to 450 volts) to 'learners' who answered questions incorrectly. It may have conflicted with their morals, but his volunteers, under his authority, proceeded as he instructed, unaware that no actual shocks were being administered.

We have hate preachers who understand the concept absolutely.

Did the Northumberland police follow this course, without thought of the 'wider context'? I am beginning to believe so. How else to explain their actions?

CHAPTER TWENTY-FOUR

Newcastle Law School: the present day, 6 February
Concerning 3 February 1931 (Day Two of the inquest)

John Kennedy, the Knowesgate road-mender and chorister, was up first the following day. The coroner asked a couple of questions about the registration numbers of Miss Foster's and Mr Herdman's cars (Herdman was next to appear), both of which contained the numbers 1 and 3: TN8135 and BR6123 respectively. Kennedy proved to be stubborn and vigilant in equal parts. It did not take long for Smirk to work up a show of righteous indignation and attempt to demolish someone he saw as a threat to the police case. But the man facing him was no one's doormat.

"Kennedy fended him off well," Bradon says. "In fact he did better than that. In not restricting himself to monosyllables, in saying it was not Herdman's motor he saw, that Herdman would not drive at anything like that pace, he took the wind out of Smirk's sails."

"So Smirk changed tack to Kennedy's credibility," Sven says. "He started to question why Kennedy had not approached the police earlier. Kennedy agreed he'd been at the scene early the next morning and said he thought he'd told the constable on duty he had seen a car the previous evening. Pressed by Smirk, he said it was 'possible' he had not mentioned it until ten days later when the police approached him. But whether it was then or earlier, what reason would he have to invent the car he'd seen, or one he hadn't? I think this was a man who didn't like the police, or authority of any kind. He must have read the papers, or listened to the wireless, but apart from making his brief visit that morning he kept quiet until the police came to him. Smirk then switched again, this time to Kennedy's statement that a man had been driving this speeding car. Kennedy confirmed it: he could see that much in the dark. Later, he was to be recalled by Bates, who must have been got at by Gordon Foster, and asked how the man appeared to have been sitting. Kennedy said he did not think he was sitting straight on. There is a note to that effect in the coroner's papers; it is highlighted but wasn't followed-up. Smirk instead, as we've seen, took the chance to frame some questions around the colour of the car and the speed it was travelling—all of them, as Peter pointed out two weeks ago, a case of smoke and mirrors if not worse. And all of them unremarked and unpunished by Dodds."

"Yes," Peter says, "between then and now I think we've dealt with Mr Kennedy. I believe, unlike Smirk and the coroner—who it seems was later to describe his evidence as remarkable—Kennedy was a reasonably honest, if reluctant, witness. I wonder why his wife was not called, as she had been walking home with him. But maybe that says it all about the selection of witnesses. Maybe Mrs Kennedy was a peaceable church-going lady whom not even Mr Smirk felt able to mug in public. Maybe it also says it all about witnesses. Half of them don't want to get involved and the other half either don't see things, or don't see them properly, or can't describe afterwards what it was they saw."

Which in a nutshell is Peter's rather jaundiced, if mostly pardonable, view on witnesses. It raises a few smiles anyway.

"Herdman next," I jog them along.

"She was a *woman*, Peter," Frances says. "And how many of those have we heard from so far? Anyway," she continues, "I find Herdman's appearance outrageous, when there were so many other useful witnesses who should have been called. He was there for one purpose only, as Matthew has said: to confirm the car John Kennedy saw was his. That idea was shot down on several fronts: first, the times they each left Kirk-whelpington were close but not close enough; second, his number plate contained a '1' and a '3' but they were wrongly positioned; third, he seems habitually to have driven at little more than walking pace; and fourth, he did not see Kennedy and his wife, both of whom he knew and to whom he would almost certainly have offered a lift."

"Game, set and match, Frances," says Peter. "And you are right; a measly three ladies from twenty-seven. Call Walter Beattie to the stand."

"Don't bother," Sven says. "Here was a man who saw no evil, heard no evil and spoke no evil. He saw nothing, as he told the coroner, even in what he described as clear moonlight; he heard nothing, certainly no one whistling or his brakes squealing; and he spoke only to the police in Hawick to tell them he had travelled past a burned car. *His* only purpose as a witness was to cast doubt on Evelyn's claim that she had heard whistling and screeching sounds. It was not even likely, albeit on a quiet road, that his would have been the first vehicle to pass by between 8.45 and 9.50 pm. Not that the police found others, or they kept mum about it if they had."

"In fact," Bradon says, "Beattie kinda destroys the police claim that Evelyn couldn't have gotten to Belsay and back in the time. This guy could have done it and stopped for coffee and cookies on the way."

Everyone laughs. Bradon, I think, has been a godsend.

Then Peter says, "But who, or what, did Evelyn hear? She wasn't clear *when* she heard these noises, except it seems to have been a short time before the bus arrived, which would certainly have fitted with Beattie pulling up. But he was a car salesman, so would surely have been attuned to car noises. When the coroner, and then a juror, raised the point, he was clear that his footbrake, the only one he used, had made no sound. So was Evelyn mistaken, or what had she heard? Someone else, who didn't come forward? Beattie himself whistling, to see if there was any response? One of the Hudson's rear tyres deflating? Or Bowler, in need of a lift, whistling down a southbound car? If she had heard these noises an hour earlier, yes, but not when she thought she did. To me, it's one of the few sub-mysteries left. I'm excluding the spinning car doors, for reasons already given, and the dratted petrol can."

"One thing needs explaining," I tell him. "Why, as you asked before, were several items said to have been found at the nearside front door, when Johnstone and others said it was the offside doors that were open? It's not clear from him and Rutherford exactly where Evelyn was lying when they found her. Johnstone said 'on the opposite side of the car from the road,' which would fit with her crawling out of the offside rear seat. But Rutherford said 'between the car and road,' which seems, if it's taken to mean the nearside, contradictory. But remembering that the car was tangential to a curve in the road, he might well have been agreeing with Johnstone, if Evelyn was lying at, say, one or two o'clock from the offside front wheel. Both seemed to agree that she was lying a few yards beyond the front of the car, so what other explanation is there? In any event, Evelyn would presumably try to crawl towards the road when she found her bearings. But if the *offside rear* door was open, it follows she must have crawled along the offside of the car to get to where the bus crew found her. So why were these items found by the *nearside front* door?"

Peter smiles. "Still thinking," he says. "I've been reprimanded before about being hasty, and don't intend to repeat the mistake."

"I think we should all think about it," Bradon says. "But what's for sure is that the coroner should have spent a lot more time on that piece of geography than he did on gas cans and their stoppers. Johnstone was asked mainly about the doors, Vasey about the gears, and Rutherford was asked nothing about anything. I know this was eighty-some years ago, but had these guys no idea of investigating crimes at all?"

"For them, and by that time," Peter says, "it was a fait accompli. It's called going through the motions, plus making sure no one else makes any wrong moves or casts serious doubt in their direction."

"Gordon Foster was next," I remind everyone, to try to stop this discussion from deteriorating into a blame game.

Thankfully, Frances takes the hint. She seems to have recovered from her premature declaration of allegiance.

"Gordon," she says, "mainly came across as a practical but solicitous older brother. He may have had a shorter fuse than his father, with the garage staff as well as Bates, but he had good antennae about when things were in danger of taking wrong turns and what the police were about. He was less easy-going than his father—nothing demonstrates it better than his reminder to Johnstone and Rutherford that they were scheduled to take the early bus to Hexham on the morning of 7 January, so had better grab their four hours sleep. He was also more suspicious, and probably as a result was given little time in the witness box. In fact, his statement had more to do with the car, retrieving it and inspecting it in the garage, than with his sister. The one thing which surprises me about Gordon is that he apparently did not make sure, when his turn came, that Bates was primed to ask him some pertinent questions. Bates as usual asked none; perhaps he'd been forewarned by Joseph Foster that he wasn't flavour of the month with Gordon. Smirk belaboured the question of gears again, and the coroner confined his input to the description Evelyn had given of the man she had picked up."

No one seems to have anything to add, but we are back on level ground. "And so we come to the police," I prompt them.

"Several points are worth noting, I think" Sven says. "First, three constables and Inspector Russell were called; no one more senior, even though more senior people had participated. Second, Shanks was not called at all, although he had been on the scene right after Fergusson, had been present at Evelyn's interview and was the most senior police officer involved until Russell's arrival the next day. Third, not one of the police who appeared gave so much as the merest hint of what they were thinking: their theory, right or wrong, to explain what happened."

"And fourth," Peter says, "Not one of these policemen, until we get to Russell, were questioned to any degree at all. Including Fergusson, and he was the only one of them who'd been present at the interview. This truly was an inquest where the truth lay more in what didn't happen and wasn't asked than in what did happen and was asked. The only point of any significance to emerge from the police was Russell's conviction that Evelyn and the car were set alight in situ. It caused a string of questions from Smirk—who else?—about whether this benighted petrol can was scorched on the inside (no); on the outside (slightly); whether its screw cap was scorched or damaged (no); whether its neck was damaged (no); whether the cap and neck were lying separately in the back of the car (yes); whether the scorching on the can but not on its accessories indicated that they must have been separated before the fire (yes); and finally, *finally*, had there been any sign of burning in the car's tracks across the moss (no)."

Peter takes a breath. "This is truly remarkable stuff," he says. "First, we hear that someone has to take its cap off in order to pour petrol from a can. What can one say to that piece of garbage? Then, we are asked to take a massive leap of logic. We are asked to believe it was impossible for Evelyn to have been set alight inside the car by lighter fuel or whatever, and then for the car to trundle all of sixty metres across frozen, wet heather and not leave traces of burning. For all his hard work, Russell's was a fatuous claim: it patently need not have burned any heather at all if the fire—at that stage many Guy Fawkes short of a conflagration—had for a minute or two been contained inside the vehicle."

"But the police," Frances says, "*had* to make sure that this point, the point about the fire starting and ending where the car came to rest, was rammed home. Their theory was that Evelyn had set it alight, so any suggestion of fire elsewhere would have destroyed them—unless the waiting world was to be asked to believe she had set herself alight then driven sixty metres. And there's another point, isn't there? The petrol can, as Goodman says, *had* to have been moved. It would hardly have suffered only slight external scorching if it had been put in the luggage box right away. It would have been thoroughly burned, inside and out. Yet Russell, on his own say-so, found the can next day resting upright and more or less undamaged on the luggage box, which was burned to ashes. So one of his constables, or Johnstone or Vasey, or a passer-by, had put it there when the fire was out. In fact, the finger of blame has to point at someone other than Fergusson, I think, and my guess would be Proud, who seems to have moved several things; scarf, purse and suspender parts among them. Fergusson says the can was upright on the luggage box at 1.00 am or just after; Proud and Vasey also have it there but on its side; Russell at that point was still hours away in Prudhoe. But whoever moved it, when its contents were poured over Evelyn hours *before*, the can would have been thrown on the ground, discarded, wouldn't it? After which, it was scorched as the heat spread, and/or residual vapour in it caught fire."

"Excellent, Frances," I tell her. "Anything else?"

They look at each other. Peter tilts his chair back.

Bradon says, "We could go on about the cap and neck being separate and so forth, but what's the point? They were moved too, and as Peter said, it would have been natural to drop them nearby once the can was opened. It would have taken someone with an extreme case of OCD to screw the cap back on with Evelyn burning to death."

"You are still sticking to the possibility that Evelyn may first have been set alight on the road, Peter?" I ask him.

He leans forward and shrugs. "The police didn't disprove it. They certainly didn't prove *she* set the car alight where it was found. I come back to an earlier point: what could Evelyn have set it alight *with*? My notion that Bowler may have set her alight on the road is still on the table, if only just. As I recall, I offered it in response to a question from Molly, but the sequence needs thought. The issues I'm wrestling with are, one, whether anyone with any sense could conceive of sexually assaulting someone if they were already burning; two, that the sanitary towel remnant was found, not on the road but on the moor; three, whether anyone, whatever their pain threshold, could faint and remain briefly unconscious whilst being licked by fire; and four, whether Evelyn could have been lying in the back, stunned, on the road, but not yet alight. It's a jigsaw. The pieces are there, but some are hiding their faces."

"In most cases," I tell him, "the answers are hidden in the details. One day soon, we need to put that jigsaw together. But let's conclude Day Two with the recalling of Joseph Foster and John Kennedy."

"Let's just conclude," Peter says, "and move on to Day Three. We've already dealt with Smirk's tricky cross-examination of Kennedy and the failure of the police to prove that Evelyn needed money, *and* that she would have received no more than a pittance in insurance from torching her car. Whether the coroner grasped it or not, Joseph bombed the police theory by the simple expedient of being honest. The jury and audience would have known what their money could buy in those days. Joseph obligingly produced Evelyn's bank statements and the insurance policies. If she'd needed money to get married, the former would have bought her a wedding reception and a house; the latter might have got her a dining room table and chairs. I believe it wasn't long before that penny dropped with the police. They never entirely discarded the idea that she planned to destroy her car and blame a mythical passenger—how could they when their pride was at stake?—but when the inquest was over it seems to have fallen into second place behind the notion that Evelyn had gone cuckoo and was seeking, thanks to Andy Warhol, what has become known as her fifteen minutes of fame. I believe in due course we will get to Fullarton James' confirmation of this radical reversal."

"And let's not forget," Frances says, "at no time did Dodds ask her parents or brother or anyone else about Evelyn's character, home life or social life. It's yet another negative that suggests bias, isn't it? All he ever asked about Evelyn Foster as a functioning human being had to do with her mental state and finances. It isn't rocket science to figure out why."

"This seems a good time to call a halt for the day," I suggest. "We are left with Day Three, including the coroner's summing-up and the jury's verdict; and its aftermath, including the police's reaction. We can then move on to our own conclusions." I give them a smile. "We seem to be nearing the end of the inquest on the inquest."

It is comforting to reflect that at least there is no trace here of any authority *I* may have had being blindly followed. Peter Maxwell, if not all of them, would laugh at the idea.

CHAPTER TWENTY-FIVE

Newcastle Law School: the present day, 10 February
Concerning 5 February 1931 (Day Three of the inquest)

As Frances said, other than oblique references during the testimonies of Margaret and Joseph Foster—Evelyn's 'worries,' her finances and the Foster's insurance policies—together with Inspector Russell's conviction that the Hudson had been set alight on the moor, nothing had openly emerged during the first days of the inquest to suggest the police had developed a theory at variance with Evelyn's version of events. The word 'fraud' had crossed no one's lips. Local people knew of that theory, and most if not all disparaged it, but as far as the formal proceedings were concerned it had become the elephant in the room.

This was to change on Day Three, but only in the sense that oblique references became less oblique and more frequent, and finally because Mr Dodds was obliged to lay the alternative theories on the line.

For the authorities the day began badly when the Chief Constable's car skidded on ice and left the road at Ottercops Farm. He and his retinue managed to climb out and get the car back onto its wheels. Carefully they drove on, just missing the start of Dr McEachran's evidence, and coolly took their places. Dr McEachran said nothing they didn't know anyway, except towards the end a juror asked if Evelyn had said she was actually knocked out by the man. 'No', the doctor replied, 'she said she became unconscious after being knocked into the back of the car.'

"So it was a case of banging her head and fainting," Peter says. "Or fainting with the shock of the onslaught. Makes sense, doesn't it?"

Everyone nods. They are still thinking through possible sequences.

Frances says, "It would have made it easier for him once she was in the back. She wouldn't have been struggling or giving him problems. He could have taken his time, dealt with her any way he wanted."

McEachran gave way to Prof McDonald, the pathologist, the man everyone wanted to hear, the man whose findings had been the cause of more speculation in the community and media than any other single element of the case, at least since the fear of Bowler's continued presence on the fells had subsided. I wondered how many people beforehand had expected McDonald's statement to be as ghastly in its details as it turned out. In any event, he had read it calmly, folded its pages, put them back in his pocket and inclined his chin in anticipation of questions.

Coroner Philip Mark Dodds was quick to set the ball rolling, and any obliqueness that had been part of his previous modus operandi was just as quick to dissipate.

"A summary, Peter?" I suggest.

"We'd be going over old ground," he says.

"Then you should be word-perfect," I tell him. "Look, I think it's important to have Dodds' questions and McDonald's replies firmly fixed. Whatever conclusions we reach must give them serious attention. In my opinion they are the main proponents of the police's case; in the absence, except arguably Russell, of the police themselves. You can be as brief as possible, but try to do so without losing inflections or nuances."

"Okay," he says and launches into (one of) his own previous modi operandi. "Question one from Dodds: was there any bruising from blows or smacking of the face as suggested by the deceased? Answer from McDonald: *I could not find any.* Two: if it had been severe, could you have found it? *I think any severe injury would have left a mark.* Three: any blow strong enough to have stunned her? *I would have expected something. As I said in my report, anything superficial would have been undetectable. I found no evidence of deep bruising.* Four: in no shape or form was there any evidence of injury or interference? *No.* Five: absolutely no sign of outrage? *None whatever.* Six: The girl says that at Wolf's Nick the man hit her and threw her over the back seat, then threw something over her, and she recalled nothing more until she was awakened by bumping. Could you tell by her burns if she had been sitting or lying in the back seat? *It is possible, but I have not heard exactly what her story was.* Seven: would there be any trace of nipping? *Her left arm was not burnt, and one would have had a good chance of seeing any severe injury. There was no such indication.* Eight: could these burns have been caused by her in the back of the car? *If she were lying forward with her chin on her chest* (the Professor demonstrates) *I could conceive of the injuries I found being produced that way.* Nine: on the other hand, assuming the car was standing where she put it and the door was open, and she threw petrol into the back and set fire to it, with her left leg on the running board, could the flames have come back that way? *I think that is possible, yes.* Ten: quite possible? *I cannot quite understand, if that were the case, why there should have been localisation of the burns.* Eleven: assuming she had upset some petrol over the lower part of her clothing and then had ignited the car, which had already been soaked with petrol, would that have been a possible cause? *Yes.* Twelve: is it not a possible solution, assuming she put the petrol on? *Yes.* And finally: if she had taken the tin and poured petrol over herself in that way, is it possible she might have got the extra splashes above the breast? *That is possible.*"

"Thank you, Peter," I say. "Which left Smirk with the minor task of tidying up. He asked the Professor to confirm Evelyn had not been, as he put it, outraged. The Professor agreed she had not. He asked if she was a virgin, to which the Professor replied that, 'the appearances I found were in every respect compatible with virginity.' And he asked if there was any evidence of Evelyn having been nipped on her arm. The Professor said he had found no such evidence.

"We can ignore Bates as being ineffectual," I continue. "Two jurors asked supplementary questions: as Peter said a week ago, the Reverend Brierley asked about facial discolouration and was told there was no evidence of it. Another juror asked if it might have faded over the period before the post mortem. He was told it could not. Now: what conclusions can we draw from the *tone* as well as the content of the exchange between Dodds and McDonald? And let me just underline before we start that, given the various rumours which had been rife in the community since January 7th, this exchange was expected to answer some serious, if not frightening, questions. Had Evelyn been raped? Had she been assaulted? Had she been targeted in some way? Was this an instance of pure bad luck, opportunism, or some pre-planned murder? Had the man she picked up burned the Hudson to destroy any evidence of what may have gone before? Was it the work of someone who had killed previously and may kill again? We have to remember that the phrase *serial killer* was not in common parlance then, and with the notable exception of the German criminologist Ernst Gennat, would not become so for several decades."

"To start with," Frances says, "if Dodds had been anywhere other than in his own courtroom, half his questions would have been overruled on grounds that they were leading the witness. This is, after all, a direct examination by Dodds, isn't it? In fact, *leading the witness* defines the whole tone of the exchange. We can't say you didn't warn us, Matthew."

Bradon says, "I see McDonald's answers as measured, making sure no one can criticise him for being hasty or unscientific. The obvious example is his insistence that superficial bruises or injuries may not have shown up. There is almost a resigned tone in his final answers to Dodds, as though he's being led down a path he'd rather not go. If what we're seeing is a true transcript, he becomes nearly monosyllabic, maybe resentful of being badgered. He seems aware of his importance, but uncomfortable, kinda defensive. His only categorical answer is in respect of Evelyn's virginity. If that's what being 'outraged' meant to him."

"I think it's interesting to consider what an impartial coroner may have asked or done," Sven says. "I think he would have made sure first that McDonald was given a transcript of Evelyn's statement. He could then have asked if there were any apparent inconsistencies between what the Professor found and what Evelyn had claimed. It's extraordinary to me that McDonald professed not to know these details. I can't make up my mind whether it was arrogance or indifference or fear that he would lose objectivity. He could have given an opinion, in context, on whether the injuries and pattern of burns he had seen were consistent with her being thrown into the back seat and set alight with petrol being thrown in her lap. He could have been asked if he was sure about the onset of her period. It would not have been within his competence to speculate, but he could have been asked if he felt the expert opinion of a psychiatrist would be helpful—I mean both in exploring Evelyn's state of mind and the possibility that evidence of menstruation would have been offensive to certain males. In fact, a psychiatrist would have been useful in order to explore the whole subject of fire-raising and its correlation with sexual excitement or rejection. There's an argument for saying that if the police believed their theory that Evelyn had set the car and herself alight, a psychiatrist *should* have been on the witness list. But unless they had a tame one, maybe they felt it would put both their theories at risk."

"And what about Evelyn's claim that she was nipped?" I ask, thinking that Sven had been pursuing the same thread as Molly.

"Well," Peter says, "what does 'nipped' mean in this context? It doesn't have to mean pinching, and even less biting or hurrying, as in nipping down to the pub. It could have meant being compressed tightly or squeezing, as in being squeezed between Bowler and the car door. That was the theory of one reporter at the time, and I have no problem with it. In any case, if Evelyn meant he was pinching her between his forefinger and thumb, would any marks have shown up through layers of clothing? As to this thing about interference, we've debated before what the word meant. Evelyn, whether or not she was a virgin, would have been totally mortified—outraged if you like—at having a complete stranger feel her up uninvited. That, whether or not it developed into attempted rape, would have been interference enough, wouldn't it? Frances?"

"Goodman says Mrs Foster would have meant rape when she used the word interference," Frances says. "*And* her mother was convinced Evelyn had understood that was what they were talking about. She told her mother she fought for her life, didn't she? But she also said, 'he hit me and burned me', *not* 'he raped me.' Would she, even *in extremis*, have used the word? Even conceding that Goodman spoke to people who are no longer available to us, including Evelyn's sisters, I doubt whether Mrs Foster's conviction was right. As Peter says, euphemisms aside, being touched up would have been quite enough for Evelyn to have felt invaded. And if we are right about Bowler taking offence at finding a sanitary towel, things would have got no further than his ripping it off and throwing it away."

"And what you're saying, Frances, is irrespective of the Professor's competence in recognising virginity or rape when he saw either," Sven adds. "Goodman suggests that saying 'the appearances I found were in every respect compatible with virginity' is a far cry from saying 'she was definitely a virgin.' If McDonald was sure, why didn't he say so without hedging? Goodman claims that all three signs of virginity must be present—an intact hymen, a normal fourchette and a narrow vagina with what he describes as rugose walls—yet given that everything around Evelyn's private parts was so badly burned, McDonald most probably would be basing his judgement solely on the appearance of the vagina."

"Conclusions?" I ask.

"McDonald was a man under pressure, and probably the wrong man for this job," Peter says bluntly.

Clearly, Peter is on the point of consigning McDonald to the same dustbin as Dodds, Bates, Smirk and the Northumberland Constabulary.

"I think we may be underestimating the Prof," Bradon says. "I've read his obituary, which records his death in Edinburgh in 1948. He is described as an attractive personality, independent, not one to follow the herd. He was, quote, an old-style morbid anatomist with a particular interest in histology, unquote—so he specialised in diseased tissues and organs, and in the microscopic structure of tissues. He comes across, back in the day, as professional, and he passed on his professionalism to his son. I think Goodman may have been too hard on him, and we should take care not to follow suit. McDonald states that 'the hymen showed no rupture or laceration' and later that 'the whole of the genital and lower urinary organs were removed in a piece.' So I think he was looking at more than the vagina, and with a relatively practised eye."

"Thank you, Bradon," I tell him. "I think that was well-argued. We shouldn't let our perhaps justified opinions of Messrs Dodds and Bates spill over onto other people. That aside, I agree with you also in saying that McDonald comes across as someone being cajoled down a route he had reservations about."

"I wonder if McDonald and Fullarton James had come into contact before in a court of law?" Peter asks, and the look in his eye suggests it is doubtful whether he has taken these last points on board.

"Maybe," Bradon says, "but I couldn't find anything when I looked. *Dodds* and Fullarton James almost surely did. Dodds was deputy coroner for south Northumberland during World War I. He was based in North Shields, and Fullarton James, as we know, was Chief Constable of the county from 1900 until 1935. The coroner in the Sun Inn case you cited a fortnight ago, Matthew, the 1913 Bedlington murders, was Dodds' senior, a Mr H T Rutherford. Dodds may have been involved in some way, as there were three deaths and a lot of other injuries. It was a complex case."

I smile at him. "You've been busy."

"Just getting the drop on Peter for once," he says. "And by the way, where did the idea that Evelyn *sat* on the running board appear from?"

"It was Dixon's boat," Peter says. "No one else floated it."

"Okay," I say. "Let's wrap up our review of the witnesses and the questions they were asked with motor engineer Jennings. Very simply, aside from all the mechanics, he was asked by Dodds whether it was feasible for Bowler to have taken hold of the steering wheel at Belsay and driven, with Evelyn beside him on his right, to Wolf's Nick. Jennings said it would be difficult, almost impossible if she resisted."

"But would she resist?" Frances asks. "*Could* she? He had made his propensity for violence quite clear by that time. And resistance would be just as difficult if she was pinioned against the door."

"Bates, for once," I add, "actually followed up on the coroner's line of questioning. He asked whether the left edge of the steering wheel was more or less central in the car and when Jennings agreed, within an inch or two, asked him if he maintained there was insufficient room to allow a person to have control over the steering with someone on his right-hand side. Jennings rather cagily said the person on the right would need to get well over to the right and the person attempting to drive would also have to lean well over. Bates asked if an experienced driver could do it and Jennings said he could, but 'it would not be by any means safe.' This probably was Bates' golden moment in the entire proceedings. But we are dealing again with equivocations."

"It's a matter of degrees, isn't it?" Frances says. "It depends just how far Evelyn was pinned against the door and handbrake, and how difficult it would be for her to move. She may have been on the plump side but she wasn't by any means a big woman. Five feet tall, McDonald said."

"So," Peter says, "all that remained after that was the jury's car park inspection of a Super-Six and the positions two people would have to adopt in order to drive it. Not even the French could have dreamed up such a farce. I'm still not fully convinced that this was how they drove, or that given her state of confusion Evelyn was not already in the back seat, but if it *was* how they did it I guarantee the car park demo would have been conducted with a lot more care than Bowler would have granted Evelyn. Maybe he was pretty well sitting on her. If I could get hold of a car with bench seats I'd be tempted to try it myself. With a good-looking female fresher, of course." He grins.

He is being droll, of course, but I have the feeling Peter is gearing up to discharge bigger cannons. I restrict myself to saying, "Which leads us on to what you've all been waiting for, I trust. The coroner's summing-up and the jury's verdict."

CHAPTER TWENTY-SIX

Newcastle Law School: the present day, 10 February
Concerning 5 February 1931 (Day Three of the inquest and aftermath)

We have sandwiches for lunch again, and are back around our table by two o'clock. On 5 February 1931, the jury had resumed their seats at just over half-past, waiting to hear what the coroner had to say.

Picture the scene, if you would. An unpretentious Village Hall, the focus of national media attention (Malcolm Campbell's new land speed record at Daytona Beach was sharing the front pages) packed to the rafters. A small bespectacled man sitting behind a table clothed in black. Acetylene gas lamps burning in the midday gloom. Spectators shuffling, trying to get comfortable on the hard, unyielding seats. The police, beside and behind their master, waiting to hear whether their case is to be successful, suspecting as they view the stern faces of George Sinclair and George MacDougall, the straight gaze of Reverend Brierley, that it will not. What could they have done, or not done, to make it better?

Of the three possible and relevant verdicts of unlawful killing, accidental death or suicide, Mr Dodds began by ruling out suicide.

"Good start," Peter mutters sardonically.

I decide to test him.

"And what today, Peter, would be the standard of proof needed in the two alternatives the jury were left with: unlawful killing on the one hand, accident or misadventure on the other?"

"The standard of proof applied at an inquest is the civil standard, the balance of probabilities," he says. "That is, the facts have led to the conclusion that it was more likely than not the death was an accident. The exceptions are unlawful killing, including murder, and suicide. If either of those verdicts is to be reached, the standard of proof is the criminal one of being proven beyond reasonable doubt, or being *sure*." He passes the test.

"Okay, so we would have two standards of proof, depending on which way the jury was thinking; a less rigorous standard in the case of accidental death. Let us look at what the coroner said:

Crimes are committed in very many ways, sometimes for obvious reasons, sometimes for reasons unknown. In this case we are dealing with the question as to whether a stranger was implicated or whether the deceased herself did it. Subject to your opinion, I think we can rule out any question of suicide.

"Mr Dodds then said there were two main points for the jury to consider," I continue. "He asked, 'was the girl murdered?' or 'did she set fire to the car and in doing so obtain the burns accidentally?' Finally, the cat was out of the bag. He told the jury if they could answer one of those questions they would have an answer to the case. He went on:

If a man was concerned in this case—without knowing who he was—he appears to me to be a homicidal maniac. Either that, or he was doing something to hide something of his own actions.

I add, "Those two sentences were, as Goodman points out, the sum total of the coroner's advice on the murder option. For the next hour he tried to persuade the jury that accidental death was their only reasonable conclusion."

"With barely a shred of evidence to support it," Frances says, "let alone the balance of probabilities or offering guidance on points of law. And it's a banal statement to have made. Incidentally, could there have been an open verdict in those days?"

"There could," I tell her. "In fact, Dodds hints at the possibility towards the end of his summing-up. We'll get to it."

"So it could have been another option," Frances says. "Okay."

"To digress briefly," I add, "verdicts of unlawful killing are not too common. Some, involving football crowds or train crashes for example, cover multiple deaths. One of the best known but least understood—due to initial BBC misreporting, eagerly swallowed and followed by the rest of the mainstream media and the establishment—concerned the deaths of Princess Diana and Dodi Fayed." I turn to Bradon. "Would you care to summarise the coroner's advice for us, warts and all?"

Bradon flicks through his notes. As usual, they look both neat and inclusive. Although the distinction between 'barrister' and 'solicitor' does not apply in the States, I think Bradon's expertise lies more in the latter.

"Okay," he says, reading. "Here we go. Dodds began by repeating his admonition about Evelyn's statement and told the jury to forget any rumours they'd heard; easier said than done, I guess. He then got into the insurance policies, saying there would be pecuniary benefit if 'the girl' wanted to burn the car and receive compensation. He referred to the policy insuring Foster's cars for £700 if they caught fire outside the garage. He failed to make clear that the £700 was a top limit, or that the amount payable was to be calculated 'according to current values.' He didn't hazard a guess as to what sum Evelyn might have received.

"He then threw the other notion into the ring, namely that there were known to have been cases in which people became obsessed with the idea of achieving notoriety by doing something abnormal. He did not elaborate." Bradon smiles. "I was interested to read that some juries in the 1930s recorded verdicts of lunacy, plain and simple. Maybe Dodds felt he'd be skating on thin ice with that one, given McEachran's view that Evelyn had been lucid and sensible."

He looks at his notes again. "Dodds went on to review the evidence as he saw it. He said he couldn't understand why the people—plural—who dropped Bowler off did so at Elishaw when they could have taken him on to Hexham and given him a better chance of connecting to a Newcastle train or bus. He referred to what he called three 'extraordinary features' of the evidence relating to Evelyn's stop in Otterburn. These were: that although Maughan and Thompson had both seen 'the girl's' car outside her father's garage (no mention of Luke) no one had seen anyone get out of it and walk through the village; that although Bowler was supposed to call in at the Percy Arms to ask about a lift, and Miss Foster was supposed to meet him there, neither of the duty staff had seen either of them; and that although it was unusual for Miss Foster to go on long journeys alone with strangers, and one of her sisters often went with her, she did so that night despite her friend Phillipson being available."

"Those," Peter says, "are three features that are not extraordinary at all. The first was down to the rubbish selection witnesses, the second was adequately explained by Bowler's presence at the bridge, and the third was answered head on by Evelyn's mother."

"For the moment, Peter," I suggest, "let Bradon continue. So far, he seems to be doing an admirable job."

"Just giving his brain a rest," Peter says.

Bradon smiles again. "Dodds began to track Evelyn's journey beyond Otterburn. He reminded the jury that the only positive sighting of the Hudson was by the bus driver Robson at Raylees, at which point it 'did not seem like a car hurrying with a passenger.' He attacked the evidence of John Kennedy, 'a man of remarkable views,' and pointed out that it was only when he was recalled that he divulged the driver seemed to be sitting sideways rather than straight on at the wheel." Bradon looks at me. "Do you mind a small diversion here?"

"Not at all." Frankly, I'd far rather it was Bradon's than Peter's.

"Goodman says if Kennedy's original statement made no mention of the driver's position, there may have been a suggestion of perjury. He suggests Smirk may have missed a trick in not asking, 'did you say this in your statement?' and then, 'why not?' which may have destroyed John Kennedy's credibility as a witness. I don't see it myself."

"No," I tell him, "and Kennedy is beyond perjury now. A lot of things are missing from witness statements but they do not amount to perjury. Joseph Foster, for example, did not divulge Evelyn's finances. Why should he? Yet he was asked about them."

"Okay," Bradon says, "but they seem to have been gunning for this guy. Anyway, Dodds then moved on to 'the girl's' allegations of having been outraged, nipped and struck, and asked if anything could be more conclusive than McDonald's report that there had been no nips, no signs of violence and, above all, that she had been a virgin."

I am conscious of Peter and Frances stirring. I wave a calming hand to stop them interrupting.

Bradon continues, "Towards the end of his review, Dodds said it could be inferred from Evelyn Foster's statement that the fire had begun on the road, but both Inspector Russell and William Jennings had said there *was* no fire until the car stopped on the moor. He invited the jury to draw 'some conclusion' from the cap being taken off the petrol can before the fire. I assume what he was getting at was the unlikelihood of Evelyn setting herself alight on the road and then driving across the moor. And he said that the pattern of burns was 'consistent with the person burned having poured petrol from a can.' This, he claimed, was supported by the burns *above* the breasts and by Evelyn Foster having her *left* foot on the running board of the car while throwing petrol inside it. McDonald, you'll recall, testified that there was limited burning above the breasts and her left foot was relatively untouched, so I'm not sure how he got to these conclusions. Dodds ended his summing-up like this:

My opinion, I must say, is that I do not think there is sufficient evidence to say these burns were caused by another person. It is for you to decide, of course— but it will be entirely improper for you to say these burns were caused by another person unless you are absolutely certain they were so caused. On the other hand, it would be equally improper for you to say these burns were caused in the way I have suggested they might have been, by her setting fire to the car and becoming accidentally alight, unless you were satisfied that was the cause. If you cannot come to a decision as to how these burns were caused, and think the evidence not definite enough, it is open for you to say so. However, that is a matter for you.

"End of," Bradon says. "The jury retired at 4.15 pm; Dodds, Smirk, Fullarton James and retinue went to the Percy Arms for tea; reporters scurried to any available phones; very few spectators left their seats in the Memorial Hall. There was some discussion in the room about the coroner's summing-up and how the jury could find against his direction, but no one seemed to expect them to take too long about it. In fact, it was 6.25 pm, over two hours later, when they returned."

"Did he say *absolutely certain* in those few choice words?" Peter asks, knowing full well he had. "What price the balance of probabilities? Where did this fellow read law? The Joseph Stalin School of Justice?"

"Patience, Peter. Please finish the proceedings off for us, Frances," I suggest to her. "I'm sure you'll enjoy it."

She says, "George MacDougall, the foreman, had told a constable, presumably Fergusson, they were ready. When they'd filed in and all the coughing and squeaking of chairs had subsided—we can imagine the anticipation in the room, and I suspect people who knew MacDougall would have an idea what was coming—Dodds asked, 'Are you agreed upon your verdict, gentlemen?' MacDougall stood: 'Yes, Mr Dodds. The verdict is wilful murder against some person or persons unknown.'

"According to the *Newcastle Daily Journal* in its next day's edition, the coroner seemed somewhat surprised. He shook his head, maybe to clear it, or more likely in disbelief that his opinion had counted for so little, and said, 'I suppose you mean that someone deliberately poured petrol over her and set her on fire?' MacDougall repeated, 'Yes.' Dodds then rephrased the verdict in official language, thus:

'We, the jury, find that Evelyn Foster died on 7 January 1931 at The Kennels, Otterburn, from shock due to burns caused by petrol being wilfully thrown over her and ignited by some person or some persons unknown.'

"MacDougall nodded. 'Correct.'

Dodds said, 'Well, that concludes the hearing.' He busied himself with his papers, not looking at the jury, and said, 'Thank you, gentlemen.'

"Mr and Mrs Foster were in tears on their way out, but Joseph stopped long enough to say, 'It's what I expected. I don't think the jury could have done anything else. The verdict vindicates my daughter. There's great relief in knowing it's all over.'

"It wasn't of course," Frances adds. "Capt. Fullarton James pushed reporters aside as he marched to his rather muddy car, saying he did not think it proper to express an opinion. He meant not there and then, but his opinion would come."

"Thank you, Frances," I say. "As clear a résumé as we could wish."

The Chief Constable's take on the verdict was to come the next morning, under headlines such as *Police and Jury Disagree*. Notable among them was the *Daily Express* and its reporter Leslie Randall, who seemed over the previous month to have had an inside track to which others could not aspire—including the premature leaking of some of McDonald's post mortem findings over a fortnight before the inquest. Randall's story included a statement attributed to Fullarton James:

We are satisfied that the motor car in which Miss Foster's supposed murderer is said to have travelled from Jedburgh does not exist. We are also satisfied that the man she described does not exist.

"We have to assume these are bona fide reports," I tell the team, "and that Randall's titbits throughout were inspired by a very high-ranking Deep Throat indeed. From what we have read, and heard earlier from Bradon, it would have been a departure from Professor McDonald's normal behaviour for him to divulge sensitive information to the press."

"You have a phrase in Britain," Sven says, "the 'royal we', I think. In this case, is Fullarton James speaking as police royalty or does he actually mean the whole of the Northumberland Constabulary?"

"Whichever, it was taken as the official stance of the Constabulary," I tell him. "Other papers followed it up and were told the Chief Constable had nothing further to add. In the absence of a denial, or even an explanation, the statement was accepted as being accurate. The Word had descended from the mountain-top. Confirmation was to come later that day when the police moved out of the Tower and went back to their normal duties. As far as they were concerned the investigation was over."

"And their troubles intensified," Frances says. "Feelings in the village began to run high. If it had not been so before, there was now a clear 'them and us' division. There were two verdicts on Evelyn Foster: those of the jury and police. One juror was to say that he and his colleagues had without doubt been in the best position to form an accurate judgement. He added something which the coroner had failed to consider: *we listened for hour after hour, we sifted every detail, every fact placed before us, and, of course, we knew something of the sterling character of the poor girl herself.* He conceded that parts of the expert evidence went against Evelyn's story, but suggested that expert evidence could be produced to support almost any argument. He went on to say: *it is preposterous that a dying girl, suffering the agony Evelyn Foster must have suffered, would readily invent such a convincing story as the one she told on her death-bed.*

"George Sinclair was to repeat that his evidence should have been taken, or read out with others that might have been useful. There is more than a hint there that others *did* know something useful. The Foster family, having believed it was over and Evelyn vindicated as her father had hoped, were thrown back into confusion, not to mention distress."

"Some things Joseph was quoted as saying did them no good," Peter points out. "He kept banging on about petrol cans as if Bowler had been carrying a substitute 2-gallon can in his jacket pocket. And John Kennedy didn't help, although no doubt he tried. He claimed, in a new revelation, that the man driving the car he saw 'knew the road.' Not only was it going fast with its lights off when it passed him, but they were switched on and off again as it negotiated a curve near Knowesgate. But does all this stuff after the event help us in reaching a view on Evelyn's death?"

"Only in so far as it gives us an idea of police thinking," I tell him pointedly. "Which was in short supply during the inquest.

"Two days after it," I continue, "Mr Foster told reporters camped outside The Kennels that he found the Chief Constable's stance hard to believe; he must either accept the jury's verdict or call a second inquest. Mr Foster said he intended to seek legal counsel and would be writing to his MP, Colonel Douglas Clifton Brown, the future Viscount Ruffside of Hexham. A couple of enterprising *Evening World* reporters got to Col.

Brown before he did. They succeeded in drawing the MP into saying he was sure 'somebody or other will carry the matter farther,' and he would 'consider very carefully and seriously whether it is my duty to raise the matter in the House.' He added, 'I personally am placed in a very difficult position because of my friendship with the Chief Constable.'

"It would be understandable if Joseph Foster's heart had sunk on reading these coded messages. He decided instead to write to the Home Secretary, John R Clynes. It was a respectful and wordy letter, written no doubt with help from his family and friends, and made the point that the inquest had contained 'many painful and scandalous innuendoes against my daughter's character'; that she had been accused of fraud and of seeking notoriety; and there had been 'not a tittle of evidence to support these shameful theories.' He said the Chief Constable had made a statement—not repudiated—to the effect that Evelyn was not murdered."

"Hear, hear," Frances says as I read these excerpts aloud.

To wrap things up, I add, "Joseph posed three questions in his letter: *(1) Was my daughter's car left unprotected for hours so that fingerprints could not be taken? (2) Is it a fact that the police made no attempt to check footprints until the ground had been trampled by curious spectators? (3) Why was the skill and experience of Scotland Yard ignored by Northumberland police?*

"These," I continue, "were fair if somewhat ill-framed questions, since although crime scenes may not have been forensically examined in 1931, the car *should* have been protected within an hour or two of Fergusson learning of the situation, a fingerprint examination *should* have been carried out, and sightseers and reporters *should* have been prohibited. So we have a series of police blunders from the get-go. I hesitate to say, given Dr McEachran's advice, that the interview should have taken place earlier that fateful night, but the idea of foul play must have occurred to both Fergusson and Shanks for them to react as they did on first hearing the news. It is just a pity that this first reaction then became a kind of inertia in the crucial hours while Bowler fled the area.

"A fortnight later Joseph was advised by the Under-Secretary at the Home Office to take the matter up with the Northumberland Joint Standing Committee, the police authority for the county."

"Plus ça change," Peter says. "The establishment closes ranks."

"It gets worse," I tell him. "The committee met a month later, on 24 March. Capt. Fullarton James denied making a statement to a reporter but admitted, 'I did have what I considered a confidential conversation with a reporter after the jury had retired.' He said the Yard had not been called in because he 'had not considered it necessary.' He ignored the points about fingerprints and footprints, but said the scene was left unprotected because 'the nearest officer was stationed six miles away.' As we know,

Kirkwhelpington, and P.C. Sinton, were three miles away. He added that there was no truth in the suggestion that the police had abandoned their investigation. 'My duty offers no alternative (but to go on),' he said.

"The Chief Constable emerged from the committee meeting without stain or censure. Tea and biscuits were served to one and all.

"The announcement of the findings was greeted in Otterburn as a whitewash job. Local people had duly noted that in the three days prior to the committee meeting there had been more police activity in Otterburn than at any time in the preceding two months, including visits by Sergeant Shanks from Bellingham and Superintendent Spratt from Alnwick. Joseph Foster, bolstered by this evidence of renewed vigour, was moved to say, 'the police have told me they are going on with the search…I wish I knew what has changed their minds.'"

"Patsy," Peter mutters.

"In the wake of the Chief Constable's statement there was talk in the village of staging a protest meeting. It didn't happen. For some months afterwards Joseph and a 'committee of friends' embarked on their own quest in search of evidence to confirm the jury's verdict. Nothing they produced drew any meaningful response from the police. Eventually they threw in the towel. Directly after the Standing Committee meeting Capt. Fullarton James instructed his troops that the Evelyn Foster proceedings were no longer to be referred to as a 'case'; they were 'the Foster affair.' He made a little joke about it:

'The affair is over. I was never particularly attracted to the girl anyway.'"

"For God's sake," Frances says.

"So there we have it," I tell my team, more or less satisfied that as far as the evidence goes we have crossed most of the 't's and dotted most of the 'i's. I think it's the best we can expect, as I'm sure total satisfaction is an unattainable Holy Grail. Short of the police re-opening the case, which I imagine would carry odds in excess of 1,000,000:1 (I am no Paddy Power, thank God), we are nearly finished. Except—

"Two things remain for us on Friday. A review of the various theories that popped up at the time and since, and our own conclusions."

"You wouldn't be forgetting the beer and wine, would you?" Peter grins. "Or Bradon's huckleberry ice cream?"

I realise, friends, that my own credibility is at stake here, and I shall need to seek assistance in order to retain it.

CHAPTER TWENTY-SEVEN

Newcastle Law School: the present day, 13 February
Theories and conclusions (1)

Today, I think to myself as I prepare the seminar room, should bring this case study to an end. I am fairly clear there will be few major surprises, although I'm not sure how much my students will have read about the other theories that were bandied about in 1931 and onwards.

What I also understand, without hard evidence or the availability of other witnesses or their long-ago statements, is that we face an impossible task in trying to produce a cast-iron explanation of everything that occurred on the night of 6 January 1931.

But three comfort zones are available. The first is the engagement of the post-graduates in this process, which is now as complete as I could have wished. The second is that we are looking at those events under the test, not of cast-iron certainty but of reasonable doubt. And the third is that unlawful killing is by definition an unreasonable act, so how can anyone be expected to apply a perfect kind of reasoning to it?

One by one they file in, Frances first, Bradon last, and we exchange good mornings. Weather-wise it is far from auspicious. It is cold and monochrome and mist-shrouded, with drips of water falling off the eaves, and could as easily be six o'clock in the morning as nine.

"I think we should start by tying up a couple of our loose ends," I begin. "I'm referring to the vexed question of items being found by Russell at the nearside front wheel, and Evelyn's vanished purse. You may recall that Julian Symons, a crime writer of note and a peer of Goodman's, says in his essay that he learned from a newspaper man here in Newcastle that an enterprising journalist had visited Wolf's Nick in the early hours of 7 January 1931. In fact, he may have been understating it. As I mentioned a fortnight ago the *Evening Chronicle* admitted two of its reporters had visited the scene in search of a scoop before 6.00 am on 7 January. They examined the car, lifted the bonnet, found Evelyn's scarf on the ground and put it over the car headlamp. They may also have left the footprint of which the police later took a mould. Symons goes on to say — he was writing circa 1960 — that 'this blunder is not officially admitted by the police.' A local policeman, by then retired, strongly denied the car had been left unguarded, which we know to be untrue. Fergusson, who left the village not too long after Evelyn's death, refused to speak to Symons at all, and the Morpeth police declined to comment. But this story seems to explain why Evelyn's scarf was on the ground when Proud saw it after

1.00 am on 7 January, but was hanging over a front headlamp when Russell retrieved it later that day. It might also explain why various items were found at the nearside front of the car. In his statement, and in the list produced later as an addendum to Prof McDonald's evidence, Russell identified several items as lying on the moor adjacent to the car's nearside front footboard or wheel; pieces of Evelyn's brown tweed coat and skirt; a piece of burned linen; burned suspender buckles; and a piece of white wadding with material attached. Part of Evelyn's sanitary towel."

"I've been tending to blame the police for why they were found in the same area," Peter says. "Proud especially."

"I think they have enough blame attached to them already, Peter," I reply. "But it can't be denied they deserved it."

"But it doesn't altogether explain *where* they were found," he says.

"No," I agree. "If both offside doors were open and had been used by Bowler in his assault when the car came to rest—including pouring the petrol on Evelyn—the fact that Russell found these things near the front nearside door, which was closed, is puzzling."

Peter says, "The fact that suspender buckles had been detached as well as the white wadding might also suggest 'interference.' But they seem to have been badly burned whereas the white wadding was not."

"It indicates to me," I tell him, "that the items were brought together by a third party or parties from different places. Brought together, that is, by the police in the early morning or by our two reporters, who may have been unmindfully stockpiling their own inventory. But you'll no doubt recall Vasey accusing P.C. Proud of picking up Evelyn's scarf, and also part of a suspender near the front wheel, which Proud later denied."

"Yes," Peter says. "That officer doth protest too much, methinks. We know on his own admission he also picked up the purse. As Frances has said, it seems he couldn't resist fingering things. And *he* was the one left in charge of the scene while the others debunked to Kirkwhelpington."

Bradon says, "We have Johnstone's word, and Rutherford's, as to where she was lying at ten o'clock. Both say she was in front of the car. It's possible she veered a bit, the state she was in, probably beating at her clothes, and that one or two bits and pieces were shed along the way."

"Probably," I reply. "And neither was asked to expand on it. I don't think we'll get further than Proud—or the reporters—on the question of the nearside items. We could sit here and make wild guesses for hours."

"Mr Symons was also helpful in confirming that Evelyn did not smoke, and carried neither a lighter nor matches," Peter adds. "Which, had she been alone, would have made the bonfire impossible."

I nod. "The answer as well as the devil may lie in these details, but we need to focus on the right details, and move on from them when we believe we have a logical explanation. Symons, let's remember, was able in 1960 to talk to many more people who knew the case than Goodman in the seventies and a hundred percent more than Dixon in the noughties, or ourselves in the here and now. So, shall we move on to the purse? Proud said he picked it up about a yard from the *rear near*side wheel."

"*About* a yard in which direction?" Frances asks. "These people are simply beyond belief. In any case, it seems to have disappeared into thin air in Kirkwhelpington."

"Yes," Peter says, "but there are two items of significance. First, the fact it still had cash in it; and second, where it was found."

"Well," Bradon says, "Proud found it very early, just after one o'clock in the morning. So we can clear any reporters or passers-by from touching it. We can also assume Bowler didn't see it or wasn't interested in cash and threw it or kicked it in disgust. I think once it went to Kirkwhelpington, it stayed there and was forgotten about. And after a while, well, Sinton wouldn't like to have admitted it was still there, would he? Even if it came to mind."

"Maybe Bowler had a look inside it for another reason," Frances says. "To see what her name was, so he could track what was going on later in the media. Her driving licences were in it. *Then* he threw it."

They think about it. Peter makes a face and shrugs. "We can't expect a beautiful line of logic," he says. "And this fellow Proud…"

"Okay," I tell them. "Let's move on. We are, I suppose, interested more in what led up to the events on the moor. Before we go further, I want to read you a definition of 'reasonable doubt' as provided by Mr Justice Darling in the case of the murder of one Leon Beron twenty years before Evelyn Foster's death. On New Year's Day 1911, in fact:

Before you say (the accused) is guilty you must be convinced that the evidence can only be explained upon the assumption that he is guilty. If upon any part of it which is necessary to the deciding of his guilt or his innocence you have a reasonable doubt, you must decide in his favour. You know without my telling you that a reasonable doubt means such a doubt…as would influence a man in his own ordinary daily affairs.

"So we are dealing with a subjective standard, but one which places a serious burden of proof on any prosecutor. Or we were then; things are slightly different now in the sense that juries in criminal courts in England are no longer customarily directed to consider whether there is reasonable doubt about a defendant's guilt. As Peter has said, they are asked instead to be sure of the defendant's guilt before they convict.

"I have read this definition to you because Evelyn Foster was, in all but name, being prosecuted in this inquest. It was not an inquiry into her death so much as an accusation that she had brought it on herself. We are looking at reasonable doubt, the standard of the day, in reverse fashion; we are testing whether there is reasonable doubt to *disbelieve* parts of her story; that the evidence can only be explained on the assumption she was lying. Let us first summarise other theories and then look at the various aspects of the case under the spotlight of the reasonable doubt test.

"Theory one was the police theory, namely that she could not have done what she claimed in the time available to her, and that she set herself alight in attempting to defraud the insurance company and blaming it on a mythical passenger. We shall come to that later.

"Theory two was that she was cuckoo, a self-seeking publicist bent on notoriety. Everything we know of her character militates against it, but we shall no doubt come to that as well. In the meantime, not content with putting his foot in it twice already, Fullarton James was quoted as saying, *I believe the girl set fire to the car herself…I have never believed that the motive was an insurance fraud. I think it more than likely, as the coroner suggested, that she was a hysterical girl who was obsessed with a desire for publicity or was suffering from some abnormality.*

"Theory three was that the jury were fired by local patriotism into returning a verdict of murder. Press reports after the inquest suggest otherwise. It seems clear they were nine conscientious citizens, making copious notes as things went along—Reverend Brierley is reported to have filled a score of foolscap sheets with them—and taking their time in reaching a considered conclusion. They were even reported, against the coroner's instructions, of having considered the possibility of suicide, but concluded that Evelyn was such a sane and easy-going person the notion was nonsensical. The good vicar told his son later that he would have staked his reputation as a parish priest that she was not a girl who would contemplate suicide—which would have been, of course, a crime.

"Theory four was that there had been a stranger involved, but he had been sparked into violence by a disagreement or a determination not to pay for his expensive ride to Ponteland. This would perhaps explain his decision to stop at Belsay, but not his decision to stay in the car and head back to Otterburn. In any event, the outcome for Evelyn would have been the same and this scenario would have been equally troublesome for the police. It would have meant accepting a third party was involved, one they had failed to find. And if they were so taken with the idea that her story was a pack of lies, should they not also have considered she may have been telling the truth, but that what Bowler told *her*, about Jedburgh and tea and so on, could just as easily have been a pack of lies?

"Theory five can be tagged as the 'imitative syndrome', with specific reference to *Rouse*, a case I talked of when we began. Two months before in Northants, Alfred Arthur Rouse had picked up a hitch-hiker and burned him in his car, hoping to pass off the corpse as his own suicide. As a commercial traveller with about eighty women on his visiting list, Rouse had ample motive to do away with himself. He had fathered several illegitimate children, his current girlfriend was pregnant, and maintenance orders were piling up like driven snow. The case received huge publicity nationally, so much so that Evelyn could well have read of it. But however much the police would have liked to, they could not introduce *Rouse* at her inquest. The case was *sub judice*, and Rouse's appeal was not dismissed until 23 February 1931; he was hanged in Bedford on 10 March. And if Evelyn might have been aware of it, so might Bowler, and that would have done the police no good at all.

"Theory six was a variation on the imitative theme, and was floated in 1977 by Goodman. In September 1933, another murder took place. A groom called Ernest Brown had an affair with the wife of his employer, Frederick Morton, the managing director of a Huddersfield firm. After a year or so Dorothy Morton, a young lady with an impressive number of notches on her bedpost, broke it off. This enraged Brown, but he followed the Mortons when they moved to Tadcaster, threw in his job when asked to mow a lawn, changed his mind, threatened Mrs Morton's life, was reinstated, and shot Morton on his return from a business trip. He then set fire to Morton's car, with Morton in it, in a garage. Goodman builds his theory that Brown may previously have killed Evelyn on several similarities: he was a groom; he dressed as Bowler would have dressed; he had spent part of his childhood at Byker, a Newcastle suburb; he travelled to horse and cattle sales in the north of England and Scotland; the modus operandi in both cases was the same; and his final words on the scaffold, at Leeds in February 1934, were heard as 'Ought to burn' or 'Otterburn.' There is another Otterburn closer to Tadcaster, but that may be coincidence. Or it may be that he had committed another crime there.

"And finally, there is Evelyn's account of her death. We can pick at these theories as we go along if anything is worth picking. I think we should now concentrate on that account while remembering that other things may just possibly have happened."

"A masterful summary, maestro, if I may say so," Peter says.

"Thank you, Peter. Very gracious of you."

"But there is another quite obvious explanation, or theory," he adds pointedly. "Which is that the police, following their default state, completely missed someone or something that was under their noses."

"You could well be right," I tell him. But let's remember what we said at the outset. We can do no better than make up our minds in respect of Evelyn's innocence or guilt. Prosecuting any third party is far beyond our reach. So let us focus on Evelyn's story. Now, Bradon, you wouldn't by chance have one of your handy lists prepared, would you?"

"I have a list," Bradon says, "or had. It contained twelve items—I was calling them 'sub-mysteries' that needed answers—but we've looked at three of them already: the items scattered at the nearside front of the car, whether Evelyn might have carried a lighter, and her purse."

"The others are in chronological order?"

"More or less."

"Then let's deal with them in that order."

"Okay," Bradon says. "One. The second car at Elishaw, the car that dropped Bowler. Did it exist, and where did it disappear to?"

"Asked and answered," Peter says. "Beach, Oliver and Townes all saw it, or if they didn't there is reasonable doubt whether the car they saw heading south from Elishaw could have been any other car." He shrugs. "They described it differently, but could the average witness today, if they saw two cars going past them at speed in the dark, distinguish between, say, a small 4x4 and a Mercedes A-Class? And it disappeared into Troughend Hall, driven by Mrs Clark, or turned right to Bellingham, driven by who knows. And who, for that matter, knows whether Bowler's story about meeting these people in Jedburgh and joining them for tea was the truth? Or that he was about to use the AA box? We have his word for it, via Evelyn. The police spent a lot of time getting nowhere in Jedburgh, interviewing people in cafés and pubs and guest houses, but for all we know now, or anyone knew then, he could have thumbed a lift. Or they could have had tea in someone's house, perhaps the cottage of these dodgy brothers Mrs Clark knew."

"So, does anyone *not* believe this part of Evelyn's story?" I ask.

"We've said before," Frances says. "It fits, witness- and time-wise."

"Two," Bradon says, looking around. "Evelyn was in the village between 7.00 and 7.15 pm or thereabouts. How come no one saw her?"

"Her mother saw her," Sven says. "Her father provided an estimate to her. Her sister Dorothy saw her, but wasn't called to testify. The only time she was in the open was for a few yards down the garden path between the Hudson and the house and at the petrol pumps by the garden wall. She would have been visible for how long? For a minute in a dark street with few people about. And several people—Thompson, Maughan, presumably Mrs Maughan, Luke—saw the car at the house."

"Does anyone have reasonable cause not to believe this part of Evelyn's story?" I ask.

"Excluding Bowler," Frances says, "even the police did. Otherwise, how could she have driven to Wolf's Nick?"

"Three," Bradon says, nodding an acknowledgement to Frances. "Her non-appearance in the Percy Arms at 7.15 pm, give or take."

"Come on, Bradon my man," Peter says. "She had no need to enter. She saw Bowler at the bridge. Sinclair saw him a hundred yards up the street before he walked down to it. Maughan may well have seen him too. Mary Ferry and Annie Carruthers saw him waiting. Both missed seeing the Hudson by a minute or two, Ferry having collected her sausages. But poor old Phillipson, coming out of the garage, saw it leaving the village."

"Does anyone have reason to disagree?" I ask.

Silence.

"Four," Bradon says. "As a follow-up to that, apart from Phillipson, why did no one else see the Hudson between the garage and bridge?"

"Maughan and his wife had passed it at the garage when it was stationary," Frances says. "Luke also saw it at there. Beach and Oliver hadn't arrived in the village by 7.15, although it's a pity the police didn't ask Tatham or Scott what time *those* two entered the hotel. Thompson had gone inside the house he was visiting, next to the one he called Tully's the shoemakers. Sinclair, having finished work at the Co-op *and* having spotted Bowler, had gone into his own house. Misses Carruthers and Ferry had cycled on their way. How many more people would have been wandering along Otterburn's main street on a cold Twelfth Night when there were decorations to take down?"

No one seems inclined to add to that crisp summary.

"Five," Bradon says, and smiles apologetically. "This one is in the nature of back-up to what we've said before, but various people, the police included, clearly believed a car could not have been driven from Raylees to Belsay and back to Wolf's Nick in eighty minutes or less."

"Your own calculations tell you it could, Bradon," Frances says. "Evelyn herself had averaged the required speed to Rochester and back. Mr Beattie tells you it could. Mr Kirsopp-Reed would tell you it could, if he knew what time it was at any given moment. Various bus drivers would tell you it could, between stops. And Kennedy confirms the car he saw — and we have no reasonable cause to doubt it was the Hudson — was travelling at high speed. That must have meant at least 25 or 30 mph."

"Does anyone have grounds for *dis*believing that the Hudson could have travelled twenty-six miles in eighty minutes, given the frosty conditions of that night?" I ask. "Assuming it would have slowed down to negotiate the hill up to Ottercops?"

Silence. Then Bradon asks, "Did anyone see *Boardwalk Empire* on TV? Or the movies *Road to Perdition* or *The Sting*? They weren't slouches, some of the cars back in the day."

Everyone smiles. No one admits to being a movie buff or TV addict; these are dedicated students of law. Bradon winks at me, as if he's been reading my mind. He has actually been doing my work for me.

"Have you all missed the second road-mender's tale in Symons' essay?" I ask. "I do not mean Kennedy."

They look blank, and then at each other.

Sven finally points a finger at me, nods and says, "Another good point, if true. Another witness who was never called."

The others are still looking blank.

"Symons writes," Sven explains, "that another road-mender heard a car turn that night outside his house near Belsay. Unfortunately, he does not say exactly where or at what time this may have occurred."

Peter snorts. "The only perjury or concealment here was by the police, and it was on a grand scale. If lying by omission is not always perjury, it certainly goes to a lack of credibility on their part."

"Six," Bradon says, having waited a beat. "Evelyn's account of the way Bowler drove back from Belsay, and its feasibility."

"Hmm," Sven says. "I think we have to say it was difficult but not impossible. If indeed it happened that way and she wasn't, as Peter has occasionally speculated, already in the back and in a state of confusion if not unconsciousness. And let's face it, she could have invented easier stories to explain that leg of the journey. She could have said she *had* fainted and was unconscious in the back throughout, or that he forced her to change seats at Belsay."

"That's one of the credible things about Evelyn's tale," Frances says. "Some things *aren't* easily explained, when she could just as easily have invented a more believable lie: Bradon's Emerson quote again. Goodman talks of a synergy in her story, a sum greater than its parts, and I agree with him. *And* I come back to what I believe is the number one question: knowing she was on the point of death, with her mother and sisters by her side, would she have persisted in a lie? *That* was the question the jury asked themselves, and which Dodds and the police totally ignored."

"Do we have a reasonable doubt yet?" I ask.

"No," Sven says. "But the driving thing is as close as we've come to a suspicion of one." He offers up his congenial crooked smile.

"And another thing," Frances says, "if anyone was tempted to believe *their* theory, how did the police explain to themselves the bits of clothing and other items around the car? Was Proud asked about his actions at the scene? Did they imagine she'd been doing a rain dance?"

This raises more smiles.

"Seven," Bradon says. "The sequence of Bowler's assault on her, and what exactly happened between the road and the moor at Wolf's Nick."

"May I?" Peter asks.

"Carry on," I tell him.

I have a feeling he's been waiting for this.

CHAPTER TWENTY-EIGHT

Newcastle Law School: the present day, 13 February
Theories and conclusions (2)

"I am going to read you out a sequence," Peter smiles. "A sub-sequence, if Bradon wishes. This is, after all, the kernel of Evelyn's story, isn't it? I am referring to the half-hour of her life from Belsay to Wolf's Nick. And let me say straight off, I am holding to the idea that here was a spurned man, spurned once at Elishaw, spurned twice at the bridge, and possibly for all we know rebuffed a third time, explicitly or implicitly, by Evelyn herself on their journey from Otterburn. So: a jilted man, a resentful man, a frustrated man, a man with an inner anger to feed, or any or all of these. Preoccupied, chain-smoking, evasive, engaging in the minimum of small talk. Few pleasantries at all. Not so much as an exchange of names."

He turns to me. "Mind if I use the whiteboard, Matthew?"

"Be my guest."

"The sequence outlined by Symons was this," he says, pinning up a flipchart pad and turning the first leaf:

1. *Belsay. Decision to turn around. First blows over EF's eye.*
2. *EF pushed against door. Bowler drives to Wolf's Nick.*
3. *Cigarette offered/declined. EF struck again, forced into back of car.*
4. *Bowler assaults her, EF resists but loses consciousness.*
5. *Bowler throws something from bottle/tin. It goes up 'in a blaze.'*
6. *EF aware of bumping, manages to open door, falls onto moor.*
7. *EF hears a car draw up, a whistle, crawls towards road.*

"It leaves something to be desired, doesn't it?" he says. "What of the bits of clothing, the sanitary towel, her near nudity from the waist down, the suspender parts, the petrol can? Let's see what Goodman makes of it:

1. *K-R's car seen. Belsay. Decision to turn around. B. creeps along seat.*
2. *First blow over EF's eye, who 'couldn't stop to phone.'*
3. *Wolf's Nick. Cigarette again. EF struck twice, knocked into back of car.*
4. *Bowler 'interferes' with EF. She fights 'for my life.'*
5. *Bowler throws something from bottle/tin. It goes up 'in a blaze.'*
6. *EF aware of bumping, it rouses her, she crawls out of car onto moor.*
7. *EF hears a car draw up, a whistle, no one comes. Something explodes.*

"We are starting to see similarities, and some slight variations," Peter comments. "The same questions remain to be answered, but it seems clear Evelyn was forced into the back of the car and first assaulted when they were parked on the road. It seems clear she was dazed. It seems clear from both accounts that Bowler had something in his pocket, something flammable that caused the first blaze; and that Evelyn lost consciousness until the car was jolting across the moor to its final resting-place. *Both* these accounts plus Dixon's, which is comparable, are drawn from a single source; Mrs Foster's testimony and the notes Fergusson took. But there is a third version, independent of Mrs Foster, from someone who was present at the interview. Dr McEachran says:

> 1. *Belsay. Decision to turn. Bowler demands the wheel. EF refuses.*
> 2. *Bowler hits her over the eye, bundles her into the back.*
> 3. *(EF questioned as to why she didn't stop or phone: no clear answer).*
> 4. *(No mention of cigarette, or of 'nipping', or even of Wolf's Nick).*
> 5. *B. takes something from his pocket and throws it over her.*
> 6. *EF roused by the bumping of the car; can't explain how it was set alight.*
> 7. *She manages to fall out of the car onto the fell and crawl away.*
> 8. *She hears the petrol tank explode, a car slow up, a whistling noise.*

"More variations, aren't there?" Peter asks, flipping over another page. "But they may be due to the doctor's attention being more on his patient's state of collapse than on her words. He was not there to take notes, but to help her. It seems to me that if he's right, he is saying Evelyn *could* have been bundled into the back at Belsay. That would be a major departure. It would remove, as we've said, this problem of the odd driving format. But it is barely credible that Bowler would have offered her a smoke at Wolf's Nick as if all was hunky-dory. So let's finally see what Mrs Foster testified to on her daughter's behalf. It was an untidy interview, and like Goodman we can only attempt to piece it together in roughly chronological order. But this is the order she gave in testimony:

> 1. *K-R's car seen. Through Belsay. Decision to turn. B. creeps along seat.*
> 2 (a) *B. says he will drive. EF objects. B. hits her over the eye; 'sand' in it.*
>   (b) *Mrs F's impression was that B. was driving/sitting close to EF.*
> 3. *Car stops; Wolf's Nick. Cigarette. B. hits EF, knocks her into back of car.*
> 4. *Bowler kept 'nipping', then 'interfering' with EF. She fights 'for my life.'*
> 5. *B. takes something from pocket: a bottle or tin. It goes up 'in a blaze.'*
> 6. *EF doesn't know how it was lit. Feels a 'bump bumping.' It rouses her.*
> 7. *She somehow gets out of Hudson, tosses off her coat 'all alight.'*
> 8. *She hears a car pull up, a whistle and a screech, but no one appears.*

"After describing this, Evelyn also confirmed that before Belsay she had no suspicions of Bowler. They talked of very little except he could drive, had a car of his own and lived in the Midlands. She told her mother 'with emphasis' that she had been unable to phone from Belsay and had not been able to 'keep hold' of the car for fear of an accident. He had struck her twice, over each eye. There was an exchange—you could call it euphemistic—between Evelyn and her mother which had to do with Evelyn's coat. Mrs Foster asked where her coat was when she got out. Evelyn replied, 'You heard, mother. I was all alight.' She said she tossed it off afterwards. Mrs Foster asked how she had known the man had taken tea with his Elishaw companions. Evelyn replied he had thanked them for it." Peter smiles. "I have repeated this because nowhere does she say the tea was taken in a café or hotel. Not even Dodds was explicit on this." Peter refers to his notes. "He said, '*He appears to have met these people at Jedburgh. He has tea with them.*' And I have repeated the part about blows being struck because it explains why her eyes were swollen, the skin discoloured, although fumes and heat or rubbing them would play a part. I have no doubt some of these signs had gone before McDonald got to her, or were superficial, or burns disguised them. And finally, you will recall Evelyn complaining of a sore back. It went unremarked by our pathologist, but could well have been sustained when she was hurled into the rear seat, twisted it and/or landed on something hard."

"An admirable summary, maestro," I smile. "But I'm sure we will all be disappointed if you cannot now tell us exactly what happened."

"I can make what I believe is a strong conjecture," he says.

"Please do."

"I have not swayed much from my first attempt of two weeks ago, the Friday Molly was with us. I have few doubts about Bowler's growing frustration, and none about his waiting in the shadows of the bridge for Evelyn to appear or being seen by our two non-witnesses, the school-teachers. As Symons says, he could well have been a criminal before this event, so from his point of view the fewer people who saw him, the better. I have no problem with Evelyn deciding not to call on George Phillipson at the bothy. By all accounts, I would not have wished to set foot in it myself. I don't understand why Bowler didn't make Evelyn switch seats at Belsay, except he may have felt safer and more in control with her forced up against the door, and may have enjoyed being further aroused by a nubile young female body pressed against his.

"So we have him striking her first at Belsay, an initial glancing blow, and then assuming this awkward driving position. For reasons aforementioned I'm inclined to go no further with Dr McEachran's take on things in this respect. I've wondered if Bowler struck Evelyn with a hand holding a cigarette, which might explain her impression of having 'sand', perhaps ash, in her eye. We have him stopping at Wolf's Nick— Evelyn said this—and offering her a cigarette. We have him suffering another refusal, losing patience, hitting her and forcing her into the back. And, Mrs Clark aside—here is my first departure from two weeks ago—we have him assaulting her there and then. We have Evelyn fighting for her life. We have him—my second—groping through her undergarments, tearing at things, pulling at her suspenders, until his fingers touch the offending sanitary towel. We have him ripping it off in disgust and throwing it behind him or on the front seat. We have Evelyn fainting, flat on her back, but as she goes under she is conscious of Bowler taking a bottle or tin from his pocket, throwing something on her—my guess would be lighter fuel—and setting it alight. Incidentally, given her description of this substance going up 'in a blaze,' I've looked at gunpowder and its derivatives, or those in use in the 1930s. I must say in theory they make more sense than sulphuric or battery acid ever did. Still, whatever medium was used, Evelyn is out of it for a minute or two.

"Bowler wants to get off the main road. He probably has little idea in the dark of the slope that faces him but he drives—at an angle of 45° according to Russell—across the road. He loses control, panics a bit, but manages—the testimony of Jennings—to get the car moving forward on four wheels. Evelyn is shaken back into semi-consciousness by the rough ground and is burning. She stirs, in more of a panic herself. Bowler senses it; the car grinds to a halt in a dry ditch, stalls in low gear. Here, Bowler—this is my third departure—decides to finish the business off. It wouldn't do for the girl to survive and tell tales, would it? Evelyn is trying to beat out the flames and perhaps to him appears to be winning. So far—please note, Messrs Russell, Jennings, Dodds and McDonald, conspirators all in the police theories—the smallish blaze has so far been contained inside the rear of the car, on Evelyn herself. If she has managed to haul herself to an upright sitting position and is trying to beat it out, the flames may even be diminishing. There is a limit, presumably, to how much energy would be generated by a thus far small fire, one that never at this stage reached the floorboards let alone the heather.

"Bowler gets out, throws the offending sanitary towel away, looks for a weapon in the luggage rack and finds the can of petrol, which in fact is not mentioned by Evelyn. In getting out, he opens the driver's offside door and reaches her via the rear offside door. He leaves both open, as testified by Beattie, Johnstone and others. There is no need to close them; he is in a hurry, and it was only after 1.00 am they began revolving. However, Evelyn is now sitting up, dazed. He unscrews the cap and directs the contents into her lap—this is my fourth departure—throwing the cap and then the can away. Let us remember at this point Russell's evidence and his replies to Smirk, and what Frances said a week ago about the can and its cap being relatively unburned. And let's consider

McDonald's evidence that her right arm was burned much more than her left. Her right arm would be nearest the offside door, exposed to petrol splashes. Bowler makes sure she is well alight and runs for the road. A few seconds later she crawls out and onto the moss, managing as she told her mother—my last departure—to shed her top coat. Which was almost burned away, so must have been near the car.

"There is a stark and simple truth in all this, isn't there? Whatever euphemisms we employ, he tried it on, found something he considered nasty and there was no way he could take it back. So he killed her."

He throws the marker pen down and says, "QED. A few sequential changes, simply to have her bundled into the back, assaulted and first set alight—a start-up fire, as it were—on the road. And he likely made off with her felt hat. To a rail station or into the blue yonder, who knows?"

"Initially, Molly had three questions," I remind him. "The feasibility of their driving position, the indistinctness of post mortem bruising, and the improbability of Bowler throwing petrol on her without burning himself. I must say your revised sequence seems to address the grey areas." I look at the others. "Beyond a reasonable doubt?"

"Only one small niggle," Sven says. "Why *not* have Bowler throw the petrol over her on the road? He assaults her there, finds the sanitary towel, knocks her out, pours petrol in her lap and drives off the road as far as he can. The fire could still be contained for that short time."

Peter grimaces. "It's possible. Either way is possible. I would only say she talked about Bowler taking a bottle or can *from his pocket*. He wouldn't have fancied driving the car with a raging fire burning behind him, and we'd still have the empty petrol can to account for. Nor would he have known the state of the ground. If it weren't for Evelyn saying he had taken something from his pocket before the 'bumping,' the whole fire thing could have taken place on the moor. And if he first came across the sanitary towel on the road, ripped it off but flung it out later on the moor, it would have been as unburned as it was found."

Sven nods. "After one of our previous discussions, I had a look at some arsonist literature. A lot of studies—Rider in 1980, Ravataheino in 1989, Douglas *et al* in 1994, Prins in 1994 and Jackson the same year—give revenge or rejection or the deriving of sexual satisfaction as motives for arson, but there are many other causes. It's a very complex crime, male-dominated, and often used to conceal another crime. It is also a good medium of expression for individuals who shirk more direct means of killing. There were items of relevance there, but nothing conclusive."

"Peter, you said these people who dropped Bowler off may not have been in a café or hotel for tea," Bradon says. "There is, though, a telling quote from the *Newcastle Evening Chronicle* on 17 January 1931. It says by then the cops had accounted for every car that passed through Jedburgh on 6 January bar one; the one that held Evelyn's assailant. It says the car's occupants were two men and a woman, who had lunch in a Jedburgh hotel and left town about four o'clock. One of the men seemed to fit the description given by Evelyn. Strangely, the police do not seem to have questioned the report's validity. So it could have been right, yes?"

Peter is surprised by this but recovers quickly. "Three hours from Jedburgh…they must have stopped for a threesome. But it's a good find, Bradon. If true, it confirms a major part of Evelyn's story. And if this trio hadn't come forward by 17 January, why would they have done so later? After a point, the police would probably have *hoped* they wouldn't. Another annoyance could have been swept under the carpet."

Frances says, "Altogether a fine summary, Peter. I applaud you. Whether or not this man was a pathological arsonist or an opportunist, it makes sense to me. If there are still question marks, we can't expect, as Matthew said, perfect reasoning of what was a totally unreasonable act. That in itself is a nice contrast to Dodds' running board scenario, which seems to be as far from reason as the unlawful killing itself, and considerably further from the established laws of physics. There were burns on her *buttocks*, for goodness' sake!"

"I believe you had two more sub-mysteries, Bradon?" I remind him.

"They're pretty much pointless now." He smiles and nods at Peter.

"Try us," I encourage him. "Your last efforts were on the money."

Bradon shrugs. "I struggled to find a definition for this word 'knut'. It means, or used to mean, an idle, upper-class man-about-town. A dude, in the old-fashioned sense. Well, I got to thinking about this guy a bit, so…number eight *would* have been: why *couldn't* the cops trace him in Jedburgh? I think the *Evening Chronicle* and Peter have given us a steer, but why did Fullarton James claim that the car Bowler 'was said to have travelled' in from Jedburgh didn't exist, and neither did he? What grounds did he have for saying so? Why so obstinate? Why no response to the *Chronicle* story three weeks before? Why no explanation?"

"Hard to say without slandering him," Peter says. "Although there is always the primary defence of truth…"

"Don't go there, Peter," I tell him.

He laughs. "The Chief Constable was of the ilk, we all know them, who think second thoughts are primary weaknesses. And did it ever cross his mind that the occupants of the car that wasn't may have been shy of coming forward because they'd been up to no good in Jedburgh or elsewhere? Or were criminals in their own right? How far did his troops pursue those lines of enquiry, if at all? This was such a thoroughly bad investigation from the start, that if some kindly soul had pointed a finger at the perpetrator I seriously doubt if the Northumberland Constabulary, in their burgeoning belief in Evelyn's guilt, would have bothered to give him a second thought. More likely, they'd have dismissed their witness as a misguided country bumpkin."

"Like it or not," Frances says, "Bowler or whoever else is long gone in every sense now, and Molly gave us a rail scenario that seems totally to have escaped these policemen. I agree with Peter; what else did they miss? It would make a great deal of sense if they'd overlooked someone or something earlier. They couldn't get Evelyn's age right, or the details of their press releases, so how could they expect people to come forward? They had various times wrong and, according to them, Evelyn had been found nearer Capheaton than Wolf's Nick. Does anyone think that *wasn't* a big error, in an age when distances meant more than going from A to B in a car? When people were born, bred and lived their lives in one area?"

"What about other theories?" I ask. "How do you feel about the 'imitative syndrome,' the idea that Bowler may have been impressionable enough to have followed a method of killing he'd read about?"

"It's possible," Sven says. "The theory that she was loopy is loopy in itself. It was contemptible for Fullarton James and Dodds to suggest it, let alone make smutty jokes. The theory that Bowler decided his fare was too high can just as easily be dismissed; he hadn't paid, but had left her purse lying on the moor, hadn't he? I think none of us believes the jury was other than painstaking, so that theory too goes by the board. But Rouse...well, let us say his case intrigues. It was in the news, and Bowler had all its elements to hand. Also, a best-seller called *The W Plan*, written in 1929 by Graham Seaton Hutchison, an army officer, a fascist and Scottish National Party supporter—which may today seem an unusual mixture—may have acted as a template for both the Rouse and Foster cases. In that book, a British spy kills a German soldier, puts the corpse in a car, drives it over an embankment and sets it on fire. So another *Rouse* imitator appeals to me more than Goodman's explanation of the Brown case. I know Goodman says Brown could drive, which was by no means common in those days, and his accent and mode of dress matched Bowler's, but it's all too neat. It would be nice to think of this man on his scaffold repenting of his 'Otterburn' crime but why, if he was wracked by remorse, wouldn't he have confessed before he reached the gallows?"

"Sven, you have a problem there," Frances says gently.

"I have?"

"Rouse himself couldn't have done it; he was in jail at the time. And if some *imitator* other than Ernest Brown was the culprit, we are still left with an unknown man. The plain fact is that *no one else* was ever fingered for Evelyn's death, or came close. I'm afraid we all have to live with it, as have members of Evelyn's family for far too long"

I look at my watch. I have a surprise for them and don't want to get my timing wrong, and there are still five minutes to kill.

"So, Bradon," I say, "you had one final sub-mystery, I think?"

"I think we've answered all we need to," he says.

"Try us," I repeat. "Indulge us."

"Well, okay, number nine *would* have been to ask how, if Evelyn *had* intended to set fire to the car herself and claim insurance, she could have explained away the missing passenger she'd told her mother about. The first thing the insurance folks would have said would have been: give us this guy's name so we can check it out, or forget it."

"It's not really a mystery, is it, Bradon?" asks Frances. "She could have said she dropped him off and had her accident on the way back. Would they have bothered tracking him then?"

"They wouldn't have coughed up if the cops said he didn't exist."

"But they would have had no reason to, would they?" Frances says.

Bradon sees the light of battle in her eyes and quickly backs down.

"It just struck me as a loose end is all," he says.

"Very well," I say soothingly. "It would be a pity to fall out when we've come this far. More to the point, there will be people who *will* fall out with some of our findings. In that case, I think we can do no better than conclude with a statement made to Goodman some forty-five years after the events of Twelfth Night 1931. It was made by Evelyn's sister Margaret a few years before she died. She said this:

We have thought about what happened ever since, but never for a moment have we doubted Evelyn was murdered. Her death was made more terrible by other people's doubts. We were just young then, but that night made us old."

I just finish speaking when there is a knock on the door. Molly walks in with a wine carrier in one hand and a carrier bag in the other.

"All done?" she asks brightly. "And the verdict is?"

"Murder by Bowler," I tell her. "Beyond any reasonable doubt, and I should add unanimously. Great timing, by the way."

She puts her burden down. "And did you identify this Bowler?"

I look at each of them. "We gave it a try, but no. Lost in the mists of time, I'm afraid. Someone, somewhere may have known, but not us."

"As expected then." Molly puts four bottles of wine on the table while I retrieve glasses. She then plonks down a carton of ice cream from the carrier bag and gives Bradon a spoon. She has been raiding my flat.

"Not the real thing, Bradon," she says, "but as close as I could get with the best of the fresh blueberries in Aldi." She smiles. "I enjoyed going around all the stores, sampling, and they seemed the pick of the bunch. It's all home-mixed, so that should count for something."

"It sure looks authentic," he says. He picks up the spoon and has a taste. "Umm…the berries are maybe not quite as crunchy, but very near the real thing. You're a star, Molly. Thank you."

"Good to see you again," Peter says, lifting his glass to her, and then to the ceiling. "We did our best, Evelyn Foster, and you have Matthew here to thank for introducing us."

"Better late than never," I say. "And the jury gave us a good steer."

"That's true," Bradon says between mouthfuls. "Do you wish some of them were still alive to tell them so? The jury, I mean?"

"No," I tell him. "Never that. They were sure in their belief. And justice, after all, is not a concept that belongs to one life, or nine. It's a concept owned by everyone."

"Oh my," Sven says. "Eat your heart out, Atticus Finch."

"But think about it," Molly says. "Think of all the thousands of conversations in living rooms and kitchens and bedrooms, in shops and pubs and workplaces, which a case like this generates down the years. Decreasing as time goes by, but still with us. Evie was the main victim, her future life, her work, marriage, children, grandchildren, torn out of her hands. Her family were close behind. But think too of all the other victims who followed. Think of the feelings of the jury at having their considered verdict cast aside. Of the witnesses who *weren't* called. Of people in isolated farmsteads and their weeks of worry. Down the years, the whole of Otterburn could be said to be a victim. If I'm not being too metaphysical, justice itself could be said to be a victim. Because of what?"

I like this little speech, which I've heard before expressed in other ways. It seems time to enjoy our drinks, and Bradon his ice cream.

"Maybe you should all go back to Otterburn," Molly suggests, "and put some flowers on her grave."

They look at each other.

"Good idea," Peter says. "Your car, I trust?"

I smile at him but my thoughts are elsewhere. I am recalling a long ago conversation with my father over a schooner of sickly-sweet sherry. I think he may have approved of this outcome, and the way it was reached.

I remember him saying, "As far as policing was concerned, it must class as one of the Top Ten worst investigations ever."

6 January 2015

ACKNOWLEDGEMENT

With special thanks to Isobelle for her encouragement and help with early drafts of this book.

www.ingramcontent.com/pod-product-compliance
Lightning Source LLC
Chambersburg PA
CBHW051510030726

47592CB00006B/2193